Bolshevism / The Enemy of Political and Industrial Democracy

John Spargo

CONTENTS

PREFACE

In the following pages I have tried to make a plain and easily understandable outline of the origin, history, and meaning of Bolshevism. I have attempted to provide the average American reader with a fair and reliable statement of the philosophy, program, and policies of the Russian Bolsheviki. In order to avoid confusion, and to keep the matter as simple and clear as possible, I have not tried to deal with the numerous manifestations of Bolshevism in other lands, but have confined myself strictly to the Russian example. With some detail—too much, some of my readers may think!—I have sketched the historical background in order that the Bolsheviki may be seen in proper perspective and fairly judged in connection with the whole revolutionary movement in Russia.

Whoever turns to these pages in the expectation of finding a sensational "exposure" of Bolshevism and the Bolsheviki will be disappointed. It has been my aim to make a deliberate and scientific study, not an *ex-parte* indictment. A great many lurid and sensational stories about the Bolsheviki have been published, the net result of which is to make the leaders of this phase of the great universal war of the classes appear as brutal and depraved monsters of iniquity. There is not a crime known to mankind, apparently, of which they have not been loudly declared to be guilty. My long experience in the Socialist movement has furnished me with too much understanding of the manner and extent to which working-class movements are abused and slandered to permit me to accept these stories as gospel truth. That experience has forced me to assume that most of the terrible stories told about the Bolsheviki are either untrue and without any foundation in fact or greatly exaggerated. The "rumor factories" in Geneva, Stockholm, Copenhagen, The Hague, and other European capitals, which were so busy during the war fabricating and exploiting for profit stories of massacres, victories, assassinations, revolutions, peace treaties, and other momentous events, which subsequent information proved never to have happened at all, seem now to have turned their attention to the Bolsheviki.

However little of a cynic one may be, it is almost impossible to refrain

4

from wondering at the fact that so many writers and journals that in the quite recent past maintained absolute silence when the czar and his minions were committing their infamous outrages against the working-people and their leaders, and that were never known to protest against the many crimes committed by our own industrial czars against our working-people and their leaders—that these writers and journals are now so violently denouncing the Bolsheviki for alleged inhumanities. When the same journals that defended or apologized for the brutal lynchings of I.W.W. agitators and the savage assaults committed upon other peaceful citizens whose only crime was exercising their lawful and moral right to organize and strike for better wages, denounce the Bolsheviki for their "brutality" and their "lawlessness" and cry for vengeance upon them, honest and sincere men become bitter and scornful.

I am not a Bolshevik or a defender of the Bolsheviki. As a Social Democrat and Internationalist of many years' standing—and therefore loyal to America and American ideals—I am absolutely opposed to the principles and practices of the Bolsheviki, which, from the very first, I have regarded and denounced as an inverted form of Czarism. It is quite clear to my mind, however, that there can be no good result from wild abuse or from misrepresentation of facts and motives. I am convinced that the stupid campaign of calumny which has been waged against the Bolsheviki has won for them the sympathy of many intelligent Americans who love fairness and hate injustice. In this way lying and abuse react against those who indulge in them.

In this study I have completely ignored the flood of newspaper stories of Bolshevist "outrages" and "crimes" which has poured forth during the past year. I have ignored, too, the remarkable collection of documents edited and annotated by Mr. Sisson and published by the United States Committee on Public Information. I do not doubt that there is much that is true in that collection of documents—indeed, there is some corroboration of some of them—but the means of determining what is true and what false are not yet available to the student. So much doubt and suspicion is reasonably and properly attached to some of the documents that the value of the whole mass is greatly impaired. To rely upon these documents to make a case against the Bolsheviki, unless and until they have been more fully investigated

5

and authenticated than they appear to have been as yet, and corroborated, would be like relying upon the testimony of an unreliable witness to convict a man serious crime.

That the Bolsheviki have been guilty of many crimes is certain. Ample evidence of that fact will be found in the following pages. They have committed many crimes against men and women whose splendid service to the Russian revolutionary movement serves only to accentuate the crimes in question. But their worst crimes have been against political and social democracy, which they have shamefully betrayed and opposed with as little scruple, and as much brutal injustice, as was ever manifested by the Romanovs. This is a terrible charge, I know, but I believe that the most sympathetic toward the Bolsheviki among my readers will, if they are candid, admit that it is amply sustained by the evidence.

Concerning that evidence it is perhaps necessary to say that I have confined myself to the following: official documents issued by the Bolshevist government; the writings and addresses of accredited Bolshevik leaders and officials—in the form in which they have been published by the Bolsheviki themselves; the declarations of Russian Socialist organizations of long and honorable standing in the international Socialist movement; the statements of equally well-known and trusted Russian Socialists, and of responsible Russian Socialist journals.

While I have indicated the sources of most of the evidence against the Bolsheviki, either in the text itself or in the foot-notes and references, I have not thought it advisable to burden my pages with such foot-notes and references concerning matters of general knowledge. To have given references and authorities for all the facts summarized in the historical outlines, for example, would have been simply a show of pedantry and served only to frighten away the ordinary reader.

I have been deeply indebted to the works of other writers, among which I may mention the following: Peter Kropotkin's *Memoirs of a Revolutionist* and *Ideals and Realities of Russian Literature*; S. Stepniak's *Underground Russia*; Leo Deutsch's *Sixteen Years in Siberia*; Alexander Ular's *Russia from Within*; William English Walling's *Russia's Message*; Zinovy N. Preev's *The Russian Riddle*; Maxim Litvinov's *The Bolshevik Revolution: Its Rise and Meaning*; M.J. Olgin's *The Soul of the Russian Revolution*; A.J. Sack's *The Birth of Russian*

Democracy; E.A. Ross's *Russia in Upheaval*; Isaac Don Levine's *The Russian Revolution*; Bessie Beatty's *The Red Heart of Russia*; Louise Bryant's *Six Red Months in Russia*; Leon Trotzky's *Our Revolution* and *The Bolsheviki and World Peace*; Gabriel Domergue's *La Russe Rouge*; Nikolai Lenine's *The Soviets at Work*; Zinoviev and Lenine's *Sozialismus und Krieg*; Emile Vandervelde's *Trois Aspects de la Révolution Russe*; P.G. Chesnais's *La Révolution et la Paix* and *Les Bolsheviks*. I have also freely availed myself of the many admirable translations of official Bolshevist documents published in *The Class Struggle*, of New York, a pro-Bolshevist magazine; the collection of documents published by *The Nation*, of New York, a journal exceedingly generous in its treatment of Bolshevism and the Bolsheviki; and of the mass of material published in its excellent "International Notes" by *Justice*, of London, the oldest Socialist newspaper in the English language, I believe, and one of the most ably edited.

Grateful acknowledgment is hereby made of friendly service rendered and valuable information given by Mr. Alexander Kerensky, former Premier of Russia; Mr. Henry L. Slobodin, of New York; Mr. A.J. Sack, Director of the Russian Information Bureau in the United States; Dr. Boris Takavenko, editor of *La Russia Nuova*, Rome, Italy; Mr. William English Walling, New York; and my friend, Father Cahill, of Bennington.

Among the Appendices at the end of the volume will be found some important documents containing some contemporary Russian Socialist judgments of Bolshevism. These documents are, I venture to suggest, of the utmost possible value and importance to the student and general reader.

John Spargo,

"Nestledown,"
Old Bennnigton, Vermont,
End of January, 1919.

BOLSHEVISM

CHAPTER I

THE HISTORICAL BACKGROUND

I

For almost a full century Russia has been the theater of a great revolutionary movement. In the light of Russian history we read with cynical amusement that in 1848, when all Europe was in a revolutionary ferment, a German economist confidently predicted that revolutionary agitation could not live in the peculiar soil of Russian civilization. August Franz von Haxthausen was in many respects a competent and even a profound student of Russian politics, but he was wrong in his belief that the amount of rural communism existing in Russia, particularly the *mir*, would make it impossible for storms of revolutionary agitation to arise and stir the national life.

As a matter of historical fact, the ferment of revolution had appeared in the land of the Czars long before the German economist made his remarkably ill-judged forecast. At the end of the Napoleonic wars many young officers of the Russian army returned to their native land full of revolutionary ideas and ideals acquired in France, Italy, and Germany, and intent upon action. At first their intention was simply to make an appeal to Alexander I to grant self-government to Russia, which at one time he had seemed disposed to do. Soon they found themselves engaged in a secret conspiratory movement having for its object the overthrow of Czarism. The story of the failure of these romanticists, the manner in which the abortive attempt at revolution in December, 1825, was suppressed, and how the leaders were punished by Nicholas I—these things are well known to most students of Russian history. The Decembrists, as they came to be called, failed, as they were bound to do, but it would be a mistake to suppose that their efforts were altogether vain. On the contrary, their inspiration was felt throughout the next thirty years and was reflected in the literature of the period. During that period Russian literature was tinged with the faith in social regeneration held by most of the cultured intellectual classes. The Decembrists were the spiritual progenitors of the Russian revolutionary movement of our time. In the writings of Pushkin—himself a Decembrist—Lermontoff, Gogol, Turgeniev, Dostoyevsky, and many others less well known, the influence of the Decembrist movement is clearly manifested.

If we are to select a single figure as the founder of the modern social revolutionary movement in Russia, that title can be applied to Alexander Herzen with greater fitness than to any other. His influence upon the movement during many years was enormous. Herzen was half-German, his mother being German. He was born at Moscow in 1812, shortly before the French occupation of the city. His parents were very rich and he enjoyed the advantages of a splendid education, as well as great luxury. At twenty-two years of age he was banished to a small town in the Urals, where he spent six years, returning to Moscow in 1840. It is noteworthy that the offense for which he had been sent into exile was the singing of songs in praise of the Decembrist martyrs. This occurred at a meeting of one of the "Students' Circles" founded by Herzen for the dissemination of revolutionary Socialist ideals among the students.

Upon his return to Moscow in 1840 Herzen, together with Bakunin and other friends, again engaged in revolutionary propaganda and in 1842 he was again exiled. In 1847, through the influence of powerful friends, he received permission to leave Russia for travel abroad. He never again saw his native land, all the remaining years of life being spent in exile. After a tour of Italy, Herzen arrived in Paris on the eve of the Revolution of 1848, joining there his friends, Bakunin and Turgeniev, and many other revolutionary leaders. It was impossible for him to participate actively in the 1848 uprising, owing to the activity of the Paris police, but he watched the Revolution with the profoundest sympathy. And when it failed and was followed by the terrible reaction his distress was almost unbounded. For a brief period he was the victim of the most appalling pessimism, but after a time his faith returned and he joined with Proudhon in issuing a radical revolutionary paper, *L'Ami du Peuple*, of which, Kropotkin tells us in his admirable study of Russian literature, "almost every number was confiscated by the police of Napoleon the Third." The paper had a very brief life, and Herzen himself was soon expelled from France, going to Switzerland, of which country he became a citizen.

In 1857 Herzen settled in London, where he published for some years a remarkable paper, called *Kolokol (The Bell)*, in which he exposed the iniquities and shortcomings of Czarism and inspired the youth of Russia with his revolutionary ideals. The paper had to be smuggled into Russia, of course, and the manner in which the smuggling was done is one of the most absorbing stories in all the tragic history of the vast land of the Czars. Herzen was a charming writer and a keen thinker, and it is impossible to exaggerate the extent of his influence. But when the freedom of the serfs, for which he so vigorously contended, was promulgated by Alexander II, and other extensive reforms were granted, his influence waned. He died in 1870 in Switzerland.

II

Alexander II was not alone in hoping that the Act of Liberation would usher in a new era of prosperity and tranquillity for Russia. Many of the most radical of the Intelligentsia, followers of Herzen, believed that Russia was destined to outstrip the older nations of western Europe in its democracy and its culture. It was not long before disillusionment came: the serfs were set free, but the manner in which the land question had been dealt with made their freedom almost a mockery. As a result there were numerous uprisings of peasants—riots which the government suppressed in the most sanguinary manner. From that time until the present the land question has been the core of the Russian problem. Every revolutionary movement has been essentially concerned with giving the land to the peasants.

Within a few months after the liberation of the serfs the revolutionary unrest was so wide-spread that the government became alarmed and instituted a policy of vigorous repression. Progressive papers, which had sprung up as a result of the liberal tendencies characterizing the reign of Alexander II thus far, were suppressed and many of the leading writers were imprisoned and exiled. Among those thus punished was that brilliant writer, Tchernyshevsky, to whom the Russian movement owes so much. His *Contemporary Review* was, during the four critical years 1858-62 the principal forum for the discussion of the problems most vital to the life of Russia. In it the greatest leaders of Russian thought discussed the land question, co-operation, communism, popular education, and similar subjects. This served a twofold purpose: in the first place, it brought to the study of the pressing problems of the time the ablest and best minds of the country; secondly, it provided these Intellectuals with a bond of union and stimulus to serve the poor and the oppressed. That Alexander II had been influenced to sign the Emancipation Act by Tchernyshevsky and his friends did not cause the authorities to spare Tchernyshevsky when, in 1863, he engaged in active Socialist propaganda. He was arrested and imprisoned in a fortress, where he wrote the novel which has so profoundly influenced two generations of discontented and protesting Russians—*What is to Be Done?* In form a novel of thrilling interest, this work was really an elaborate treatise upon Russian social conditions. It dealt with the vexed problems of marriage and divorce, the land question, co-operative production, and other similar matters, and the solutions it suggested for these problems became widely accepted as the program of revolutionary Russia. Few books in any literature have ever produced such a profound impression, or exerted as much influence upon the life of a nation. In the following year, 1864, Tchernyshevsky was exiled to hard labor in Siberia, remaining there until 1883, when he returned to Russia. He lived only six years longer, dying in 1889.

The attempt made by a young student to assassinate Alexander II, on April 4, 1866, was seized upon by the Czar and his advisers as an excuse for instituting a policy of terrible reaction. The most repressive measures were taken against the Intelligentsia and all the liberal reforms which had been introduced were practically destroyed. It was impossible to restore serfdom, of course, but the condition of the peasants without land was even worse than if they had remained serfs. Excessive taxation, heavy redemption charges, famine, crop failures, and other ills drove the people to desperation. Large numbers of students espoused the cause of the peasants and a new popular literature appeared in which the sufferings of the people were portrayed with fervor and passion. In 1868-69 there were numerous demonstrations and riots by way of protest against the reactionary policy of the government.

It was at this time that Michael Bakunin, from his exile in Switzerland, conspired with Nechaiev to bring about a great uprising of the peasants, through the Society for the Liberation of the People. Bakunin advised the students to leave the universities and to go among the people to teach them and, at the same time, arouse them to revolt. It was at this time, too, that Nicholas Tchaykovsky and his friends, the famous Circle of Tchaykovsky, began to distribute among students in all parts of the Empire books dealing with the condition of the peasants and proposing remedies therefor. This work greatly influenced the young Intelligentsia, but the immediate results among the peasants were not very encouraging. Even the return from Switzerland, by order of the government, of hundreds of students who were disciples of Bakunin and Peter Lavrov did not produce any great success.

Very soon a new organization appeared. The remnant of the Circle Tchaykovsky, together with some followers of Bakunin, formed a society called the Land and Freedom Society. This society, which was destined to exert a marked influence upon revolutionary Russia, was the most ambitious revolutionary effort Russia had known. The society had a constitution and a carefully worked out program. It had one special group to carry on propaganda among students; another to agitate among the peasants; and a third to employ armed force against the government and against those guilty of treachery toward the society. The basis of the society was the conviction that Russia needed an economic revolution; that only an economic revolution, starting with the producers, could overthrow Czarism and establish the ideal state of society.

The members of this Land and Freedom Society divided their work into four main divisions: (1) Agitation—passive and active. Passive agitation included strikes, petitions for reforms, refusal to pay taxes, and so on. Active agitation meant riots and uprisings. (2) Organization—the formation of a fighting force prepared to bring about a general uprising. (3) Education—the spreading of revolutionary knowledge and ideas, a continuation of the work of the Tchaykovsky Circle. (4) Secularization—the carrying on of systematic work against the Orthodox Church through special channels. One of the early leaders of this society was George Plechanov, who later founded the

13

Russian Social Democracy and gave to the Russian revolutionary movement its Marxian character, inspiring such men as Nikolai Lenine and Leon Trotzky, among many others. The society did not attain any very great amount of success in its efforts to reach the peasants, and it was that fact more than any other which determined Plechanov's future course.

III

When the failure of the Land and Freedom methods became evident, and the government became more and more oppressive, desperate individuals and groups resorted to acts of terrorism. It was thus that Vera Zasulich attempted the assassination of the infamous Chief of Police Trepov. The movement to temper Czarism by assassination systematically pursued was beginning. In 1879 the Land and Freedom Society held a conference for the purpose of discussing its program. A majority favored resorting to terroristic tactics; Plechanov and a few other well-known revolutionists were opposed—favoring the old methods. The society split, the majority becoming known as the Will of the People and adopting a terroristic program. This organization sentenced Czar Alexander II to death and several unsuccessful attempts were made to carry out the sentence. The leaders believed that the assassination of the Czar would give rise to a general revolution throughout the whole of Russia. In February, 1880, occurred the famous attempt to blow up the Winter Palace. For a time it seemed that the Czar had learned the lesson the Will of the People sought to teach him, and that he would institute far-reaching reforms. Pursuing a policy of vacillation and fear, however, Alexander II soon fell back into the old attitude. On March 1, 1881, a group of revolutionists, among them Sophia Perovskaya, made another attempt upon his life, succeeding, at first, only in damaging the bottom of the Czar's carriage and wounding a number of Cossack soldiers. "Thank God, I am untouched," said the Czar, in response to the inquiry of an officer of his guard. "It's too soon to thank God!" cried N.I. Grinevitsky, hurling a bomb at the Czar. Within a short time Alexander II and his assailant were both dead.

The assassination of Alexander II was a tragic event for Russia. On the very morning of his death the ill-fated monarch had approved a plan for extensive reforms presented by the liberal Minister, Loris-Melikoff. It had been decided to call a conference three days later and to invite a number of well-known public men to co-operate in introducing the reforms. These reforms would not have been far-reaching enough to satisfy the revolutionists, but they would certainly have improved the situation and given Russia a new hope. That hope died with Alexander II. His son, Alexander III, had always been a pronounced reactionary and had advised his father against making any concessions to the agitators. It was not surprising, therefore, that he permitted himself to be advised against the liberals by the most reactionary bureaucrats in the Empire, and to adopt the most oppressive policies.

The new Czar was greatly influenced by his former tutor, the reactionary bureaucrat Pobiedonostzev. At first it was believed that out of respect for his father's memory Alexander III would carry out the program of reforms formulated by Loris-Melikoff, as his father had promised to do. In a Manifesto issued on the 29th of April, 1881, Alexander III promised to do this, but in the same document there were passages which could only be interpreted as meaning that all demands for constitutional reform would be resisted and Absolutism upheld at all cost. Doubtless it was due to the influence of Pobiedonostzev, Procurator of the Holy Synod, that Alexander III soon abandoned all intention of carrying out his father's wishes in the matter of reform and instituted such reactionary policies that the peasants feared that serfdom was to be restored. A terrible persecution of the Jews was begun, lasting for several years. The Poles, too, felt the oppressive hand of Pobiedonostzev. The latter was mastered by the Slavophil philosophy that the revolutionary unrest in Russia was traceable to the diversity of races, languages, and religions. He believed that Nihilism, Anarchism, and Socialism flourished because the people were cosmopolitan rather than nationalistic in experience and feeling, and that peace and stability could come only from the persistent and vigorous development of the three principles of Nationality, Orthodoxy, and Autocracy as the basis of the state.

In this doctrine we have the whole explanation of the reactionary policy of Alexander III. In the Manifesto of April 29th was announced the Czar's determination to strengthen and uphold autocracy. That was the foundation stone. To uphold orthodoxy was the next logical necessity, for autocracy and orthodoxy were, in Russia, closely related. Hence the non-orthodox sects—such as the Finnish Protestants, German Lutherans, Polish Roman Catholics, the Jews, and the Mohammedans—were increasingly restricted in the observance of their religion. They might not build new places of worship; their children could not be educated in the faith of their parents. In many cases children were taken away from their parents in order to be sent to schools where they would be inculcated with the orthodox faith. In a similar way, every attempt was made to suppress the use of languages other than Russian.

Along with this attempt to force the whole population into a single mold went a determined resistance to liberalism in all its forms. All this was accompanied by a degree of efficiency in the police service quite unusual in Russia, with the result that the terroristic tactics of the Will of the People party were unavailing, except in the cases of a few minor officials. Plots to assassinate the Czar were laid, but they were generally betrayed to the police. The most serious of these plots, in March, 1887, led to the arrest of all the conspirators.

In the mean time there had appeared the first definite Marxian Social Democratic group in Russia. Plechanov, Vera Zasulich, Leo Deutsch, and other Russian revolutionists in Switzerland formed the organization known as the Group for the Emancipation of Labor. This organization was based upon the principles and tactics of Marxian Socialism and sought to create a purely proletarian movement. As we have seen, when revolutionary terrorism was at its height Plechanov and his disciples had proclaimed its futility and pinned their faith to the nascent class of industrial wage-workers. In the early 'eighties this class was so small in Russia that it seemed to many of the best and clearest minds of the revolutionary movement quite hopeless to rely upon it. Plechanov was derided as a mere theorist and closet philosopher, but he never wavered in his conviction that Socialism must come in Russia as the natural outcome of capitalist development. By means of a number of scholarly polemics against the principles and tactics of the Will of the People party, Plechanov gathered to his side of the controversy a group of very brilliant and able disciples, and so laid the basis for the Social Democratic Labor party. With the relatively rapid expansion of capitalism, beginning with the year 1888, and the inevitable increase of the city proletariat, the Marxian movement made great progress. A strong labor-union movement and a strong political Socialist movement were thus developed side by side.

At the same time there was a revival of terrorism, the one available reply of the oppressed to brutal autocracy. While the Marxian movement made headway among the industrial workers, the older terroristic movement made headway among the peasants. Various groups appeared in different parts of the country. When Alexander III died, at the end of 1894, both movements had developed considerable strength. Working in secret and subject to terrible measures of repression, their leaders being constantly imprisoned and exiled, these two wings of the Russian revolutionary movement were gathering strength in preparation for an uprising more extensive and serious than anything that had hitherto been attempted.

Whenever a new Czar ascended the throne in Russia it was the fashion to hope for some measure of reform and for a degree of liberality. Frequently, as in the case of Alexander III, all such hopes were speedily killed, but repeated experiences of the kind did not prevent the birth of new hopes with the death of successive Czars. When, therefore, Alexander III was succeeded by his son, Nicholas II, liberal Russia expectantly awaited the promulgation of constitutional reforms. In this they were doomed to disappointment, just as they had been on the occasion of the accession of the new Czar's immediate predecessor. Nicholas II was evidently going to be quite as reactionary as his father was. This was made manifest in a number of ways. When a deputation from one of the zemstvos, which congratulated him upon his ascension to the throne, expressed the hope that he would listen to "the voice of the people and the expression of its desires," the reply of the new Czar was a grim warning of what was to come. Nicholas II told the zemstvos that he intended to follow the example of his father and uphold the principles of Absolutism, and that any thought of participation by the zemstvos or other organizations of the people in state affairs was a senseless dream. More significant still, perhaps, was the fact that the hated Pobiedonostzev was retained in power.

The revolutionists were roused as they had not been for a decade or more. Some of the leaders believed that the new reign of reaction would prove to be the occasion and the opportunity for bringing about a union of all the revolutionary forces, Anarchists and Socialists alike, peasants and

17

industrial workers. This hope was destined to fail, but there was an unmistakable revolutionary awakening. In the latter part of January, 1895, an open letter to Nicholas II was smuggled into the country from Switzerland and widely distributed. It informed the Czar that the Socialists would fight to the bitter end the hateful order of things which he was responsible for creating, and menacingly said, "It will not be long before you find yourself entangled by it."

IV

In one respect Nicholas II differed from Alexander III—he was by nature more humane and sentimental. Like his father, he was thoroughly dominated by Pobiedonostzev's theory that Russia, in order to be secure and stable, must be based upon Nationality, Orthodoxy, and Autocracy. He wanted to see Holy Russia homogeneous and free from revolutionary disturbances. But his sensitive nature shrank from the systematic persecution of the non-orthodox sects and the Jews, and he quietly intimated to the officials that he would not approve its continuance. At the same time, he was not willing to face the issue squarely and openly announce a change of policy or restore religious freedom. That would have meant the overthrow of Pobiedonostzev and the Czar's emancipation from his sinister influence, and for that Nicholas II lacked the necessary courage and stamina. Cowardice and weakness of the will characterized his reign from the very beginning.

When the officials, in obedience to their ruler's wishes, relaxed the severity which had marked the treatment of the Jews and the non-orthodox Christian sects, the change was soon noted by the victims and once more there was a revival of hope. But the efforts of the Finns to secure a modification of the Russification policy were quite fruitless. When a deputation was sent from Finland to represent to the Czar that the rights and privileges solemnly reserved to them at the time of the annexation were being denied to the people of Finland, Nicholas II refused to grant the deputation an audience. Instead of getting relief, the people of Finland soon found that the oppression steadily increased. It was evident that Finnish nationality was to be crushed out, if possible, in the interest of Russian homogeneity.

It soon became apparent, moreover, that Pobiedonostzev was to enjoy even more power than he had under Alexander III. In proportion as the character of Nicholas II was weaker than that of his father, the power of the Procurator of the Holy Synod was greater. And there was a superstitious element in the mentality of the new Czar which Pobiedonostzev played upon with infinite cunning. He ruled the weak-willed Czar and filled the ministries with men who shared his views and upon whom he could rely. Notwithstanding the Czar's expressed wishes, he soon found ways and means to add to the persecutions of the Jews and the various non-orthodox Christian sects. In his determination to hammer the varied racial groups into a homogeneous nation, he adopted terrible measures and so roused the hatred of the Finns, Armenians, Georgians, and other subject peoples, stirring among them passionate resentment and desire for revolutionary action. It is impossible to conceive of a policy more dangerous to the dynasty than was conceived and followed by this fanatical Russophil. The Poles were persecuted and forced, in sheer despair, and by self-interest, into the revolutionary movement. Armenians were persecuted and their church lands and church funds confiscated; so they, too, were forced into the revolutionary current.

Worse than all else was the cruel persecution of the Jews. Not only were they compelled to live within the Pale of Settlement, but this was so reduced that abominable congestion and poverty resulted. Intolerable restrictions were placed upon the facilities for education in the secondary schools, the gymnasia, and in the universities. It was hoped in this way to destroy the intellectual leadership of the Jews. Pogroms were instigated, stirring the civilized world to protest at the horrible outrages. The Minister of the Interior, Von Plehve, proclaimed his intention to "drown the Revolution in Jewish blood," while Pobiedonostzev's ambition was "to force one-third of the Jews to conversion, another third to emigrate"—to escape persecution. The other third he expected to die of hunger and misery. When Leo Tolstoy challenged these infamies, and called upon the civilized world on behalf of the victims, the Holy Synod denounced Tolstoy and his followers as a sect "especially dangerous for the Orthodox Church and the state." Later, in 1900, the Holy Synod excommunicated Tolstoy from the Orthodox Church.

The fatal logic of fanatical fury led to attacks upon the zemstvos. These local organizations had been instituted in 1864, by Alexander II, in the liberal years of his reign. Elected mainly by the landlords and the peasants, they were a vital part of the life of the nation. Possessing no political powers or functions, having nothing to do with legislation, they were important agencies of local government. The representatives of each county constituted a county-zemstvo and the representatives elected by all the county-zemstvos in a province constituted a province-zemstvo. Both types concerned themselves with much the same range of activities. They built roads and telegraph stations; they maintained model farms and agricultural experiment stations similar to those maintained by our state governments. They maintained schools, bookstores, and libraries: co-operative stores; hospitals and banks. They provided the peasants with cheap credit, good seeds, fertilizers, agricultural implements, and so forth. In many cases they provided for free medical aid to the peasants. In some instances they published newspapers and magazines.

It must be remembered that the zemstvos were the only representative public bodies elected by any large part of the people. While the suffrage was quite undemocratic, being so arranged that the landlords were assured a majority over the peasants at all times, nevertheless they did perform a great democratic service. But for them, life would have been well-nigh impossible for the peasant. In addition to the services already enumerated, these civic bodies were the relief agencies of the Empire, and when crop failures brought famine to the peasants it was always the zemstvos which undertook the work of relief. Hampered at every point, denied the right to control the schools they created and maintained, inhibited by law from discussing political questions, the zemstvos, nevertheless, became the natural channels for the spreading of discontent and opposition to the régime through private communication and discussion.

To bureaucrats of the type of Pobiedonostzev and Von Plehve, with their fanatical belief in autocracy, these organizations of the people were so many plague spots. Not daring to suppress them altogether, they determined to restrict them at every opportunity. Some of the zemstvos were suspended and disbanded for certain periods of time. Individual members were exiled for utterances which Von Plehve regarded as dangerous. The power of the zemstvos themselves was lessened by taking from them such important functions as the provisioning of famine-stricken districts and by limiting in the most arbitrary manner the amount of the budget permitted to each zemstvo. Since every decision of the zemstvos was subject to veto by the governors of the respective provinces, the government had at all times a formidable weapon at hand to use in its fight against the zemstvos. This weapon Von Plehve used with great effect; the most reasonable actions of the zemstvos were vetoed for no other reason than hatred of any sort of representative government.

V

The result of all this was to drive the zemstvos toward the revolutionary movements of the peasants and the city workers. That the zemstvos were not naturally inclined to radicalism and revolution needs no demonstration. Economic interest, tradition, and environment all conspired to keep these popular bodies conservative. Landowners were always in the majority and in general the zemstvos reflected the ideas and ideals of the enlightened wealthy and cultivated classes. The peasant representatives in the zemstvos were generally peasants of the most successful and prosperous type, hating the revolutionists and all their works. By means of a policy incredibly insane these conservatively inclined elements of the population were goaded to revolt. The newspapers and magazines of the zemstvos became more and more critical of the government, more and more outspoken in denunciation of existing conditions. Presently, the leaders of the zemstvos followed the example of the revolutionists and held a secret convention at which a program for common action was agreed upon. Thus they were resorting to illegal methods, exactly as the Socialists had done. Finally, many of the liberal zemstvo leaders formed themselves into a political party—the Union of Liberation—with a special organ of its own, called *Emancipation*. This organ, edited by the brilliant and courageous Peter Struve, was published in Stuttgart, Germany, and, since its circulation in Russia was forbidden, it had to be smuggled into the country and secretly circulated, just as the revolutionary Socialist journals were. Thus another bond was established between two very different movements.

As was inevitable, revolutionary terrorism enormously increased. In the cities the working-men were drawn mainly into the Social Democratic

Working-men's party, founded by Plechanov and others in 1898, but the peasants, in so far as they were aroused at all, rallied around the standard of the Socialist-Revolutionists, successors to the Will of the People party. This party was peculiarly a party of the peasants, just as the party of Plechanov was peculiarly a party of industrial workers. It emphasized the land question above all else. It naturally scorned the view, largely held by the Marxists in the other party, that Russia must wait until her industrial development was perfected before attempting to realize Socialism. It scorned the slow, legalistic methods and resolutely answered the terrorism of Czarism by a terrorism of the people. It maintained a special department for carrying on this grim work. Its Central Committee passed sentences of death upon certain officials, and its decrees were carried out by the members of its Fighting Organization. To this organization within the party belonged many of the ablest and most consecrated men and women in Russia.

A few illustrations will suffice to make clear the nature of this terroristic retaliation: In March, 1902, Sypiagin, the Minister of the Interior, was shot down as he entered his office by a member of the Fighting Organization, Stephen Balmashev, who was disguised as an officer. Sypiagin had been duly sentenced to death by the Central Committee. He had been responsible for upward of sixty thousand political arrests and for the suffering of many exiles. Balmashev went to his death with heroic fortitude. In May, 1903, Gregory Gershuni and two associates executed the reactionary Governor of Ufa. Early in June, 1904, Borikov, Governor-General of Finland, was assassinated by a revolutionist. A month later, July 15th, the infamous Von Plehve, who had been judged by the Central Committee and held responsible for the Kishinev pogrom, was killed by a bomb thrown under the wheels of his carriage by Sazanov, a member of the Fighting Force. The death of this cruel tyrant thrilled the world. In February, 1905, Ivan Kaliaiev executed the death sentence which had been passed upon the ruthless Governor-General of Moscow, the Grand-Duke Serghei Alexandrovich.

There was war in Russia—war between two systems of organized terrorism. Sometimes the Czar and his Ministers weakened and promised concessions, but always there was speedy reaction and, usually, an increased vigor of oppression. The assassination of Von Plehve, however, for the first time really weakened the government. Czarism was, in fact, already toppling. The new Minister of the Interior, Von Plehve's successor, Prince Svyatpolk-Mirski, sought to meet the situation by a policy of compromise. While he maintained Von Plehve's methods of suppressing the radical organizations and their press, and using provocative agents to entrap revolutionary leaders, he granted a certain degree of freedom to the moderate press and adopted a relatively liberal attitude toward the zemstvos. By this means he hoped to avert the impending revolution.

Taking advantage of the new conditions, the leaders of the zemstvos organized a national convention. This the government forbade, but it had lost much of its power and the leaders of the movement ignored the order and proceeded to hold the convention. At this convention, held at St. Petersburg, November 6, 1904, attended by many of the ablest lawyers, doctors, professors, scientists, and publicists in Russia, a resolution was adopted demanding that the government at once call representatives of the people together for the purpose of setting up a constitutional government in Russia. It was a revolutionary act, a challenge to the autocracy, which the latter dared not accept. On the contrary, in December the Czar issued an ambiguous ukase in which a number of concessions and reforms were promised, but carefully avoiding the fundamental issues at stake.

VI

Meanwhile the war with Japan, unpopular from the first, had proved to be an unbroken series of military defeats and disasters for Russia. From the opening of the war in February to the end of the year the press had been permitted to publish very little real news concerning it, but it was not possible to hide for long the bitter truth. Taxes mounted higher and higher, prices rose, and there was intense suffering, while the loss of life was enormous. News of the utter failure and incompetence of the army and the navy seeped through. Here was Russia with a population three times as large as that of Japan, and with an annual budget of two billions as against Japan's paltry sixty millions, defeated at every turn. What did this failure signify? In the first place, it signified the weakness and utter incompetence of the régime. It meant that imperialist expansion, with a corresponding strengthening of the old régime, was out of the question. Most intelligent Russians, with no lack of real patriotism, rejoiced at the succession of defeats because it proved to the masses the unfitness of the bureaucracy.

It signified something else, also. There were many who remembered the scandals of the Turkish War, in 1877, when Bessarabia was recovered. At that time there was a perfect riot of graft, corruption, and treachery, much of which came under the observation of the zemstvos of the border. High military officials trafficked in munitions and food-supplies. Food intended for the army was stolen and sold—sometimes, it was said, to the enemy. Materials were paid for, but never delivered to the army at all. The army was demoralized and the Turks repulsed the Russians again and again. Now similar stories began to be circulated. Returning victims told stories of brutal treatment of the troops by officers; of wounded and dying men neglected; of lack of hospital care and medical attention. They told worse stories, too, of open treachery by military officials and others; of army supplies stolen; of shells ordered which would fit no guns the Russian army ever had, and so on. It was suggested, and widely believed, that Germany had connived at the systematic corruption of the Russian bureaucracy and the Russian army, to serve its own imperialistic and economic ends.

Such was the state of Russia at the end of the year 1904. Then came the tragic events of January, 1905, which marked the opening of the Revolution. In order to counteract the agitation of the Social Democrats among the city workers, and the formation by them of trades-unions, the government had caused to be formed "legal" unions—that is, organizations of workmen approved by the government. In order to give these organizations some semblance to real labor-unions, and thereby the better to deceive the workers, strikes were actually inspired by agents of the government from time to time. On more than one occasion strikes thus instigated by the government spread beyond control and caused great alarm. The Czar and his agents were playing with fire.

Among such unions was the Gathering of Industrial Working-men of St. Petersburg, which had for its program such innocent and non-revolutionary objects as "sober and reasonable pastimes, aimed at physical, intellectual, and moral improvement; strengthening of Russian national ideas; development of sensible views concerning the rights and

24

duties of working-men and improvement of labor conditions and mutual assistance." It was founded by Father Gapon, who was opposed to the revolutionary movement, and was regarded by the Socialists as a Czarist tool.

On January 3d—Russian calendar—several thousand men belonging to the Gathering of Industrial Workin-gmen of St. Petersburg went out on strike. By the 6th the strike had assumed the dimensions of a general strike. It was estimated that on the latter date fully one hundred and forty thousand men were out on strike, practically paralyzing the industrial life of the city. At meetings of the strikers speeches were made which had as much to do with the political demands for constitutional government as with the original grievances of the strikers. The strike was fast becoming a revolution. On the 9th Father Gapon led the hosts to the Winter Palace, to present a petition to the Czar asking for reforms. The text of the petition was widely circulated beforehand. It begged the Czar to order immediately "that representatives of all the Russian land, of all classes and groups, convene." It outlined a moderate program which had the support of almost the entire nation with the exception of the bureaucracy:

Let every one be equal and free in the right of election; order to this end that election for the Constituent Assembly be based on general, equal, direct, and secret suffrage. This is our main request; in it and upon it everything is founded; this is the only ointment for our painful wounds; and in the absence of this our blood will continue to flow constantly, carrying us swiftly toward death.

But this measure alone cannot remedy all our wounds. Many others are necessary, and we tell them to you, Sire, directly and openly, as to our Father. We need:

I. *Measures to counteract the ignorance and legal oppression of the Russian people*:

(1) Personal freedom and inviolability, freedom of speech and the press, freedom of assemblage, freedom in religious affairs;

(2) General and compulsory public education at the expense of the state;

(3) Responsibility of the Ministers to the people, and guarantees of lawfulness in administration;

(4) Equality before the law for all without exemption;

(5) Immediate rehabilitation of those punished for their convictions.

(6) Separation of the Church from the state.

II. Measures against the poverty of the people:

(1) Abolition of indirect taxes and introduction of direct income taxes on a progressive scale;

(2) Abolition of the redemption payments, cheap credit, and gradual transferring of the land to the people;

(3) The orders for the naval and military Ministers should be filled in Russia and not abroad;

(4) The cessation of the war by the will of the people.

III. Measures against oppression of labor by capital:

(1) Protection of labor by legislation;

(2) Freedom of consumers' and producers' leagues and trades-unions;

(3) An eight-hour workday and a regulation of overtime;

(4) Freedom of struggle against capital (freedom of labor strikes);

(5) Participation of labor representatives in the framing of a bill concerning state insurance of working-men;

(6) Normal wages.

Those are, Sire, the principal wants with which we have come to you. Let your decree be known, swear that you will satisfy them, and you will make Russia happy and glorious, and your name will be branded in our hearts and in the hearts of our posterity for ever and ever. If, however, you will not reply to our prayer, we shall die here, on the place before your palace. We have no other refuge and no other means. We have two roads before us, one to freedom and happiness, the other to the grave. Tell us, Sire, which, and we will follow obediently, and if it be the road of death, let our lives be a sacrifice for suffering-wearied Russia. We do not regret the sacrifice; we bring it willingly.

Led on by the strange, hypnotic power of the mystical Father Gapon, who was clad in the robes of his office, tens of thousands of working-people marched that day to the Winter Palace, confident that the Czar would see them, receive their petitions, and harken to their prayers. It was not a revolutionary demonstration in the accepted sense of that term; the marchers did not carry red flags nor sing Socialist songs of revolt. Instead, they bore pictures of the Czar and other members of the royal family and sang "God

Save the Czar" and other well-known religious hymns. No attempt was made to prevent the procession from reaching the square in front of the Winter Palace. Suddenly, without a word of warning, troops appeared from the courtyards, where they were hidden, and fired into the crowded mass of human beings, killing more than five hundred and wounding nearly three thousand. All who were able to do so turned and fled, among them Father Gapon.

Bloody Sunday, as the day is known in Russian annals, is generally regarded as the beginning of the First Revolution. Immediately people began to talk of armed resistance. On the evening of the day of the tragedy there was a meeting of more than seven hundred Intellectuals at which the means for carrying on revolution was the topic discussed. This was the first of many similar gatherings which took place all over Russia. Soon the Intellectuals began to organize unions, ostensibly for the protection of their professional interests, but in reality for political purposes. There were unions of doctors, writers, lawyers, engineers, professors, editors, and so on. Quietly, and almost without design, there was being effected another and more important union, namely, the union of all classes against autocracy and despotism.

The Czar gave from his private purse fifty thousand rubles for the relief of the families of the victims of Bloody Sunday. On the 19th of January he received a deputation of carefully selected "loyal" working-men and delivered to them a characteristic homily, which infuriated the masses by its stupid perversion of the facts connected with the wanton massacre of Bloody Sunday. Then, at the end of the month, he proclaimed the appointment of a commission to "investigate the causes of labor unrest in St. Petersburg and its suburbs and to find means of avoiding them in the future." This commission was to consist of representatives of capital and labor. The working-men thereupon made the following demands:

(1) That labor be given an equal number of members in the commission with capital;

(2) That the working-men be permitted to freely elect their own representatives;

(3) That the sessions of the commission be open to the public;

(4) That there be complete freedom of speech for the representatives of labor in the commission;

(5) That all the working-people arrested on January 9th be released.

These demands of the working-men's organizations were rejected by the government, whereupon the workers agreed to boycott the commission and refuse to have anything to do with it. At last it became evident to the government that, in the circumstances, the commission could not accomplish any good, and it was therefore abandoned. The Czar and his advisers were desperate and vacillating. One day they would adopt a conciliatory attitude toward the workers, and the next day follow it up with fresh measures of repression and punishment.

Little heeding the stupid charge by the Holy Synod that the revolutionary leaders were in the pay of the Japanese, the workers went on organizing and striking. All over Russia there were strikes, the movement had spread far beyond the bounds of St. Petersburg. General strikes took place in many of the large cities, such as Riga, Vilna, Libau, Warsaw, Lodz, Batum, Minsk, Tiflis, and many others. Conflicts between strikers and soldiers and police were common. Russia was aflame with revolution. The movement spread to the peasants in a most surprising manner. Numerous extensive and serious revolts of peasants occurred in different parts of Russia, the peasants looting the mansions of the landowners, and indulging in savage outbreaks of rioting.

While this was going on the army was being completely demoralized. The terrible defeat of the Russian forces by the Japanese—the foe that had been so lightly regarded—at Mukden was a crushing blow which greatly impaired the morale of the troops, both those at home and those at the front. Disaster followed upon disaster. May saw the destruction of the great Russian fleet. In June rebellion broke out in the navy, and the crew of the battle-ship *Potyamkin*, which was on the Black Sea, mutinied and hoisted the red flag. After making prisoners of their officers, the sailors hastened to lend armed assistance to striking working-men at Odessa who were in conflict with soldiers and police.

VII

It was a time of turbulent unrest and apparent utter confusion. It was not easy to discern the underlying significance and purpose of some of the most important events. On every hand there were strikes and uprisings, many of them without any sort of leadership or plan. Strikes which began over questions of wages and hours became political demonstrations in favor of a Constituent Assembly. On the other hand, political demonstrations became transformed, without any conscious effort on the part of anybody, into strikes for immediate economic betterment. There was an intense class conflict going on in Russia, as the large number of strikes for increased wages and shorter hours proved, yet the larger political struggle dwarfed and obscured the class struggle. For the awakened proletariat of the cities the struggle in which they were engaged was economic as well as political. They wisely regarded the political struggle as part of the class struggle, as Plechanov and his friends declared it to be. Yet the fact remained that the capitalist class against which the proletariat was fighting on the economic field was, for the most part, fighting against autocracy, for the overthrow of Czarism and the establishment of political democracy, as earnestly, if less violently, than the proletariat was. The reason for this was the recognition by the leading capitalists of Russia of the fact that industrial progress was retarded by the old régime, and that capitalist development requires popular education, a relatively high standard of living, political freedom, and stability and order in government. It was perfectly natural, therefore, for the great associations of manufacturers and merchants to unite in urging the government to grant extensive political reforms so long as the class conflict was merely incidental.

What had begun mainly as a class war had become the war of all classes against autocracy. Of course, in such a merging of classes there necessarily appeared many shadings and degrees of interest. Not all the social groups and classes were as radical in their demands as the organized peasants and city workers, who were the soul of the revolutionary movement. There were, broadly speaking, two great divisions of social life with which the Revolution was concerned—the political and the economic. With regard to the first there was practical unanimity; he would be a blind slave to theoretical formulæ who sought to maintain the thesis that class interests divided masses and classes here. All classes, with the exception of the bureaucracy, wanted the abolition of Czarism and Absolutism and the establishment of a constitutional government, elected by the people on a basis of universal suffrage, and directly responsible to the electorate.

Upon the economic issue there was less agreement, though all parties and classes recognized the need of extensive change. It was universally recognized that some solution of the land question must be found. There can never be social peace or political stability in Russia until that problem is settled. Now, it was easy for the Socialist groups, on the one hand, and the moderate groups, upon the other, to unite in demanding that the large estates be divided among the peasants. But while the Socialist groups—those of the peasants as well as those of city workers—demanded that the land be taken without compensation, the bourgeois elements, especially the leaders of the zemstvos, insisted that the state should pay compensation for the land taken. Judgment upon this vital question has long been embittered by the experience of the peasants with the "redemption payments" which were established when serfdom was abolished. During the period of greatest intensity, the summer of 1905, a federation of the various revolutionary peasants' organizations was formed and based its policy upon the middle ground of favoring the payment of compensation *in some cases*.

All through this trying period the Czar and his advisers were temporizing and attempting to obtain peace by means of petty concessions. A greater degree of religious liberty was granted, and a new representative body, the Imperial Duma, was provided for. This body was not to be a parliament in any real sense, but a debating society. It could *discuss* proposed legislation, but it had no powers to *enact* legislation of any kind. Absolutism was dying hard, clinging to its powers with remarkable tenacity. Of course, the concessions did not satisfy the revolutionists, not even the most moderate sections, and the net result was to intensify rather than to diminish the flame.

On the 2d of August—10th, according to the old Russian calendar—the war with Japan came to an end with the signing of the Treaty of Portsmouth. Russia had experienced humiliating and disastrous defeat at the hands of a nation far inferior in population and wealth, but infinitely superior in military capacity and morale. The news of the conditions of peace intensified the ardor and determination of the revolting Russian people and, on the other hand, added to the already great weakness of the government. September witnessed a great revival of revolutionary agitation, and by the end of the month a fresh epidemic of strikes had broken out in various parts of the country. By the middle of October the whole life of Russia, civil, industrial, and commercial, was a chaos. In some of the cities the greater part of the population had placed themselves in a state of siege, under revolutionary leadership.

On the 17th of October—Russian style—the Czar issued the famous Manifesto which acknowledged the victory of the people and the death of Absolutism. After the usual amount of pietistic verbiage by way of introduction the Manifesto said:

We make it the duty of the government to execute our firm will:

(1) To grant the people the unshakable foundations of civic freedom on the basis of real personal inviolability, freedom of conscience, of speech, of assemblage of unions.

(2) To admit now to participation in the Imperial Duma, without stopping the pending elections and in so far as it is feasible in the short time remaining before the convening of the Duma, all the classes of the population, *leaving the farther development of the principle of universal suffrage to the new legislative order.*

(3) *To establish as an unshakable rule that no law can become binding without the consent of the Imperial Duma, and that the representatives of the people must be guaranteed a real participation in the control over the lawfulness of the authorities appointed by us.*

We call upon all faithful sons of Russia to remember their duty to their fatherland, to aid in putting an end to the unprecedented disturbances, and to exert with us all their power to restore quiet and peace in our native land.

VIII

The Czar's Manifesto rang through the civilized world. In all lands it was hailed as the end of despotism and the triumph of democracy and freedom. The joy of the Russian people was unbounded. At last, after fourscore years of heroic struggle and sacrifice by countless heroes, named and nameless, the goal of freedom was attained. Men, women, and children sang in the streets to express their joy. Red flags were displayed everywhere and solemnly saluted by the officers and men of the Czar's army. But the rejoicing was premature, as the events of a few hours clearly proved. With that fatal vacillation which characterized his whole life, Nicholas II had no sooner issued his Manifesto than he surrendered once more to the evil forces by which he was surrounded and harked back to the old ways. The day following the issuance of the Manifesto, while the people were still rejoicing, there began a series of terrible pogroms. The cry went forth, "Kill the Intellectuals and the Jews!"

There had been organized in support of the government, and by its agents, bodies of so-called "patriots." These were, in the main, recruited from the underworld, a very large number of them being criminals who were released from the prison for the purpose. Officially known as the Association of the Russian People and the Association to Combat the Revolution, these organizations were popularly nicknamed the Black Hundreds. Most of the members were paid directly by the government for their services, while others were rewarded with petty official positions. The Czar himself accepted membership in these infamous organizations of hired assassins. Within three weeks after the issuance of the Manifesto more than a hundred organized pogroms took place, the number of killed amounting to nearly four thousand; the wounded to more than ten thousand, according to the most competent authorities. In Odessa alone more than one thousand persons were killed and many thousands wounded in a four-days' massacre. In all the bloody pages of the history of the Romanovs there is nothing comparable to the frightful terror of this period.

Naturally, this brutal vengeance and the deception which Nicholas II and his advisers had practised upon the people had the immediate effect of increasing the relative strength and prestige of the Socialists in the revolutionary movement as against the less radical elements. To meet such brutality and force only the most extreme measures were deemed adequate. The Council of Workmen's Deputies, which had been organized by the proletariat of St. Petersburg a few days before the Czar issued his Manifesto, now became a great power, the central guiding power of the Revolution. Similar bodies were organized in other great cities. The example set by the city workers was followed by the peasants in many places and Councils of

Peasants' Deputies were organized. In a few cases large numbers of soldiers, making common cause with these bodies representing the working class, formed Councils of Soldiers' Deputies. Here, then, was a new phenomenon; betrayed by the state, weary of the struggle to democratize and liberalize the political state, the workers had established a sort of revolutionary self-government of a new kind, entirely independent of the state. We shall never comprehend the later developments in Russia, especially the phenomenon of Bolshevism, unless we have a sympathetic understanding of these Soviets—autonomous, non-political units of working-class self-government, composed of delegates elected directly by the workers.

As the revolutionary resistance to the Black Hundreds increased, and the rapidly growing Soviets of workmen's, peasants' and soldiers' delegates asserted a constantly increasing indifference to the existing political state, the government again tried to stem the tide by making concessions. On November 3d—new style—in a vain attempt to appease the incessant demand for the release of the thousands of political prisoners, and to put an end to the forcible release of such prisoners by infuriated mobs, a partial amnesty was declared. On the 16th a sop was thrown to the peasants in the shape of a decree abolishing all the remaining land-redemption payments. Had this reform come sooner it might have had the effect of stemming the tide of revolt among the peasants, but in the circumstances it was of no avail. Early in December the press censorship was abolished by decree, but that was of very little importance, for the radical press had thrown off all its restraints, simply ignoring the censorship. The government of Nicholas II was quite as helpless as it was tyrannical, corrupt, and inefficient. The army and navy, demoralized by the defeat suffered at the hands of Japan, and especially by knowledge of the corruption in high places which made that defeat inevitable, were no longer dependable. Tens of thousands of soldiers and marines had joined with the workmen in the cities in open rebellion. Many more indulged themselves in purposeless rioting.

The organization of the various councils of delegates representing factory-workers and peasants, inevitable as it seemed to be, had one disastrous effect, the seriousness of which cannot be overstated. As we have seen, the cruel, blundering policy of the government had united all classes against it in a revolutionary movement of unexampled magnitude. Given the conditions prevailing in Russia, and especially the lack of industrial development and the corresponding numerical weakness of the industrial proletariat, it was evident that the only chance of success in the Revolution lay in the united effort of all classes against the old régime. Nothing could have better served the autocracy, and therefore injured the revolutionary cause, than the creation of a division in the ranks of the revolutionists.

This was exactly what the separate organizations of the working class accomplished. All the provocative agents of the Czar could not have contrived anything so serviceable to the reaction. *Divide et impera* has been the guiding principle of cunning despots in all ages, and the astutest advisers of Nicholas II must have grinned with Satanic glee when they realized how seriously the forces they were contending against were dividing. Stupid oppression had driven into one united force the wage-earning and wage-paying classes. Working-men and manufacturers made common cause against that stupid oppression. Now, however, as the inevitable result of the organization of the Soviets, and the predominance of these in the Revolution, purely economic issues came to the front. In proportion as the class struggle between employers and employed was accentuated the common struggle against autocracy was minimized and obscured. Numerous strikes for increased wages occurred, forcing the employers to organize resistance. Workers in one city—St. Petersburg, for example—demanded the immediate introduction of an eight-hour workday, and proclaimed it to be in force, quite regardless of the fact that longer hours prevailed elsewhere and that, given the competitive system, their employers were bound to resist a demand that would be a handicap favoring their competitors.

As might have been foreseen, the employers were forced to rely upon the government, the very government they had denounced and conspired to overthrow. The president of the Council of Workmen's Deputies of St. Petersburg, Chrustalev-Nosar, in his *History of the Council of Workmen's Deputies,* quotes the order adopted by acclamation on November 11th—new style—introducing, from November 13th, an eight-hour workday in all shops and factories "in a revolutionary way." By way of commentary, he quotes a further order, adopted November 25, repealing the former order and declaring:

The government, headed by Count Witte, *in its endeavor to break the vigor*

34

of the revolutionary proletariat, came to the support of capital, thus turning the question of an eight-hour workday in St. Petersburg into a national problem. The consequence has been that the working-men of St. Petersburg are unable now, apart from the working-men of the entire country, to realize the decree of the Council. The Council of Workmen's Deputies, therefore, deems it necessary to *stop temporarily the immediate and general establishment of an eight-hour workday by force.*

The Councils inaugurated general strike after general strike. At first these strikes were successful from a revolutionary point of view. Soon, however, it became apparent that the general strike is a weapon which can only be used effectively on rare occasions. It is impossible to rekindle frequently and at will the sacrificial passion necessary to make a successful general strike. This the leaders of the proletariat of Russia overlooked. They overlooked, also, the fact that the masses of the workers were exhausted by the long series of strikes in which they had engaged and were on the verge of starvation. The consequence was that most of the later strikes failed to accomplish anything like the ends sought.

Naturally, the government was recovering its confidence and its courage in proportion to the class divisions and antagonisms of the opposition. It once more suppressed the revolutionary press and prohibited meetings. Once more it proclaimed martial law in many cities. With all its old-time assurance it caused the arrest of the leaders of the unions of workmen and peasants, broke up the organizations and imprisoned their officers. It issued a decree which made it a crime to participate in strikes. With the full sanction of the government, as was shown by the publication of documentary evidence of unquestioned authenticity, the Black Hundreds renewed their brutality. The strong Council of Workmen's Deputies of St. Petersburg, with which Witte had dealt as though it were part of the government itself, was broken up and suppressed. Witte wanted constitutional government on the basis of the October Manifesto, but he wanted the orderly development of Russian capitalism. In this attitude he was supported, of course, by the capitalist organizations. The very men who in the summer of 1905 had demanded that the government grant the demands of the workers and so end the strikes, and who worked in unison with the workers to secure the much-desired political freedom, six months later were

35

demanding that the government suppress the strikes and exert its force to end disorder.

Recognition of these facts need not imply any lack of sympathy with the proletariat in their demands. The class struggle in modern industrial society is a fact, and there is abundant justification—the justification of necessity and of achievement—for aggressive class consciousness and class warfare. But it is quite obvious that there are times when class interests and class warfare must be set aside in favor of larger social interests. It is obviously dangerous and reactionary—and therefore wrong—to insist upon strikes or other forms of class warfare in moments of great calamity, as, for example, during disasters like the Johnstown flood and the Messina earthquake, or amid the ravages of a pestilential plague. Marx, to whom we owe the formulation of the theory of class struggle which has guided the Socialist movement, would never have questioned this important truth; he would never have supported class separatism under conditions such as those prevailing in Russia at the end of 1905. Only doctrinaires, slaves to formulæ, but blind to reality, could have sanctioned such separatism. But doctrinaires always abound in times of revolution.

By December the government was stronger than it had been at any time since the Revolution began. The zemstvos were no longer an active part of the revolutionary movement. Indeed, there had come over these bodies a great change, and most of them were now dominated by relatively reactionary landowners who, hitherto apathetic and indifferent, had been stirred to defensive action by the aggressive class warfare of the workers. Practically all the bourgeois moderates had been driven to the more or less open support of the government. December witnessed a new outburst in St. Petersburg, Moscow, and other cities. Barricades were raised in the streets in many places. In Moscow, where the most bitter and sanguinary struggles took place, more than a thousand persons were killed. The government was better prepared than the workers; the army had recovered no little of its lost morale and did not refuse to shoot down the workers as it had done on previous occasions. The strikes and insurrections were put down in bloody vengeance and there followed a reign of brutal repression indescribably horrible and savage. By way of protest and retaliation, there were individual acts of terrorism, such as the execution of the Governor of Tambov by Marie

Spiridonova, but these were of little or no avail. The First Revolution was drowned in blood and tears.

CHAPTER II

FROM REVOLUTION TO REVOLUTION

I

No struggle for human freedom was ever wholly vain. No matter how vast and seemingly complete the failure, there is always something of enduring good achieved. That is the law of progress, universal and immutable. The First Russian Revolution conformed to the law; it had failed and died in a tragic way, yet its failure was relative and it left something of substantial achievement as the foundation for fresh hope, courage, and effort. Czarism had gathered all its mighty black forces and seemed, at the beginning of 1906, to be stronger than at any time in fifty years. The souls of Russia's noblest and best sons and daughters were steeped in bitter pessimism. And yet there was reason for hope and rejoicing; out of the ruin and despair two great and supremely vital facts stood in bold, challenging relief.

The first of these facts was the new aspect of Czarism, its changed status. Absolutism as a legal institution was dead. Nothing that Nicholas II and his advisers were able to do could undo the constitutional changes effected when the imperial edict made it part of the fundamental law of the nation that "no law can become binding without the consent of the Imperial Duma," and that the Duma, elected by the people, had the right to control the actions of the officials of the government, even when such officials were appointed by the Czar himself. Absolutism was illegal now. Attempts might be made to reintroduce it, and, indeed, that was the real significance of the policy pursued by the government, but Absolutism could no longer possess the moral strength that inheres in the sanctity of law. In fighting it the Russian people now had that strength upon their side.

The second vital and hopeful fact was likewise a moral force. Absolutism with all its assumed divine prerogatives, in the person of the Czar, had declared its firm will "to grant the people the unshakable foundations of civic freedom on the basis of real personal inviolability, freedom of conscience, of speech, of assemblage and of unions." This civic freedom Absolutism had sanctioned. By that act it gave the prestige of legality to such assemblages, discussions, and publications as had always hitherto been forced to accept risks and disabilities inseparable from illegal conduct. Civic freedom had long been outlawed, a thing associated with lawlessness and crime, and so long as that condition remained many who believed in civic freedom itself, who wanted a free press, freedom of public assemblage and of conscience in matters pertaining to religion, were kept from participation in the struggle. Respect for law, as law, is deeply rooted in civilized mankind—a fact which, while it makes the task of the revolutionist hard, and at times impedes progress, is, nevertheless, of immense value to human society.

Civic freedom was not yet a fact. It seemed, as a reality, to be as far away as ever. Meetings were forbidden by officials and broken up by soldiers and police; newspapers were suppressed, as of old; labor-unions, and even the unions of the Intellectuals, were ruthlessly persecuted and treated as conspiracies against the state. All this and more was true and discouraging. Yet there was substantial gain: civic freedom as a practical fact did not exist, but civic freedom as a lawful right lived in the minds of millions of people—the greatest fact in Russia. The terms of the Manifesto of October 17th—Absolutism's solemn covenant with the nation—had not been repealed, and the nation knew that the government did not dare to repeal it. Not all the Czar's armies and Black Hundreds could destroy that consciousness of the lawful right to civic freedom. Nothing could restore the old condition. Whereas in the past the government, in suppressing the press and popular assemblages, could say to the people, "We uphold the law!" now when the government attempted these things, the people defiantly cried out, "You break the law!" Absolutism was no longer a thing of law.

Nicholas II and all his bureaucrats could not return the chicken to the egg from which it had been hatched. They could not unsay the fateful words which called into being the Imperial Duma. The Revolution had put into their souls a terrible fear of the wrath of the people. The Czar and his government had to permit the election of the Duma to proceed, and yet, conscious of the fact that the success of the Duma inevitably meant the end

39

of the old régime, they were bound, in self-protection, to attempt to kill the Duma in the hope that thereby they would kill, or at least paralyze, the Revolution itself. Thus it was, while not daring to forbid the elections for the Duma to proceed, the government adopted a Machiavellian policy.

The essentials of that policy were these: on the one hand, the Duma was not to be seriously considered at all, when it should assemble. It would be ignored, if possible, and no attention paid to any of its deliberations or attempts to legislate. A certain amount of latitude would be given to it as a debating society, a sort of safety-valve, but that was all. If this policy could not be carried out in its entirety, if, for example, it should prove impossible to completely ignore the Duma, it would be easy enough to devise a mass of hampering restrictions and regulations which would render it impotent, and yet necessitate no formal repudiation of the October Manifesto. On the other hand, there was the possibility that the Duma might be captured and made a safe ally. The suffrage upon which the elections were to be based was most undemocratic and unjust, giving to the landlords and the prosperous peasants, together with the wealthy classes in the cities, an enormous preponderance in the electorate. By using the Black Hundreds to work among the electors—bribing, cajoling, threatening, and coercing, as the occasion might require—it might be possible to bring about the election of a Duma which would be a pliant and ready tool of the government.

One of the favorite devices of the Black Hundreds was to send agents among the workers in the cities and among the peasants to discredit the Duma in advance, and to spread the idea that it would only represent the bourgeoisie. Many of the most influential Socialist leaders unfortunately preached the same doctrine. This was the natural and logical outcome of the separate action of the classes in the Revolution, and of the manner in which the proletariat had forced the economic struggle to the front during the political struggle. In the vanguard of the fight for the Duma were the Constitutional Democrats, led by Miliukov, Prince Lvov, and many prominent leaders of the zemstvos. The divorce between the classes represented by these men and the proletariat represented by the Social Democrats was absolute. It was not surprising that the leaders of the Social Democratic party should be suspicious and distrustful of the Constitutional Democrats and refuse to co-operate with them.

But many of the Social Democrats went much farther than this, and, in the name of Socialism and proletarian class consciousness, adopted the same attitude toward the Duma itself as that which the agents of the Black Hundreds were urging upon the people. Among the Socialist leaders who took this position was Vladimir Ulyanov, the great propagandist whom the world knows to-day as Nikolai Lenine, Bolshevik Prime Minister and Dictator. Lenine urged the workers to boycott the Duma and to refuse to participate in the elections in any manner whatever. At a time when only a united effort by all classes could be expected to accomplish anything, and when such a victory of the people over the autocratic régime as might have been secured by united action would have meant the triumph of the Revolution, Lenine preached separatism. Unfortunately, his influence, even at that time, was very great and his counsels prevailed with a great many Socialist groups over the wiser counsels of Plechanov and others.

It may be said, in explanation and extenuation of Lenine's course, that the boycotting of the elections was the logical outcome of the class antagonism and separatism, and that the bourgeois leaders were just as much responsible for the separatism as the leaders of the proletariat were. All this is true. It is quite true to say that wiser leadership of the manufacturing class in the critical days of 1905 would have made concessions and granted many of the demands of the striking workmen. By so doing they might have maintained unity in the political struggle. But, even if so much be granted, it is poor justification and defense of a Socialist policy to say that it was neither better nor worse, neither more stupid nor more wise, than that of the bourgeoisie! In the circumstances, Lenine's policy was most disastrous for Russia. It is not necessary to believe the charge that was made at the time and afterward that Lenine was in the pay of the government and a tool of the Black Hundreds. Subsequent incidents served to fasten grave suspicion upon him, but no one ever offered proof of corruption. In all probability, he was then, and throughout the later years, honest and sincere—a fanatic, often playing a dangerous game, unmoral rather than immoral, believing that the end he sought justified any means.

II

When the elections for the Duma were held, in March, 1906, the failure of the government's attempt to capture the body was complete. It was overwhelmingly a progressive parliament that had been elected. The Constitutional Democrats, upon a radical program, had elected the largest number of members, 178. Next came the representatives of the peasants' organizations, with a program of moderate Socialism, numbering 116. This group became known in the Duma as the Labor Group. A third group consisted of 63 representatives of border provinces, mostly advanced Liberals, called Autonomists, on account of their special interest in questions concerning local autonomy. There were only 28 avowed supporters of the government. Finally, despite the Socialist boycott of the elections, there were almost as many Socialists elected as there were supporters of the government.

Once more Russia had spoken for democracy in no uncertain voice. And once more Czarism committed the incredible folly of attempting to stem the tide of democracy by erecting further measures of autocracy as a dam. Shortly before the time came for the assembling of the newly elected Duma, the Czar's government announced new fundamental laws which limited the powers of the Duma and practically reduced it to a farce. In the first place, the Imperial Council was to be reconstituted and set over the Duma as an upper chamber, or Senate, having equal rights with the Duma. Half of the members of the Imperial Council were to be appointed by the Czar and the other half elected from universities, zemstvos, bourses, and by the clergy and the nobility. In other words, over the Duma was to be set a body which could always be so manipulated as to insure the defeat of any measure displeasing to the old régime. And the Czar reserved to himself the power to summon or dissolve the Duma at will, as well as the power to declare war and to make peace and to enter into treaties with other nations. What a farce was this considered as a fulfilment of the solemn assurances given in October, 1905!

But the reactionary madness went even farther; believing the revolutionary movement to have been crushed to such a degree that it might act with impunity, autocracy took other measures. Three days before the assembling of the Duma the Czar replaced his old Ministry by one still more reactionary. At the head of the Cabinet, as Prime Minister, he appointed the notorious reactionary bureaucrat, Goremykin. With full regard for the bloody traditions of the office, the infamous Stolypin, former Governor of Saratov,

42

was made Minister of the Interior. At the head of the Department of Agriculture, which was charged with responsibility for dealing with agrarian problems, was placed Stishinsky, a large landowner, bitterly hostile to, and hated by, the peasants. The composition of the new Ministry was a defiance of the popular will and sentiment, and was so interpreted.

The Duma opened on April 27th, at the Taurida Palace. St. Petersburg was a vast armed camp that day. Tens of thousands of soldiers, fully armed, were massed at different points in readiness to suppress any demonstrations by the populace. It was said that provocateurs moved among the people, trying to stir an uprising which would afford a pretext for action by the soldiers. The members of the Duma were first received by the Czar at the Winter Palace and addressed by him in a pompous speech which carefully avoided all the vital questions in which the Russian people were so keenly interested. It was a speech which might as well have been made by the first Czar Nicholas. But there was no need of words to tell what was in the mind of Nicholas II; that had been made quite evident by the new laws and the new Ministry. Before the Duma lay the heavy task of continuing the Revolution, despite the fact that the revolutionary army had been scattered as chaff is scattered before the winds.

The first formal act of the Duma, after the opening ceremonies were finished, was to demand amnesty for all the political prisoners. The members of the Duma had come to the Taurida Palace that day through streets crowded with people who chanted in monotonous chorus the word "Amnesty." The oldest man in the assembly, I.I. Petrunkevitch, was cheered again and again as he voiced the popular demand on behalf of "those who have sacrificed their freedom to free our dear fatherland." There were some seventy-five thousand political prisoners in Russia at that time, the flower of Russian manhood and womanhood, treated as common criminals and, in many instances, subject to terrible torture. Well might Petrunkevitch proclaim: "All the prisons of our country are full. Thousands of hands are being stretched out to us in hope and supplication, and I think that the duty of our conscience compels us to use all the influence our position gives us to see that the freedom that Russia has won costs no more sacrifices ... I think, gentlemen ... we cannot refrain just now from expressing our deepest feelings, the cry of our heart—that free Russia demands the liberation of all

43

prisoners." At the end of the eloquent appeal there was an answering cry of: "Amnesty!" "Amnesty!" The chorus of the streets was echoed in the Duma itself.

There was no lack of courage in the Duma. One of its first acts was the adoption of an address in response to the speech delivered by the Czar to the members at the reception at the Winter Palace. The address was in reality a statement of the objects and needs of the Russian people, their program. It was a radical document, but moderately couched. It demanded full political freedom; amnesty for all who had been imprisoned for political reasons or for violations of laws in restriction of religious liberty; the abolition of martial law and other extraordinary measures; abolition of capital punishment; the abolition of the Imperial Council and democratization of the laws governing elections to the Duma; autonomy for Finland and Poland; the expropriation of state and private lands in the interest of the peasants; a comprehensive body of social legislation designed to protect the industrial workers. In a word, the program of the Duma was a broad and comprehensive program of political and social democracy, which, if enacted, would have placed Russia among the foremost democracies of the world.

The boldness of the Duma program was a direct challenge to the government and was so interpreted by the Czar and his Ministers. By the reactionary press it was denounced as a conspiracy to hand the nation over to the Socialists. That it should have passed the Duma almost unanimously was an indication of the extent to which the liberal bourgeoisie represented by the Constitutional Democrats was prepared to go in order to destroy autocracy. No wonder that some of the most trusted Marxian Socialists in Russia were urging that it was the duty of the Socialists to co-operate with the Duma! Yet there was a section of the Marxists engaged in a constant agitation against the Duma, preaching the doctrine of the class struggle, but blind to the actual fact that the dominant issue was in the conflict between the democracy of the Duma and the autocracy of Czarism.

The class consciousness of the old régime was much clearer and more intelligent. The Czar refused to receive the committee of the Duma, appointed to make formal presentation of the address. Then, on May 12th, Goremykin, the Prime Minister, addressed the Duma, making answer to its demands. On behalf of the government he rebuked the Duma for its unpatriotic conduct in a speech full of studied insult and contemptuous defiance. He made it quite clear that the government was not going to grant any reforms worthy of mention. More than that, he made it plain to the entire nation that Nicholas II and his bureaucracy would never recognize the Duma as an independent parliamentary body. Thus the old régime answered the challenge of the Duma.

For seventy-two days the Duma worked and fought, seventy-two days of parliamentary history for which there is no parallel in the annals of parliamentary government. For. the sake of the larger aims before it, the Duma carried out the demands of the government that it approve certain petty measures placed before it for the formality of its approval. On the other hand, it formulated and passed numerous measures upon its own initiative and demanded that they be recognized as laws of the land. Among the measures thus adopted were laws guaranteeing freedom of assemblage; equality of all citizens before the law; the right of labor organizations to exist and to conduct strikes; reform of judicial procedure in the courts; state aid for peasants suffering from crop failure and other agrarian reforms; the abolition of capital punishment. In addition to pursuing its legislative program, the Duma members voiced the country's protest against the shortcomings of the government, subjecting the various Ministers to searching interpellation, day after day.

Not a single one of the measures adopted by the Duma received the support of the Imperial Council. This body was effectively performing the task for which it had been created. To the interpellations of the Duma the Czar's Ministers made the most insulting replies, when they happened to take any notice of them at all. All the old iniquities were resorted to by the government, supported, as always, by the reactionary press. The homes of members of the Duma were entered and searched by the police and every parliamentary right and privilege was flouted. Even the publication of the speeches delivered in the Duma was forbidden.

The Duma had from the first maintained a vigorous protest against "the infamy of executions without trial, pogroms, bombardment, and imprisonment." Again and again it had been charged that pogroms were carried out under the protection of the government, in accordance with the old policy of killing the Jews and the Intellectuals. The answer of the government was—another pogrom of merciless savagery. On June 1st, at Byalostock, upward of eighty men, women, and children were killed, many more wounded, and scores of women, young and old, brutally outraged. The Duma promptly sent a commission to Byalostock to investigate and report upon the facts, and presently the commission made a report which proved beyond question the responsibility of the government for the whole brutal and bloody business. It was shown that the inflammatory manifestos calling upon the "loyal" citizens to make the attack were printed in the office of the Police Department; that soldiers in the garrison had been told days in advance when the pogrom would take place; and that in the looting and sacking of houses and shops, which occurred upon a large scale, officers of the garrison had participated. These revelations made a profound impression in Russia and throughout Europe.

III

The Duma finally brought upon itself the whole weight of Czarism when it addressed a special appeal to the peasants of the country in which it dealt with candor and sincerity with the great agrarian problems which bore upon the peasants so heavily. The appeal outlined the various measures which the Duma had tried to enact for the relief of the peasants, and the attitude of the Czar's Ministers. The many strong peasants' organizations, and their numerous representatives in the Duma, made the circulation of this appeal an easy matter. The government could not close these channels of communication, nor prevent the Duma's strong plea for lawful rights and against lawlessness by government officials from reaching the peasants. Only one method of defense remained to the Czar and his Ministers: On July 9th, like a thunderbolt from the sky, came a new Manifesto from the Czar, dissolving the Duma. In the Manifesto all the old arrogance of Absolutism reappeared. A more striking contrast to the Manifesto of the previous October could not be readily imagined. The Duma was accused of having exceeded its rights by "investigating the actions of local authorities appointed by the Emperor," notwithstanding the fact that in the October Manifesto it had been solemnly covenanted "that the representatives of the people must be guaranteed a real participation in the control over the lawfulness of the

46

authorities appointed by us." The Duma was condemned for "finding imperfections in the fundamental laws which can be altered only by the monarch's will" and for its "overtly lawless act of appealing to the people." The Manifesto charged that the growing unrest and lawlessness of the peasants were due to the failure of the Duma to ameliorate their conditions—and this in spite of the record!

When the members of the Duma arrived at the Taurida Palace next day they found the place filled with troops who prevented their entrance. They were powerless. Some two hundred-odd members adjourned to Viborg, whence they issued an appeal to the people to defend their rights. These men were not Socialists, most of them belonging to the party of the Constitutional Democrats, but they issued an appeal to the people to meet the dissolution of the Imperial Duma by a firm refusal to pay taxes, furnish recruits for the army, or sanction the legality of any loans to the government. This was practically identical with the policy set forth in the Manifesto of the Executive Committee of the St. Petersburg Council of Workmen's Deputies at the beginning of the previous December, before the elections to the Duma. Now, however, the Socialists in the Duma—both the Social Democrats and the Socialist-Revolutionists—together with the semi-Socialist Labor Group, decided that it was not enough to appeal for passive resistance; that only an armed uprising could accomplish anything. They therefore appealed to the city proletariat, the peasants, the army, and the navy to rise in armed strength against the tyrannical régime.

Neither appeal produced any noteworthy result. The response to the Viborg appeal was far less than that which followed the similar appeal of the St. Petersburg workmen in December. The signers of the appeal were arrested, sentenced to three months' imprisonment, and deprived of their electoral rights. To the appeal of the Duma Socialists there was likewise very little response, either from city workers, peasants, soldiers, or marines. Russia was struggle-weary. The appeals fell upon the ears of a cowed and beaten populace. The two documents served only to emphasize one fact, namely, that capacity and daring to attempt active and violent resistance was still largely confined to the working-class representatives. In appealing to the workers to meet the attacks of the government with armed resistance, the leaders of the peasants and the city proletariat were ready to take their places in the vanguard of the fight. On the other hand, the signers of the Viborg appeal for passive resistance manifested no such determination or desire, though they must have known that passive resistance could only be a temporary phase, that any concerted action by the people to resist the collection of taxes and recruiting for the army would have led to attack and counter-attack-to a violent revolution.

Feeling perfectly secure, the government, while promising the election of another Duma, carried on a policy of vigorous repression of all radical and revolutionary agitation and organization. Executions without trial were almost daily commonplaces. Prisoners were mercilessly tortured, and, in many cases, flogged to death. Hundreds of persons, of both sexes, many of them simple bourgeois-liberals and not revolutionists in any sense of the word, were exiled to Siberia. The revolutionary organizations of the workers were filled with spies and provocateurs, an old and effective method of destroying their morale. In all the provinces of Russia field court martial was proclaimed. Field court martial is more drastic than ordinary court martial and practically amounts to condemnation without trial, for trials under it are simply farcical, since neither defense nor appeal is granted. Nearly five hundred revolutionists were put to death under this system, many of them without even the pretense of a trial.

The Black Hundreds were more active than ever, goaded on by the Holy Synod. Goremykin resigned as Premier and his place was taken by the unspeakably cruel and bloodthirsty Stolypin, whose "hemp neckties," as the grim jest of the masses went, circled the necks of scores of revolutionists swinging from as many gallows. There were many resorts to terrorism on the part of the revolutionists during the summer of 1906, many officials paying for the infamies of the government with their lives. How many of these "executions" were genuine revolutionary protests, and how many simple murders instigated or committed by provocative agents for the purpose of discrediting the revolutionists and affording the government excuses for fresh infamies, will perhaps never be known. Certainly, in many cases, there was no authorization by any revolutionary body.

In February, 1907, the elections for the Second Duma were held under a reign of terror. The bureaucracy was determined to have a "safe and sane" body this time, and resorted to every possible nefarious device to attain that end. Whole masses of electors whose right to vote had been established at the previous election were arbitrarily disfranchised. While every facility was given to candidates openly favoring the government, including the Octobrists, every possible obstacle was placed in the way of radical candidates, especially Socialists. The meetings of the latter were, in hundreds of cases, prohibited; in other hundreds of cases they were broken up by the Black Hundreds and the police. Many of the most popular candidates were arrested and imprisoned without trial, as were members of their campaign committees. Yet, notwithstanding all these things, the Second Duma was, from the standpoint of the government, worse than the first. The Socialists, adopting the tactics of Plechanov, against the advice of Lenine, his former pupil and disciple, had decided not to boycott the elections this time, but to participate in them. When the returns were published it was found that the Social Democrats and the Socialist-Revolutionists had each elected over sixty deputies, the total being nearly a third of the membership—455. In addition there were some ninety members in the peasants' Labor Group, which were semi-Socialist. There were 117 Constitutional Democrats. The government supporters, including the Octobrists, numbered less than one hundred.

From the first the attitude of the government toward the new Duma was one of contemptuous arrogance. "The Czar's Hangman," Stolypin, lectured the members as though they were naughty children, forbidding them to invite experts to aid them in framing measures, or to communicate with any of the zemstvos or municipal councils upon any questions whatsoever. "The Duma was not granted the right to express disapproval, reproach, or mistrust of the government," he thundered. To the Duma there was left about as much real power as is enjoyed by the "governments" of our "juvenile republics."

As a natural consequence of these things, the Second Duma paid less attention to legislation than the First Duma had done, and gave its time largely to interpellations and protests. Partly because of the absence of some of the most able leaders they had had in the First Duma, and partly to the aggressive radicalism of the Socialists, which they could only half-heartedly approve at best, the Constitutional Democrats were less influential than in the former parliament. They occupied a middle ground—always a difficult position. The real fight was between the Socialists and the reactionaries,

49

supporters of the government. Among the latter were perhaps a score of members belonging to the Black Hundreds, constituting the extreme right wing of the reactionary group. Between these and the Socialists of the extreme left the assembly was kept at fever pitch. The Black Hundreds, for the most part, indulged in violent tirades of abuse, often in the most disgusting profanity. The Socialists replied with proletarian passion and vigor, and riotous scenes were common. The Second Duma was hardly a deliberative assembly!

On June 1st Stolypin threw a bombshell into the Duma by accusing the Social Democrats of having conspired to form a military plot for the overthrow of the government of Nicholas II. Evidence to this effect had been furnished to the Police Department by the spy and provocative agent, Azev. Of course there was no secret about the fact that the Social Democrats were always trying to bring about revolt in the army and the navy. They had openly proclaimed this, time and again. In the appeal issued at the time of the dissolution of the First Duma they had called upon the army and navy to rise in armed revolt. But the betrayal of their plans was a matter of some consequence. Azev himself had been loudest and most persistent in urging the work on. Stolypin demanded that all the Social Democrats be excluded permanently from the Duma and that sixteen of them be handed over to the government for imprisonment. The demand was a challenge to the whole Duma, since it called into question the right of the Duma to determine its own membership. Obviously, if members of parliament are to be dismissed whenever an autocratic government orders it, there is an end of parliamentary government. The demand created a tremendous sensation and gave rise to a long and exciting debate. Before it was ended, however, Nicholas II ordered the Duma dissolved. On June 3d the Second Duma met the fate of its predecessor, having lasted one hundred days.

IV

As on the former occasion, arrangements were at once begun to bring about the election of another and more subservient Duma. It is significant that throughout Nicholas II and his Cabinet recognized the imperative necessity of maintaining the institution in form. They dared not abolish it, greatly as they would have liked to do so. On the day that the Duma was dissolved the Czar, asserting his divine right to enact and repeal laws at will, disregarding again the solemn assurances of the October Manifesto, by edict changed the electoral laws, consulting neither the Duma nor the Imperial Council. This new law greatly decreased the representation of the city workers and the peasants in the Duma and correspondingly increased the representation of the rich landowners and capitalists. A docile and "loyal" Duma was thus made certain, and no one was very much surprised when the elections, held in September, resulted in an immense reactionary majority. When the Third Duma met on December 14, 1907, the reactionaries were as strong as the Socialist and Labor groups had been in the previous Duma, and of the reactionaries the group of members of the Black Hundreds was a majority.

In the mean time there had been the familiar rule of brutal reaction. Most of the Social Democratic members of the Second Duma were arrested and condemned for high treason, being sent to prison and to Siberia. New laws and regulations restricting the press were proclaimed and enforced with increasing severity. By comparison with the next two years, the period from 1905 to 1907 was a period of freedom. After the election of the Third Duma the bureaucracy grew ever bolder. Books and leaflets which had been circulated openly and with perfect freedom during 1905 and 1906 were forbidden, and, moreover, their authors were arrested and sentenced to long terms of imprisonment. While the law still granted freedom of assemblage and the right to organize meetings, these rights did not exist as realities. Everywhere the Black Hundreds held sway, patronized by the Czar, who wore their emblem and refused to permit the punishment of any of their members, even though they might be found guilty by the courts.

It is not necessary to dwell upon the work of the Third Duma. This is not a history of Russia, and a detailed study of the servile parliament of Nicholas II and Stolypin would take us too far afield from our special study—the revolutionary movement. Suffice it, therefore, to say that some very useful legislation, necessary to the economic development of Russia, was enacted, and that, despite the overwhelming preponderance of reactionaries, it was not an absolutely docile body. On several occasions the Third Duma exercised the right of criticism quite vigorously, and on two or three

51

occasions acted in more or less open defiance of the wishes of the government. A notable instance of this was the legislation of 1909, considerably extending freedom of religious organization and worship, which was, however, greatly curtailed later by the Imperial Council—and then nullified by the government.

The period 1906-14 was full of despair for sensitive and aspiring souls. The steady and rapid rise in the suicide-rate bore grim and eloquent testimony to the character of those years of dark repression. The number of suicides in St. Petersburg increased during the period 1905-08 more than 400 per cent.; in Moscow about 800 per cent.! In the latter city two-fifths of the suicides in 1908 were of persons less than twenty years old! And yet, withal, there was room for hope, the soul of progress was not dead. In various directions there was a hopeful and promising growth. First among these hopeful and promising facts was the marvelous growth of the Consumers' Co-operatives. After 1905 began the astonishing increase in the number of these important organizations, which continued, year after year, right up to the Revolution of 1917. In 1905 there were 4,479 such co-operatives in Russia; in 1911 there were 19,253. Another hopeful sign was the steadily increasing literacy of the masses. Statistics upon this point are almost worthless. Russian official statistics are notoriously defective and the figures relating to literacy are peculiarly so, but the leaders of Russian Socialism have attested to the fact. In this connection it is worthy of note that, according to the most authentic official records, the number of persons subscribing to the public press grew in a single year, from 1908 to 1909, fully 25 per cent. Education and organization were going on, hand in hand.

Nor was agitation dead. In the Duma the Socialist and Labor parties and groups, knowing that they had no chance to enact their program, made the Duma a rostrum from which to address the masses throughout the nation. Sometimes, indeed, the newspapers were forbidden to print their speeches, but as a rule they were published, at least by the liberal papers, and so disseminated among the masses. In these speeches the Social Democrats, Socialist-Revolutionaries, Laborites, and more daring of the Constitutional Democrats mercilessly exposed the bureaucracy, so keeping the fires of discontent alive.

V

Of vast significance to mankind was the controversy that was being waged within the Socialist movement of Russia during these years, for this was the period in which Bolshevism was shaping itself and becoming articulate. The words "Bolsheviki" and "Bolshevism" first made their appearance in 1903, but it was not until 1905 that they began to acquire their present meaning. At the second convention of the Social Democratic party, held in 1903, the party split in two factions. The majority faction, headed by Lenine, adopted the name Bolsheviki, a word derived from the Russian word "bolshinstvo," meaning "majority." The minority faction, which followed Plechanov, though he did not formally join it, was called, in contradistinction, the "Mensheviki"—that is, the minority. No question of principle was involved in the split, the question at issue being simply whether there should be more or less centralization in the organization. There was no thought on either side of leaving the Social Democratic party. It was simply a factional division in the party itself and did not prevent loyal co-operation. Both the Bolsheviki and the Mensheviki remained Social Democrats—that is, Socialists of the school of Marx.

During the revolutionary struggle of 1905-06 the breach between the two factions was greatly widened. The two groups held utterly irreconcilable conceptions of Socialist policy, if not of Socialism as an ideal. The psychology of the two groups was radically different. By this time the Lenine faction was no longer the majority, being, in fact, a rather small minority in the party. The Plechanov faction was greatly in the majority. But the old names continued to be used. Although a minority, the Lenine faction was still called the Bolsheviki, and the Plechanov faction called the Mensheviki, despite the fact that it was the majority. Thus Bolshevism no longer connoted the principles and tactics of the majority. It came to be used interchangeably with Leninism, as a synonym. The followers of Vladimir Ulyanov continued to regard themselves as part of the Social Democratic party, its radical left wing, and it was not until after the Second Revolution, in 1917, that they manifested any desire to be differentiated from the Social Democrats.

Vladimir Ulyanov was born in 1870, at Simbirsk, in central Russia.

There is no mystery about his use of the alias, Nikolai Lenine, which he has made world-famous and by which he chooses to be known. Almost every Russian revolutionist has had to adopt various aliases for self-protection and for the protection of other Russian Socialists. Ulyanov has followed the rule and lived and worked under several aliases, and his writings under the name "Nikolai Lenine" made him a great power in the Russian Socialist movement.

Lenine's father was a governmental official employed in the Department of Public Instruction. It is one of the many anomalies of the life of the Russian Dictator that he himself belongs by birth, training, culture, and experience to the bourgeoisie against which he fulminates so furiously. Even his habits and tastes are of bourgeois and not proletarian origin. He is an Intellectual of the Intellectuals and has never had the slightest proletarian experience. As a youth still in his teens he entered the University of St. Petersburg, but his stay there was exceedingly brief, owing to a tragedy which greatly embittered his life and gave it its direction. An older brother, who was also a student in the university, was condemned to death, in a secret trial, for complicity in a terrorist plot to assassinate Alexander III. Shortly afterward he was put to death. Lenine himself was arrested at the same time as his brother, but released for lack of evidence connecting him with the affair. It is said, however, that the arrest caused his expulsion from the university. Lenine was not the only young man to be profoundly impressed by the execution of the youthful Alexander Ulyanov; another student, destined to play an important rôle in the great tragedy of revolutionary Russia, was stirred to bitter hatred of the system. That young student was Alexander Kerensky, whose father and the father of the Ulyanovs were close friends.

Lenine's activities brought him into conflict with the authorities several times and forced him to spend a good deal of time in exile. As a youth of seventeen, at the time of the execution of his brother, he was dismissed from the Law School in St. Petersburg. A few years later he was sent to Siberia for a political "crime." Upon various occasions later he was compelled to flee from the country, living sometimes in Paris, sometimes in London, but more often in Switzerland. It was through his writings mainly that he acquired the influence he had in the Russian movement. There is nothing unusual or remarkable about this, for the Social Democratic party of Russia was practically directed from Geneva. Lenine was in London when the

Revolution of 1905 broke out and caused him to hurry to St. Petersburg.

As a young man Lenine, like most of the Intelligentsia of the period, gave up a good deal of his spare time to teaching small groups of uneducated working-men the somewhat abstract and intricate theories and doctrines of Socialism. To that excellent practice, no doubt, much of Lenine's skill as a lucid expositor and successful propagandist is due. He has written a number of important works, most of them being of a polemical nature and dealing with party disputations upon questions of theory and tactics. The work by which he was best known in Socialist circles prior to his sensational rise to the Premiership is a treatise on *The Development of Capitalism in Russia*. This work made its appearance in 1899, when the Marxian Socialist movement was still very weak. In it Lenine defended the position of the Marxians, Plechanov and his group, that Russia was not an exception to the general law of capitalist development, as was claimed by the leaders of the People's party, the *Narodniki*. The book gave Lenine an assured position among the intellectual leaders of the movement, and was regarded as a conclusive defense of the position of the Plechanov group, to which Lenine belonged. Since his overthrow of the Kerensky régime, and his attempt to establish a new kind of social state in Russia, Lenine has been frequently confronted by his own earlier reasoning by those who believe his position to be contrary to the true Marxian position.

From 1903 to 1906 Lenine's views developed farther and farther away from those of his great teacher, George Plechanov. His position in the period of the First Duma can best be stated, perhaps, in opposition to the position of Plechanov and the Mensheviki. Accepting the Marxian theory of historical development, Plechanov and his followers believed that Russia must pass through a phase of capitalist development before there could be a social—as distinguished from a merely political—revolution. Certainly they believed, an intensive development of industry, bringing into existence a strong capitalist class, on the one hand, and a strong proletariat, on the other hand, must precede any attempt to create a Social Democratic state. They believed, furthermore, that a political revolution, creating a democratic constitutional system of government, must come before the social revolution could be achieved. They accepted the traditional Marxian view that the achievement of this political revolution must be mainly the task of the bourgeoisie, and that the proletariat, and especially the Socialists, should co-operate with the enlightened bourgeoisie in attaining that political revolution without which there could never be a Socialist commonwealth.

Plechanov was not blind to the dangers of compromise which must be faced in basing the policy of a movement of the masses upon this reasoning. He argued, however, that there was no choice in the matter at all; that the iron law of historical inevitability and necessity determined the matter. He pointed out that the bourgeoisie, represented by the Constitutional Democrats in the political struggle, were compelled to wage relentless war upon Absolutism, the abolition of which was as absolutely essential to the realization of their class aims as it was to the realization of the class aims of the proletariat. Hence, in this struggle, the capitalist class, as yet too weak to accomplish the overthrow of autocracy and Czarism, and the proletariat, equally dependent for success upon the overthrow of autocracy and Czarism, and equally too weak to accomplish it unaided, had to face the fact that historical development had given the two classes which were destined to wage a long conflict an immediate unity of interest. Their imperative needs at the moment were not conflicting needs, but identical ones. To divide their forces, to refuse to co-operate with each other, was to play the game of the Czar and his associates, argued Plechanov.

The Mensheviki favored participation in the Duma elections and co-operation with the liberal and radical bourgeoisie parties, in so far as might be necessary to overthrow the autocracy, and without sacrificing Socialist principles. They pointed out that this position was evidently feared by the bureaucracy far more than the position of the extremists among the Social Democrats and the Socialist-Revolutionists, who refused to consider such co-operation, and pointed to the fact that provocateurs in large numbers associated themselves with the latter in their organizations and preached the same doctrine of absolute isolation and exclusiveness.

It will be seen that the position of the Mensheviki was one of practical political opportunism, an opportunism, however, that must be sharply distinguished from what Wilhelm Liebknecht used to call "political cow-trading." No man in the whole history of international Socialism ever more thoroughly despised this species of political opportunism than George Plechanov. To those who are familiar with the literature of international

Socialism it will be unnecessary to say that Plechanov was not the man to deprecate the importance of sound theory as a guide to the formulation of party policies. For many years he was rightly regarded as one of the greatest theoreticians of the movement. Certainly there was only one other writer in the whole international movement who could be named as having an equal title to be considered the greatest Socialist theorist since Marx—Karl Kautsky.

But Plechanov[1]—like Marx himself—set reality above dogma, and regarded movement as of infinitely greater importance than theory. The Mensheviki wanted to convene a great mass convention of representatives of the industrial proletariat during the summer of 1906. "It is a class movement," they said, "not a little sectarian movement. How can there be a *class* movement unless the way is open to all the working class to participate?" Accordingly, they wanted a convention to which all the factory-workers would be invited to send representatives. There should be no doctrinal tests, the sole qualification being membership in the working class. It did not matter to the advocates of this policy whether a man belonged to the Social Democratic party or to any party; whether he called himself a revolutionist or anything else. It was, they said, a movement of the working class, not the movement of a sect within the working class.

They knew, of course, that in such a great mass movement there would probably be some theoretical confusion, more or less muddled thinking. They recognized, too, that in the great mass convention they proposed some Social Democratic formulations might be rejected and some others adopted which did not accord with the Marxian doctrines. But, quoting Marx to the effect that "One step of real movement is worth a thousand programs," they contended that if there was anything at all in the Marxian theory of progress through class struggles, and the historic rule of the working class, it must follow that, while they might make mistakes and go temporarily astray, the workers could not go far wrong, their class interests being a surer guide than any amount of intellectualism could produce.

Lenine and his friends, the Bolsheviki, bitterly opposed all this reasoning and took a diametrically opposite position upon every one of the questions involved. They absolutely opposed any sort of co-operation with bourgeois parties of any kind, for any purpose whatever. No matter how progressive a particular bourgeois party might be, nor how important the reform aimed at, they believed that Social Democrats should remain in "splendid isolation," refusing to make any distinction between more liberal and less liberal, progressive and reactionary, groups in the bourgeoisie. Trotzky, who did not at first formally join the Bolsheviki, but was a true Bolshevik in his intellectual convictions and sympathies, fully shared this view.

Now, Lenine and Trotzky were dogmatic Marxists, and as such they could not deny the contention that capitalism must attain a certain development before Socialism could be attained in Russia. Nor could they deny that Absolutism was an obstacle to the development both of capitalist industry and of Socialism. They contended, however, that the peculiar conditions in Russia, resulting from the retardation of her economic development for so long, made it both possible and necessary to create a revolutionary movement which would, at one and the same time, overthrow both autocracy and capitalism. Necessarily, therefore, their warfare must be directed equally against autocracy and all political parties of the landlord and capitalist classes. They were guided throughout by this fundamental conviction. The policy of absolute and unqualified isolation in the Duma, which they insisted the Social Democrats ought to pursue, was based upon that conviction.

VI

All this is quite clear and easily intelligible. Granted the premise, the logic is admirable. It is not so easy, however, to see why, even granting the soundness of their opposition to *co-operation* with bourgeois parties and groups in the Duma, there should be no political *competition* with them—which would seem to be logically implied in the boycott of the Duma elections. Non-participation in the elections, consistently pursued as a proletarian policy, would leave the proletariat unrepresented in the legislative body, without one representative to fight its battles on what the world universally regards as one of the most important battle-fields of civilization.

And yet, here, too, they were entirely logical and consistent—they did not believe in parliamentary government. As yet, they were not disposed to emphasize this overmuch, not, apparently, because of any lack of candor and good faith, but rather because the substitute for parliamentary government had not sufficiently shaped itself in their minds. The desire not to be confused with the Anarchists was another reason. Because the Bolsheviki and the Anarchists both oppose parliamentary government and the political state, it has been concluded by many writers on the subject that Bolshevism is simply Anarchism in another guise. This is a mistake. Bolshevism is quite different from and opposed to Anarchism. It requires strongly centralized government, which Anarchism abhors.

Parliamentary government cannot exist except upon the basis of the will of the majority. Whoever enters into the parliamentary struggle, therefore, must hope and aim to convert the majority. Back of that hope and aim must be faith in the intellectual and moral capacity of the majority. At the foundation of Bolshevist theory and practice lies the important fact that there is no such faith, and, consequently, neither the hope nor the aim to convert the majority and with its strength make the Revolution. Out of the adult population of Russia at that time approximately 85 per cent. were peasants and less than 5 per cent. belonged to the industrial proletariat. At that time something like 70 per cent. of the people were illiterate. Even in St. Petersburg—where the standard of literacy was higher than in any other city—not more than 55 per cent. of the people could sign their own names in 1905, according to the most authentic government reports. When we contemplate such facts as these can we wonder that impatient revolutionaries should shrink from attempting the task of converting a majority of the population to an intelligent acceptance of Socialism?

There was another reason besides this, however. Lenine—and he personifies Bolshevism—was, and is, a doctrinaire Marxist of the most dogmatic type conceivable. As such he believed that the new social order must be the creation of that class which is the peculiar product of modern capitalism, the industrial proletariat. To that class alone he and his followers pinned all their faith and hope, and that class was a small minority of the population and bound to remain a minority for a very long period of years. Here, then, we have the key. It cannot be too strongly stressed that the

59

Bolsheviki did not base their hope upon the working class of Russia, and did not trust it. The working class of Russia—if we are to use the term with an intelligent regard to realities—was and is mainly composed of peasants; the industrial proletariat was and is only a relatively small part of the great working class of the nation. *But it is upon that small section, as against the rest of the working class, that Bolshevism relies.*

Lenine has always refused to include the peasants in his definition of the working class. With almost fanatical intensity he has insisted that the peasant, together with the petty manufacturer and trader, would soon disappear; that industrial concentration would have its counterpart in a great concentration of landownings and agriculture; that the small peasant holdings would be swallowed up by large, modern agricultural estates, with the result that there would be an immense mass of landless agricultural wage-workers. This class would, of course, be a genuinely proletarian class, and its interests would be identical with those of the industrial proletariat. Until that time came it would be dangerous to rely upon the peasants, he urged, because their instincts are bourgeois rather than proletarian. Naturally, he has looked askance at the peasant Socialist movements, denying that they were truly Socialist at all. They could not be Socialist movements in the true sense, he contended, because they lacked the essential quality of true Socialists, namely, proletarian class consciousness.

Naturally, too, Lenine and his followers have always regarded movements which aimed to divide the land among the peasants, and so tend to give permanence to a class of petty agriculturists, as essentially reactionary. The exigencies of the struggle have forced them into some compromises, of course. For example, at first they were not willing to admit that the peasants could be admitted into their group at all, but later on they admitted some who belonged to the poorest class of peasants. Throughout, however, they have insisted that the peasant class as a whole was a class of petty bourgeoisie and that its instincts and interests would inevitably lead it to side with the bourgeoisie as against the proletariat. Of course, this is a very familiar phase of Socialist evolution in every country. It lasted in Germany many years. In Russia, however, the question assumed an importance it never had in any other country, owing to the vast preponderance of peasants in the population. Anything more un-Russian than this theorizing cannot be well conceived. It runs counter to every fact in Russian experience, to the very basis of her economic life at this stage of her history. Lenine is a Russian, but his dogmas are not Russian, but German. Bolshevism is the product of perverted German scholasticism.

Even the industrial workers as a whole, in their present stage of development, were not to be trusted, according to the Bolshevist leaders. They frankly opposed the Mensheviki when the latter proposed to hold their great convention of industrial workers, giving as their reason the fear that the convention majority would not consist of class-conscious revolutionary Marxian Socialists. In other words, they feared that the majority would not be on their side, and they had not the time or the patience to convert them. There was no pretense of faith in the majority of the industrial proletariat, much less of faith in the entire working class of Russia. The industrial proletariat was a minority of the working class, and the Bolsheviki pinned their faith to a minority of that minority. They wanted to establish, not democracy, but dictatorship of Russia by a small, disciplined, intelligent, and determined minority of working-men.

The lines of cleavage between the Mensheviki and the Bolsheviki were thus clearly drawn. The former, while ready to join in mass uprisings and armed insurrections by the masses, believed that the supreme necessity was education and organization of all the working-people. Still relying upon the industrial proletariat to lead the struggle, they nevertheless recognized that the peasants were indispensable. The Bolsheviki, on the other hand, relied exclusively upon armed insurrection, initiated and directed by desperate minorities. The Mensheviki contended that the time for secret, conspiratory action was past; that Russia had outgrown that earlier method. As far as possible, they carried the struggle openly into the political field. They organized unions, educational societies, and co-operatives, confident that through these agencies the workers would develop cohesion and strength, which, at the right time, they would use as their class interests dictated. The Bolsheviki, on the other hand, clung to the old conspiratory methods, always mastered by the idea that a sudden *coup* must some day place the reins of power in the hands of a revolutionary minority of the workers and enable them to set up a dictatorship. That dictatorship, it must be understood, was not to be permanent; democracy, possibly even political democracy, would come later.

As we have already noted, into the ranks of the terrorist Socialist-Revolutionaries and the Bolsheviki spies and provocative agents wormed their way in large numbers. It is the inevitable fate of secret, conspiratory movements that this should be so, and also that it should result in saturating the minds of all engaged in the movements with distrust and suspicion. More than once the charge of being a provocateur was leveled at Lenine and at Trotzky, but without justification, apparently. There was, indeed, one incident which placed Lenine in a bad light. It belongs to a somewhat later period than we have been discussing, but it serves admirably to illustrate conditions which obtained throughout the whole dark period between the two great revolutions. One of Lenine's close friends and disciples was Roman Malinovsky, a fiery speaker of considerable power, distinguished for his bitter attacks upon the bourgeois progressive parties and upon the Mensheviki. The tenor of his speeches was always the same—only the interest of the proletariat should be considered; all bourgeois political parties and groups were equally reactionary, and any co-operation with them, for any purpose, was a betrayal of Socialist principle.

Malinovsky was trusted by the Bolsheviki. He was elected to the Fourth Duma, where he became the leader of the little group of thirteen Social Democrats. Like other members of the Bolshevik faction, he entered the Duma, despite his contempt for parliamentary action, simply because it afforded him a useful opportunity for agitation and demonstrations. In the Duma he assailed even a portion of the Social Democratic group as belonging to the bourgeoisie, succeeding in splitting it in two factions and becoming the leader of the Bolshevik faction, numbering six. This blatant demagogue, whom Lenine called "the Russian Bebel," was proposed for membership in the International Socialist Bureau, the supreme council of the International Socialist movement, and would have been sent as a delegate to that body as a representative of Russian Socialist movement but for the discovery of the fact that he was a secret agent of the Czar's government!

It was proved that Malinovsky was a provocateur in the pay of the Police Department, and that many, if not all, of his speeches had been prepared for him in the Police Department by a former director named Beletzky. The exposure made a great sensation in Russian Socialist circles at the time, and the fact that it was Nikolai Lenine who had proposed that Malinovsky be chosen to sit in the International Socialist Bureau naturally caused a great deal of unfriendly comment. It cannot be denied that the incident placed Lenine in an unfavorable light, but it must be admitted that nothing developed to suggest that he was guilty of anything more serious than permitting himself to be outwitted and deceived by a cunning trickster. The incident serves to show, however, the ease with which the extreme fanaticism of the Bolsheviki played into the hands of the autocracy.

VII

While Bolsheviki and Mensheviki wrangled and disputed, great forces were at work among the Russian people. By 1910 the terrible pall of depression and despair which had settled upon the nation as a result of the failure of the First Revolution began to break. There was a new generation of college students, youthful and optimistic spirits who were undeterred by the failure of 1905-06, confident that they were wiser and certain to succeed. Also there had been an enormous growth of working-class organizations, large numbers of unions and co-operative societies having been formed in spite of the efforts of the government. The soul of Russia was once more stirring.

The end of 1910 and the beginning of 1911 witnessed a new series of strikes, such as had not occurred since 1905. The first were students' strikes, inaugurated in support of their demand for the abolition of capital punishment. These were quickly followed by important strikes in the industrial centers for economic ends—better wages and shorter working-hours. As in the period immediately preceding the First Revolution, the industrial unrest soon manifested itself in political ways. Without any conscious leadership at all this would have been inevitable in the existing circumstances. But there was leadership. Social Democrats of both factions, and Socialists of other groups as well, moved among the workers, preaching the old, yet ever new, gospel of revolt. Political strikes followed the strikes for immediate economic ends. Throughout the latter part of 1911 and the whole of 1912 the revolutionary movement once more spread among the masses.

The year 1913 was hardly well begun when revolutionary activities assumed formidable proportions. January 9th—Russian calendar—anniversary of Bloody Sunday, was celebrated all over the country by great demonstrations which were really demonstration-strikes. In St. Petersburg fifty-five thousand workers went out—and there were literally hundreds of other smaller "strikes" of a similar nature throughout the country. In April another anniversary of the martyrdom of revolting working-men was similarly celebrated in most of the industrial centers, hundreds of thousands of workers striking as a manifestation against the government. The 1st of May was celebrated as it had not been celebrated since 1905. In the various industrial cities hundreds of thousands of workmen left their work to march through the streets and hold mass meetings, and so formidable was the movement that the government was cowed and dared not attempt to suppress it by force. There was a defiant note of revolution in this great uprising of the workers. They demanded an eight-hour day and the right to organize unions and make collective bargains. In addition to these demands, they protested against the Balkan War and against militarism in general.

Had the great war not intervened, a tragic interlude in Russia's long history of struggle, the year 1914 would have seen the greatest struggle for the overthrow of Czarism in all that history. Whether it would have been more successful than the effort of 1905 can never be known, but it is certain that the working-class revolutionary movement was far stronger than it was nine years before. On the other hand, there would not have been the same degree of support from the other classes, for in the intervening period class lines had been more sharply drawn and the class conflict greatly intensified. Surging through the masses like a mighty tide was the spirit of revolt, manifesting itself much as it had done nine years before. All through the early months of the year the revolutionary temper grew. The workers became openly defiant and the government, held in check, doubtless, by the delicate balance of the international situation, dared not resort to force with sufficient vigor to stamp out the agitation. Mass meetings were held in spite of all regulations to the contrary; political strikes occurred in all parts of the country. In St. Petersburg and Moscow barricades were thrown up in the streets as late as July. Then the war clouds burst. A greater passion than that of revolution swept over the nation and it turned to present a united front to

64

the external foe.

CHAPTER III

THE WAR AND THE PEOPLE

I

The war against Austria and Germany was not unpopular. Certainly there was never an occasion when a declaration of war by their rulers roused so little resentment among the Russian people. Wars are practically never popular with the great mass of the people in any country, and this is especially true of autocratically governed countries. The heavy burdens which all great wars impose upon the laboring class, as well as upon the petty bourgeoisie, cause even the most righteous wars to be regarded with dread and sorrow. The memory of the war with Japan was too fresh and too bitter to make it possible for the mass of the Russian people to welcome the thought of another war. It cannot, therefore, in truth be said that the war with the Central Empires was popular. But it can be said with sincerity and the fullest sanction that the war was not unpopular; that it was accepted by the greater part of the people as a just and, moreover, a necessary war. Opposition to the war was not greater in Russia than in England or France, or, later, in America. Of course, there were religious pacifists and Socialists who opposed the war and denounced it, as they would have denounced any other war, on general principles, no matter what the issues involved might be, but their number and their influence were small and quite unimportant.

The one great outstanding fact was the manner in which the sense of peril to the fatherland rallied to its defense the different races, creeds, classes, and parties, the great tidal wave of genuine and sincere patriotism sweeping everything before it, even the mighty, passionate revolutionary agitation. It can hardly be questioned or doubted that if the war had been bitterly resented by the masses it would have precipitated revolution instead of retarding it. From this point of view the war was a deplorable disaster. That no serious attempt was made to bring about a revolution at that time is the best possible evidence that the declaration of war did not enrage the people. If not a popular and welcome event, therefore, the declaration of war by the Czar was not an unpopular one. Never before since his accession to the throne had Nicholas II had the support of the nation to anything like the same extent.

Take the Jews, for example. Bitterly hated and persecuted as they had been, despised and humiliated beyond description; victims of the knout and the pogrom; tortured by Cossacks and Black Hundreds; robbed by official extortions; their women shamed and ravaged and their babies doomed to rot and die in the noisome Pale—the Jews owed no loyalty to the Czar or even to the nation. Had they sought revenge in the hour of Russia's crisis, in howsoever grim a manner, it would have been easy to understand their action and hard indeed to regard it with condemnation. It is almost unthinkable that the Czar could have thought of the Jews in his vast Empire in those days without grave apprehension and fear.

Yet, as all the world knows, the Jews resolutely overcame whatever suggestion of revenge came to them and, with marvelous solidarity, responded to Russia's call without hesitation and without political intrigue or bargaining. As a whole, they were as loyal as any of the Czar's subjects. How shall we explain this phenomenon?

The explanation is that the leaders of the Jewish people, and practically the whole body of Jewish Intellectuals, recognized from the first that the war was more than a war of conflicting dynasties; that it was a war of conflicting ideals. They recognized that the Entente, as a whole, notwithstanding that it included the autocracy of Russia, represented the generous, democratic ideals and principles vital to every Jew in that they must be securely established before the emancipation of the Jew could be realized. Their hatred of Czarism was not engulfed by any maudlin sentiment; they knew that they had no "fatherland" to defend. They were not swept on a tide of jingoism to forget their tragic history and proclaim their loyalty to the infamous oppressor. No. Their loyalty was to the Entente, not to the Czar. They were guided by enlightened self-interest, by an intelligent understanding of the meaning to them of the great struggle against Teutonic militarist-imperialism.

67

Every intelligent and educated Jew in Russia knew that the real source of the brutal anti-Semitism which characterized the rule of the Romanovs was Prussian and not Russian. He knew that it had long been one of the main features of Germany's foreign policy to instigate and stimulate hatred and fear of the Jews by Russian officialdom. There could not be a more tragic mistake than to infer from the ruthless oppression of the Jews in Russia that anti-Semitism is characteristically Russian. Surely, the fact that the First Duma was practically unanimous in deciding to give equal rights to the Jews with all the rest of the population proves that the Russian people did not hate the Jews. The ill-treatment of the Jews was part of the policy by which Germany, for her own ends, cunningly contrived to weaken Russia and so prevent the development of her national solidarity. Racial animosity and conflict was an ideal instrument for attaining that result. Internal war and abortive revolutionary outbreaks which kept the country unsettled, and the energies of the government taxed to the uttermost, served the same end, and were, therefore, the object of Germany's intrigues in Russia, equally with hostility to the Jews, as we shall have occasion to note.

German intrigue in Russia is an interesting study in economic determinism. Unless we comprehend it we shall strive in vain to understand Russia's part in the war and her rôle in the history of the past few decades. A brief study of the map of Europe by any person who possesses even an elementary knowledge of the salient principles of economics will reveal Germany's interest in Russia and make quite plain why German statesmen have so assiduously aimed to keep Russia in a backward economic condition. As a great industrial nation it was to Germany's interest to have Russia remain backward industrially, predominantly an agricultural country, quite as surely as it was to her interest as a military power to have weakness and inefficiency, instead of strength and efficiency, in Russia's military organization. As a highly developed industrial nation Russia would of necessity have been Germany's formidable rival—perhaps her most formidable rival—and by her geographical situation would have possessed an enormous advantage in the exploitation of the vast markets in the far East. As a feudal agricultural country, on the other hand, Russia would be a great market for German manufactured goods, and, at the same time, a most convenient supply-depot for raw materials and granary upon which Germany could rely for raw materials, wheat, rye, and other staple grains—a supply-depot and granary, moreover, accessible by overland transportation not subject to naval attack.

For the Russian Jew the defeat of Germany was a vital necessity. The victory of Germany and her allies could only serve to strengthen Prussian influence in Russia and add to the misery and suffering of the Jewish population. That other factors entered into the determination of the attitude of the Jews, such as, for example, faith in England as the traditional friend of the Jew, and abhorrence at the cruel invasion of Belgium, is quite true. But the great determinant was the well-understood fact that Germany's rulers had long systematically manipulated Russian politics and the Russian bureaucracy to the serious injury of the Jewish race. Germany's militarist-imperialism was the soul and inspiration of the oppression which cursed every Jew in Russia.

II

The democratic elements in Russia were led to support the government by very similar reasoning. The same economic and dynastic motives which had led Germany to promote racial animosities and struggles in Russia led her to take every other possible means to uphold autocracy and prevent the establishment of democracy. This had been long recognized by all liberal Russians, no matter to what political school or party they might belong. It was as much part of the common knowledge as the fact that St. Petersburg was the national capital. It was part of the intellectual creed of practically every liberal Russian that there was a natural affinity between the great autocracies of Germany and Russia, and that a revolution in Russia which seriously endangered the existence of monarchical absolutism would be suppressed by Prussian guns and bayonets reinforcing those of loyal Russian troops. It was generally believed by Russian Socialists that in 1905 the Kaiser had promised to send troops into Russia to crush the Revolution if called upon for that aid. Many German Socialists, it may be added, shared that belief. Autocracies have a natural tendency to combine forces against revolutionary movements. It would have been no more strange for Wilhelm II to aid Nicholas II in quelling a revolution that menaced his throne than it was for Alexander I to aid in putting down revolution in Germany; or than it was for Nicholas I to crush the Hungarian Revolution in 1849, in the interest of Francis Joseph; or than it was for Bismarck to rush to the aid of Alexander II in putting down the Polish insurrection in 1863.

The democrats of Russia knew, moreover, that, in addition to the natural affinity which served to bind the two autocracies, the Romanov and Hohenzollern dynasties had been closely knit together in a strong union by years and years of carefully planned and strongly wrought blood ties. As Isaac Don Lenine reminds us in his admirable study of the Russian Revolution, Nicholas II was more than seven-eighths German, less than one-eighth of his blood heritage being Romanov. Catherine the Great, wife of Peter III, was a Prussian by birth and heritage and thoroughly Prussianized her court. After her—from 1796 to 1917—six Czars reigned in Russia, five of whom married German wives. As was inevitable in such circumstances, the Russian court had long been notoriously subject to German influences and strongly pro-German in its sympathies—by no means a small matter in an autocratic country. Fully aware of their advantage, the Kaiser and his Ministers increased the German influence and power at the Russian court by encouraging German nobles to marry into Russian court circles. The closing decade of the reign of Nicholas II was marked by an extraordinary increase of Prussian influence in his court, an achievement in which the Kaiser was greatly assisted by the Czarina, who was, it will be remembered, a German princess.

Naturally, the German composition and character of the Czar's court was reflected in the diplomatic service and in the most important departments of the Russian government, including the army. The Russian Secret Service was very largely in the hands of Germans and Russians who had married German wives. The same thing may be said of the Police Department. Many of the generals and other high officers in the Russian army were either of German parentage or connected with Germany by marriage ties. In brief, the whole Russian bureaucracy was honeycombed by German influence.

Outside official circles, much the same condition existed among the great landowners. Those of the Baltic provinces were largely of Teutonic descent, of course. Many had married German wives. The result was that the nobility of these provinces, long peculiarly influential in the political life of

70

Russia, was, to a very large degree, pro-German. In addition to these, there were numerous large landowners of German birth, while many, probably a big majority, of the superintendents of the large industrial establishments and landed estates were German citizens. It is notorious that the principal factories upon which Russia had to rely for guns and munitions were in charge of Germans, who had been introduced because of their high technical efficiency.

In view of these facts, and a mass of similar facts which might be cited, it was natural for the democrats of Russia to identify Germany and German intrigue and influence with the hated bureaucracy. It was as natural as it was for the German influence to be used against the democratic movement in Russia, as it invariably was. Practically the entire mass of democratic opinion in Russia, including, of course, all the Socialist factions, regarded these royal, aristocratic, and bureaucratic German influences as a menace to Russia, a cancer that must be cut out. With the exception of a section of the Socialists, whose position we shall presently examine, the mass of liberal-thinking, progressive, democratic Russians saw in the war a welcome breaking of the German yoke. Believing that the victory of Germany would restore the yoke, and that her defeat by Russia would eliminate the power which had sustained Czarism, they welcomed the war and rallied with enthusiasm at the call to arms. They were loyal, but to Russia, not to the Czar. They felt that in warring against Prussian militarist-imperialism they were undermining Russian Absolutism.

That the capitalists of Russia should want to see the power of Germany to hold Russia in chains completely destroyed is easy to understand. To all intents and purposes, from the purely economic point of view, Russia was virtually a German colony to be exploited for the benefit of Germany. The commercial treaties of 1905, which gave Germany such immense trade advantages, had become exceedingly unpopular. On the other hand, the immense French loan of 1905, the greater part of which had been used to develop the industrial life of Russia, had the effect of bringing Russian capitalists into closer relations with French capitalists. For further capital Russia could only look to France and England with any confident hope. Above all, the capitalists of Russia wanted freedom for economic development; they wanted stability and national unity, the very things

71

Germany was preventing. They wanted efficient government and the elimination of the terrible corruption which infested the bureaucracy. The law of economic evolution was inexorable and inescapable; the capitalist system could not grow within the narrow confines of Absolutism.

For the Russian capitalist class, therefore, it was of the most vital importance that Germany's power should not be increased, as it would of necessity be if the Entente submitted to her threats and permitted Serbia to be crushed by Austria, and the furtherance of the Pan-German *Mitteleuropa* designs. It was vitally necessary to Russian capitalism that Germany's strangle-hold upon the inner life of Russia should be broken. The issue was not the competition of capitalism, as that is commonly understood; it was not the rivalry for markets like that which animates the capitalist classes of all lands. The Russian capitalist class was animated by no fear of German competition in the sense in which the nations of the world have understood that term. They had their own vast home market to develop. The industrialization of the country must transform a very large part of the peasantry into factory artisans living in cities, having new needs and relatively high wages, and, consequently, more money to spend. For many years to come their chief reliance must be the home market, constantly expanding as the relative importance of manufacturing increased and forced improved methods of agriculture upon the nation in the process, as it was bound to do.

It was Germany as a persistent meddler in Russian government and politics that the capitalists of Russia resented. It was the unfair advantage that this underhand political manipulation gave her in their own home field that stirred up the leaders of the capitalist class of Russia. That, and the knowledge that German intrigue by promoting divisions in Russia was the mainstay of the autocracy, solidified the capitalist class of Russia in support of the war. There was a small section of this class that went much farther than this and entertained more ambitious hopes. They realized fully that Turkey had already fallen under the domination of Germany to such a degree that in the event of a German victory in the war, or, what really amounted to the same thing, the submission of the Entente to her will, Germany would become the ruler of the Dardanelles and European Turkey be in reality, and perhaps in form, part of the German Empire.

Such a development could not fail, they believed, to have the most disastrous consequences for Russia. Inevitably, it would add to German prestige and power in the Russian Empire, and weld together the Hohenzollern, Habsburg, and Romanov autocracies in a solid, reactionary mass, which, under the efficient leadership of Germany, might easily dominate the entire world. Moreover, like many of the ablest Russians, including the foremost Marxian Socialist scholars, they believed that the normal economic development of Russia required a free outlet to the warm waters of the Mediterranean, which alone could give her free access to the great ocean highways. Therefore they hoped that one result of a victorious war by the Entente against the Central Empires, in which Russia would play an important part, would be the acquisition of Constantinople by Russia. Thus the old vision of the Czars had become the vision of an influential and rising class with a solid basis of economic interest.

III

As in every other country involved, the Socialist movement was sharply divided by the war. Paradoxical as it seems, in spite of the great revival of revolutionary hope and sentiment in the first half of the year, the Socialist parties and groups were not strong when the war broke out. They were, indeed, at a very low state. They had not yet recovered from the reaction. The manipulation of the electoral laws following the dissolution of the Second Duma, and the systematic oppression and repression of all radical organizations by the administration, had greatly reduced the Socialist parties in membership and influence. The masses were, for a long time, weary of struggle, despondent, and passive. The Socialist factions meanwhile were engaged in an apparently interminable controversy upon theoretical and tactical questions in which the masses of the working-people, when they began to stir at last, took no interest, and which they could hardly be supposed to understand. The Socialist parties and groups were subject to a very great disability in that their leaders were practically all in exile. Had a revolution broken out, as it would have done but for the war, Socialist leadership would have asserted itself.

As in all other countries, the divisions of opinion created by the war among the Socialists cut across all previous existing lines of separation and made it impossible to say that this or that faction adopted a particular view. Just as in Germany, France, and England, some of the most revolutionary Socialists joined with the more moderate Socialists in upholding the war, while extremely moderate Socialists joined with Socialists of the opposite extreme in opposing it. It is possible, however, to set forth the principal features of the division with tolerable accuracy:

A majority of the Socialist-Revolutionary party executive issued an anti-war Manifesto. There is no means of telling how far the views expressed represented the attitude of the peasant Socialists as a whole, owing to the disorganized state of the party and the difficulties of assembling the members. The Manifesto read:

There is no doubt that Austrian imperialism is responsible for the war with Serbia. But is it not equally criminal on the part of Serbs to refuse autonomy to Macedonia and to oppress smaller and weaker nations?

It is the protection of this state that our government considers its "sacred duty." What hypocrisy! Imagine the intervention of the Czar on behalf of poor Serbia, whilst he martyrizes Poland, Finland and the Jews, and behaves like a brigand toward Persia.

Whatever may be the course of events, the Russian workers and peasants will continue their heroic fight to obtain for Russia a place among civilized nations.

This Manifesto was issued, as reported in the Socialist press, prior to the actual declaration of war. It was a threat of revolution made with a view to preventing the war, if possible, and belongs to the same category as the similar threats of revolution made by the German Socialists before the war to the same end. The mildness of manner which characterizes the Manifesto may be attributed to two causes—weakness of the movement and a resulting lack of assurance, together with a lack of conviction arising from the fact that many of the leaders, while they hated the Czar and all his works, and could not reconcile themselves to the idea of making any kind of truce with their great enemy, nevertheless were pro-Ally and anxious for the defeat of German imperialism. In other words, these leaders shared the national feeling against Germany, and, had they been free citizens of a democratically governed country, would have loyally supported the war.

When the Duma met, on August 8th, for the purpose of voting the war credits, the Social Democrats of both factions, Bolsheviki and Mensheviki, fourteen in number,[2] united upon a policy of abstention from voting. Valentin Khaustov, on behalf of the two factions, read this statement:

A terrible and unprecedented calamity has broken upon the people of the entire world. Millions of workers have been torn away from their labor, ruined, and swept away by a bloody torrent. Millions of families have been delivered over to famine.

War has already begun. While the governments of Europe were preparing for it, the proletariat of the entire world, with the German workers at the head, unanimously protested.

The hearts of the Russian workers are with the European proletariat.

This war is provoked by the policy of expansion for which the ruling classes of all countries are responsible.

The proletariat will defend the civilization of the world against this attack.

The conscious proletariat of the belligerent countries has not been sufficiently powerful to prevent this war and the resulting return of barbarism.

But we are convinced that the working class will find in the international solidarity of the workers the means to force the conclusion of peace at an early date. The terms of that peace will be dictated by the people themselves, and not by the diplomats.

We are convinced that this war will finally open the eyes of the great masses of Europe, and show them the real causes of all the violence and oppression that they endure, and that therefore this new explosion of barbarism will be the last.

As soon as this declaration was read the fourteen members of the Social Democratic group left the chamber in silence. They were immediately followed by the Laborites and Socialist-Revolutionists representing the peasant Socialists, so that none of the Socialists in the Duma voted for the war credits. As we shall see later on, the Laborites and most of the Socialist-Revolutionists afterward supported the war. The declaration of the Social Democrats in the Duma was as weak and as lacking in definiteness of policy as the Manifesto of the Socialist-Revolutionists already quoted. We know now that it was a compromise. It was possible to get agreement upon a statement of general principles which were commonplaces of Socialist propaganda, and to vaguely expressed hopes that "the working class will find in the international solidarity of the workers the means to force the conclusion of peace at an early date." It was easy enough to do this, but it would have been impossible to unite upon a definite policy of resistance and opposition to the war. It was easy to agree not to vote for the war credits, since there was no danger that this would have any practical effect, the voting of the credits—largely a mere form—being quite certain. It would have been impossible to get all to agree to vote *against* the credits.

Under the strong leadership of Alexander Kerensky the Labor party soon took a decided stand in support of the war. In the name of the entire group of the party's representatives in the Duma, Kerensky read at an early session a statement which pledged the party to defend the fatherland. "We firmly believe," said Kerensky, "that the great flower of Russian democracy, together with all the other forces, will throw back the aggressive enemy and *will defend their native land.*" The party had decided, he said, to support the war "in defense of the land of our birth and of our civilization created by the blood of our race.... We believe that through the agony of the battle-field the brotherhood of the Russian people will be strengthened and a common desire created to free the land from its terrible internal troubles." Kerensky declared that the workers would take no responsibility for the suicidal war into which the governments of Europe had plunged their peoples. He strongly criticized the government, but ended, nevertheless, in calling upon the peasants and industrial workers to support the war:

"The Socialists of England, Belgium, France, and Germany have tried to protest against rushing into war. We Russian Socialists were not able at the last to raise our voices freely against the war. But, deeply convinced of the brotherhood of the workers of all lands, we send our brotherly greetings to all who protested against the preparations for this fratricidal conflict of peoples. Remember that Russian citizens have no enemies among the working classes of the belligerents! *Protect your country to the end against aggression by the states whose governments are hostile to us, but remember that there would not have been this terrible war had the great ideals of democracy, freedom, equality, and brotherhood been directing the activities of those who control the destinies of Russia and other lands!* As it is, our authorities, even in this terrible moment, show no desire to forget internal strife, grant no amnesty to those who have fought for freedom and the country's happiness, show no desire for reconciliation with the non-Russian peoples of the Empire.

"And, instead of relieving the condition of the laboring classes of the people, the government puts on them especially the heaviest load of the war expenses, by tightening the yoke of indirect taxes.

"Peasants and workers, all who want the happiness and well-being of Russia in these great trials, harden your spirit! Gather all your strength and, having defended your land, free it; and to you, our brothers, who are shedding blood for the fatherland, a profound obeisance and fraternal greetings."

Kerensky's statement was of tremendous significance. Made on behalf of the entire group of which he was leader, it reflected the sober second thought of the representatives of the peasant Socialists and socialistically inclined radicals. Their solemnly measured protest against the reactionary policy of the government was as significant as the announcement that they would support the war. It was a fact that at the very time when national unity was of the most vital importance the government was already goading the people into despairing revolt.

That a section of the Bolsheviki began a secret agitation against the war, aiming at a revolt among the soldiers, regardless of the fact that it would mean Russia's defeat and Germany's triumph, is a certainty. The government soon learned of this movement and promptly took steps to crush it. Many Russian Socialists have charged that the policy of the Bolsheviki was inspired by provocateurs in the employ of the police, and by them betrayed. Others believe that the policy was instigated by German provocateurs, for very obvious purposes. It was not uncommon for German secret agents to worm their way into the Russian Socialist ranks, nor for the agents of the Russian police to keep the German secret service informed of what was going on in Russian Socialist circles. Whatever truth there may be in the suspicion that the anti-war Bolshevik faction of the Social Democrats were the victims of the Russian police espionage system, and were betrayed by one whom they had trusted, as the Socialist-Revolutionists had been betrayed by Azev, the fact remains that the government ordered the arrest of five of the Bolshevist Social Democratic members of the Duma, on November 17th. Never before had the government disregarded the principle of parliamentary immunity. When members of the First Duma, belonging to various parties, and members of the Second Duma, belonging to the Social Democratic party, were arrested it was only after the Duma had been formally dissolved. The arrest of the five Social Democrats while the Duma was still sitting evoked a strong protest, even from the conservatives.

The government based its action upon the following allegations, which appear to have been substantially correct: in October arrangements were made to convoke a secret conference of delegates of the Social Democratic organization to plan for a revolutionary uprising. The police learned of the plan, and when at last, on November 17th, the conference was held at Viborg, eight miles from Petrograd—as the national capital was now called—a detachment of police found eleven persons assembled, including five members of the Imperial Duma, Messrs. Petrovsky, Badavev, Mouranov, Samoelov, and Chagov. The police arrested six persons, but did not arrest the Duma members, on account of their parliamentary position. An examining magistrate, however, indicted the whole eleven who attended the conference, under Article No. 102 of the Penal Code, and issued warrants for their arrest. Among those arrested was Kamanev, one of Lenine's closest friends, who behaved so badly at his trial, manifesting so much cowardice, that he was censured by his party.

At this conference, according to the government, arrangements were made to circulate among the masses a Manifesto which declared that "from the viewpoint of the working class and of the laboring masses of all the nations of Russia, the defeat of the monarchy of the Czar and of its armies would be of extremely little consequence." The Manifesto urged the imperative necessity of *carrying on on all sides the propaganda of the social revolution among the army and at the theater of the war, and that weapons should be directed not against their brothers, the hired slaves of other countries, but against the reactionary bourgeois governments.* The Manifesto went on, according to the government, to favor the organization of a similar propaganda in all languages, among all the armies, with the aim of creating republics in Russia, Poland, Germany, Austria, and all other European countries, these to be federated into a republican United Stares of Europe.

The declaration that the defeat of the Russian armies would be "of extremely little consequence" to the workers became the key-note of the anti-war agitation of the Bolsheviki. Lenine and Zinoviev, still in exile, adopted the view that the defeat of Russia was *actually desirable* from the point of view of the Russian working class. "We are Russians, and for that very reason we want Czarism to be defeated," was the cry.[3] In his paper, the *Social Democrat*, published in Switzerland, Lenine advocated Russian defeat, to be brought about through treachery and revolt in the army, as the best means of furthering revolutionary progress. The majority of the Bolshevik faction made common cause with the extreme left-wing Socialists of the Socialist-Revolutionary party, who shared their views and became known as "Porazhentsi"—that is, advocates of defeat. Naturally, the charge was made that they were pro-German, and it was even charged that they were in the pay of Germany. Possibly some of them were, but it by no means follows that because they desired Russia's defeat they were therefore consciously pro-German. They were not pro-German, but anti-Czarists. They believed quite honestly, most of them, that Russia's defeat was the surest and quickest way of bringing about the Revolution in Russia which would overthrow Czarism. In many respects their position was quite like that of those Irish rebels who desired to see England defeated, even though it meant Germany's triumph, not because of any love for Germany, but because they hated England and believed that her defeat would be Ireland's opportunity. However short-sighted and stupid such a policy may be judged to be, it is quite comprehensible and should not be misrepresented. It is a remarkable fact that the Bolsheviki, while claiming to be the most radical and extreme internationalists, were in practice the most narrow nationalists. They were exactly as narrow in their nationalism as the Sinn-Feiners of Ireland. They were not blind to the terrible wrongs inflicted upon Belgium, or to the fact that Germany's victory over Russia would make it possible for her to crush the western democracies, France and England. But neither to save Belgium nor to prevent German militarism crushing French and English workers under its iron heel would they have the Russian workers make any sacrifice. They saw, and cared only for, what they believed to be *Russian* interests.

IV

But during the first months of the war the Porazhentsi—including the Bolsheviki—were a very small minority. The great majority of the Socialist-Revolutionists rallied to the support of the Allied cause. Soon after the war began a Socialist Manifesto to the laboring masses of Russia was issued. It bore the signature of many of the best-known Russian Socialists, representing all the Socialist factions and groups except the Bolsheviki. Among the names were those of George Plechanov, Leo Deutsch, Gregory Alexinsky, N. Avksentiev, B. Vorovonov, I. Bunakov, and A. Bach—representing the best thought of the movement in practically all its phases. This document is of the greatest historical importance, not merely because it expressed the sentiments of Socialists of so many shades, but even

80

more because of its carefully reasoned arguments why Socialists should support the war and why the defeat of Germany was essential to Russian and international social democracy. Despite its great length, the Manifesto is here given in its entirety:

We, the undersigned, belong to the different shades of Russian Socialistic thought. We differ on many things, but we firmly agree in that the defeat of Russia in her struggle with Germany would mean her defeat in her struggle for freedom, and we think that, guided by this conviction, our adherents in Russia must come together for a common service to their people, in the hour of the grave danger the country is now facing.

We address ourselves to the politically conscious working-men, peasants, artisans, clerks—to all of those who earn their bread in the sweat of their brow, and who, suffering from the lack of means and want of political rights, are struggling for a better future for themselves, for their children, and for their brethren.

We send them our hearty greeting, and persistently say to them: Listen to us in this fatal time, when the enemy has conquered the Western strongholds of Russia, has occupied an important part of our territory and is menacing Kiev, Petrograd, and Moscow, these most important centers of our social life.

Misinformed people may tell you that in defending yourselves from German invasion you support our old political régime. These people want to see Russia defeated because of their hatred of the Czar's government. Like one of the heroes of our genius of satire, Shchedrin, they mix fatherland with its temporary bosses. But Russia belongs not to the Czar, but to the Russian working-people. In defending Russia, the working-people defend themselves, defend the road to their freedom. As we said before, the inevitable consequences of German victory would be the strengthening of our old régime.

The Russian reactionaries understand this very thoroughly. *In a faint, half-hearted manner they are defending Russia from Germany.* The Ministers who resigned recently, Maklakov and Shcheglovitov, presented a secret report to the Czar, in November, 1914, in which they explained how advantageous it would be for the Czar to make a separate peace with Germany. *They*

81

understand that the defeat of Germany would be a defeat of the principles of monarchism, so dear to all our European reactionaries.

Our people will never forget *the failure of the Czar's government to defend Russia.* But if the progressive, the politically conscious people will not take part in the struggle against Germany, the Czar's government will have an excuse for saying: "It is not our fault that Germany defeats us; it is the fault of the revolutionists who have betrayed their country," and this will vindicate the government in the eyes of the people.

The political situation in Russia is such that only across the bridge of national defense can we reach freedom. Remember, *we do not tell you, first victory against the external enemy and then revolution against the internal, the Czar's government.*

In the course of events the defeat of the Czar's government may serve as a necessary preliminary condition for, and even as a guaranty of, the elimination of the German danger. The French revolutionists of the end of the eighteenth century would never have been able to have overcome the enemy, attacking France on all sides, had they not adopted such tactics only when the popular movement against the old régime became mature enough to render their efforts effective.

Furthermore, you must not be embarrassed by the arguments of those who believe that every one who defends his country refuses thereby to take part in the struggle of the classes. These persons do not know what they are talking about. In the first place, in order that the struggle of the classes in Russia should be successful, certain social and political conditions must exist there. *These conditions will not exist if Germany wins.*

In the second place, if the working-man of Russia cannot but defend himself against the exploitation of the Russian landed aristocrat and capitalist it seems incomprehensible that he should remain inactive when the lasso of exploitation is being drawn around his neck by the German landed aristocracy (the *Junker*) and the German capitalist who are, unfortunately, at the present time *supported by a considerable part of the German proletariat that has turned traitor to its duty of solidarity with the proletariat of other countries.*

By striving to the utmost to cut this lasso of German imperialistic exploitation, the proletariat of Russia will continue the struggle of the classes in that form which at the present moment is most appropriate, fruitful, and effective.

It has been our country's fate once before to suffer from the bloody horrors of a hostile invasion. But never before did it have to defend itself against an enemy so well armed, so skilfully organized, so carefully prepared for his plundering enterprise as he is now.

The position of the country is dangerous to the highest degree; therefore upon all of you, upon all the politically conscious children of the working-people of Russia, lies an enormous responsibility.

If you say to yourselves that it is immaterial to you and to your less developed brothers as to who wins in this great international collision going on now, and if you act accordingly, Russia will be crushed by Germany. And when Russia will be crushed by Germany, it will fare badly with the Allies. This does not need any demonstration.

But if, on the contrary, you become convinced that the defeat of Russia will reflect badly upon the interests of the working population, and if you will help the self-defense of our country with all your forces, our country and her allies will escape the terrible danger menacing them.

Therefore, go deeply into the situation. You make a great mistake if you imagine that it is not to the interests of the working-people to defend our country. In reality, nobody's interests suffer more terribly from the invasion of an enemy than the interests of the working-population.

Take, for instance, the Franco-Prussian War of 1870-71. When the Germans besieged Paris and the cost of all the necessaries of life rose enormously, it was clear that the poor suffered much more than the rich. In the same way, when Germany exacted five billions of contribution from vanquished France, this same, in the final count, was paid by the poor; for paying that contribution indirect taxation was greatly raised, the burden of which nearly entirely falls on the lower classes.

More than that. The most dangerous consequence to France, due to her defeat in 1870-71, was the retardation of her economic development. In other words, the defeat of France badly reflected upon the contemporary interests of her people, and, even more, upon her entire subsequent development.

The defeat of Russia by Germany will much more injure our people than the defeat of France injured the French people. The war now exacts incredibly large expenditures. It is more difficult for Russia, a country economically backward, to bear that expenditure than for the wealthy states of western Europe. Russia's back, even before the war, was burdened with a heavy state loan. Now this debt is growing by the hour, and vast regions of Russia are subject to wholesale devastation.

If the Germans will win the final victory, they will demand from us an enormous contribution, in comparison with which the streams of gold that poured into victorious Germany from vanquished France, after the war of 1871, will seem a mere trifle.

But that will not be all. The most consequent and outspoken heralds of German imperialism are even now saying that it is necessary to exact from Russia the cession of important territory, which should be cleared from the present population for the greater convenience of German settlers. Never before have plunderers, dreaming of despoiling a conquered people, displayed such cynical heartlessness!

But for our vanquishers it will not be enough to exact an unheard-of enormous contribution and to tear up our western borderlands. Already, in 1904, Russia, being in a difficult situation, was obliged to conclude a commercial treaty with Germany, very disadvantageous to herself. The treaty hindered, at the same time, the development of our agriculture and the progress of our industries. It affected, with equal disadvantage, the interests of the farmers as well as of those engaged in industry. It is easy to imagine what kind of a treaty victorious German imperialism would impose upon us. In economic matters, Russia would become a German colony. Russia's further economic development would be greatly hindered if not altogether stopped. Degeneration and deprivation would be the result of German victory for an important part of the Russian working-people.

What will German victory bring to western Europe? After all we have already said, it is needless to expatiate on how many of the unmerited economic calamities it will bring to the people of the western countries allied to Russia. We wish to draw your attention to the following: England, France, even Belgium and Italy, are, in a political sense, far ahead of the German Empire, which has not as yet grown up to a parliamentary régime. German victory over these countries would be the victory of the old over the new, and if the democratic ideal is dear to you, you must wish success to our Western Allies.

Indifference to the result of this war would be, for us, equal to political suicide. The most important, the most vital interests of the proletariat and of the laboring peasantry demand of you an active participation in the defense of the country. Your watchword must be victory over the foreign enemy. In an active movement toward such victory, the live forces of the people will become free and strong.

Obedient to this watchword, you must be as wise as serpents. Although in your hearts may burn the flame of noble indignation, in your heads must reign, invariably, cold political reckoning. You must know that zeal without reason is sometimes worse than complete indifference. Every act of agitation in the rear of the army, fighting against the enemy, would be equivalent to high treason, as it would be a service to the foreign enemy.

The thunders of the war certainly cannot make the Russian manufacturers and merchants more idealistic than they were in time of peace. In the filling of the numerous orders, inevitable during the mobilization of industry for war needs, the capitalists will, as they are accustomed to, take great care of the interests of capital, and will not take care of the interests of hired labor. You will be entirely right if you wax indignant at their conduct. But in all cases, whenever you desire to answer by a strike, you must first think whether such action would not be detrimental to the cause of the defense of Russia.

The private must be subject to the general. The workmen of every factory must remember that they would commit, without any doubt, the gravest mistake if, considering only their own interests, they forget how severely the interests of the entire Russian proletariat and peasantry would suffer from German victory.

The tactics which can be defined by the motto, "All or nothing," are the tactics of anarchy, fully unworthy of the conscious representatives of the proletariat and peasantry. The General Staff of the German Army would greet with pleasure the news that we had adopted such tactics. *Believe us that this Staff is ready to help all those who would like to preach it in our country.* They want trouble in Russia, they want strikes in England, they want everything that would facilitate the achievement of their conquering schemes.

But you will not make them rejoice. You will not forget the words of our great fabulist: "What the enemy advises is surely bad." You must insist that all your representatives take the most active part in all organizations created now, under the pressure of public opinion, for the struggle with the foe. Your representatives must, if possible, take part not only in the work of the special technical organizations, such as the War-Industrial Committees which have been created for the needs of the army, but also in all other organizations of social and political character.

The situation is such that we cannot come to freedom in any other way than by the war of national defense.

That the foregoing Manifesto expressed the position of the vast majority of Russian Socialists there can be no doubt whatever. Between this position and that of the Porazhentsi with their doctrine that Russia's defeat by Germany was desirable, there was a middle ground, which was taken by a not inconsiderable number of Socialists, including such able leaders as Paul Axelrod. Those who took up this intermediate position were both anti-Czarists and anti-German-imperialists. They were pro-Ally in the large sense, and desired to see the Allies win over the Central Empires, if not a "crushing" victory, a very definite and conclusive one. But they regarded the alliance of Czarism with the Allies as an unnatural marriage. They believed that autocratic Russia's natural alliance was with autocratic Germany and Austria. Their hatred of Czarism led them to wish for its defeat, even by Germany, provided the victory were not so great as to permit Germany to extend her domain over Russia or any large part of it. Their position became embodied in the phrase, "Victory by the Allies on the west and Russia's defeat on the east." This was, of course, utterly unpractical theorizing and bore no relation to reality.

V

Thanks in part to the vigorous propaganda of such leaders as Plechanov, Deutsch, Bourtzev, Tseretelli, Kerensky, and many others, and in part to the instinctive good sense of the masses, support of the war by Socialists of all shades and factions—except the extreme Bolsheviki and the so-called "Internationalist" sections of Mensheviki and Socialist-Revolutionists—became general. The anti-war minority was exceedingly small and had no hold upon the masses. Had the government

86

been both wise and honestly desirous of presenting a united front to the foe, and to that end made intelligent and generous concessions to the democratic movement, it is most unlikely that Russia would have collapsed. As it was, the government adopted a policy which could not fail to weaken the military force of the nation—a policy admirably suited to German needs.

Extremes meet. On the one hand there were the Porazhentsi Socialists, contending that the interests of progress would be best served by a German victory over Russia, and plotting to weaken and corrupt the morale of the Russian army and to stir up internal strife to that end. On the other hand, within the royal court, and throughout the bureaucracy, reactionary pro-German officials were animated by the belief that the victory of Germany was essential to the permanence of Absolutism and autocratic government. They, too, like the Socialist "defeatists," aimed to weaken and corrupt the morale of the army and to divide the nation.

These Germanophiles in places of power realized that they had unconscious but exceedingly useful allies in the Socialist intransigents. Actuated by motives however high, the latter played into the hands of the most corrupt and reactionary force that ever infested the old régime. This force, the reactionary Germanophiles, had from the very first hoped and believed that Germany would win the war. They had exerted every ounce of pressure they could command to keep the Czar from maintaining the treaty with France and entering into the war on her side against Germany and Austria. When they failed in this, they bided their time, full of confidence that the superior efficiency of the German military machine would soon triumph. But when they witnessed the great victorious onward rush of the Russian army, which for a time manifested such a degree of efficiency as they had never believed to be possible, they began to bestir themselves. From this quarter came the suggestion, very early in the war, as Plechanov and his associates charged in their Manifesto, that the Czar ought to make an early peace with Germany.

They went much farther than this. Through every conceivable channel they contrived to obstruct Russia's military effort. They conspired to disorganize the transportation system, the hospital service, the food-supply, the manufacture of munitions. They, too, in a most effective manner, were plotting to weaken and corrupt the morale of the army. There was universal uneasiness. In the Allied chancelleries there was fear of a treacherous separate peace between Russia and Germany. It was partly to avert that catastrophe by means of a heavy bribe that England undertook the forcing of the Dardanelles. All over Russia there was an awakening of the memories of the graft that ate like a canker-worm at the heart of the nation. Men told once more the story of the Russian general in Manchuria, in 1904, who, when asked why fifty thousand men were marching barefoot, answered that the boots were in the pocket of Grand-Duke Vladimir! They told again the story of the cases of "shells" for the Manchurian army which were intercepted in the nation's capital, *en route* to Moscow, and found to contain—paving-stones! How General Kuropatkin managed to amass a fortune of over six million rubles during the war with Japan was remembered. Fear that the same kind of treason was being perpetrated grew almost to the panic point.

So bad were conditions in the army, so completely had the Germanophile reactionaries sabotaged the organization, that the people themselves took the matter in hand. Municipalities all over the country formed a Union of Cities to furnish food, clothes, and other necessaries to the army. The National Union of Zemstvos did the same thing. More than three thousand institutions were established on the different Russian fronts by the National Union of Zemstvos. These institutions included hospitals, ambulance stations, feeding stations for troops on the march, dental stations, veterinary stations, factories for manufacturing supplies, motor transportation services, and so on through a long catalogue of things which the administration absolutely failed to provide. The same great organization furnished millions of tents and millions of pairs of boots and socks. Civil Russia was engaged in a great popular struggle to overcome incompetence, corruption, and sabotage in the bureaucracy. For this work the civilian agencies were not thanked by the government. Instead, they were oppressed and hindered. Against them was directed the hate of the dark forces of the "occult government" and at the same time the fierce opposition and scorn of men who called themselves Socialists and champions of proletarian freedom!

There was treachery in the General Staff and throughout the War Department, at the very head of which was a corrupt traitor, Sukhomlinov. It was treachery in the General Staff which led to the tragic disasters in East Prussia. The great drive of the Austrian and German armies in 1915, which led to the loss of Poland, Lithuania, and large parts of Volhynia and Courland, and almost entirely eliminated Russia from the war, was unquestionably brought about by co-operation with the German General Staff on the part of the sinister "occult government," as the Germanophile reactionary conspiracy in the highest circles came to be known.

No wonder that Plechanov and his friends in their Manifesto to the Russian workers declared that the reactionaries were defending Russia from subjugation by Germany in "a half-hearted way," and that "our people will never forget the failure of the Czar's government to defend Russia." They were only saying, in very moderate language, what millions were thinking; what, a few months later, many of the liberal spokesmen of the country were ready to say in harsher language. As early as January, 1915, the Duma met and cautiously expressed its alarm. In July it met again, many of the members coming directly from the front, in uniform. Only the fear that a revolution would make the continuance of the war impossible prevented a revolution at that time. The Duma was in a revolutionary mood. Miliukov, for example, thundered:

" ... In January we came here with ... the feeling of patriotic alarm. We then kept this feeling to ourselves. Yet in closed sessions of committees we told the government all that filled the soul of the people. The answer we received did not calm us; it amounted to saying that the government could get along without us, without our co-operation. To-day we have convened in a grave moment of trial for our fatherland. The patriotic alarm of the people has proved to be well founded, to the misfortune of our country. Secret things have become open, and the assertions of half a year ago have turned out to be mere words. Yet the country cannot be satisfied with words. *The people wish to take affairs into their own hands and to correct what has been neglected. The people look upon us as legal executors of their will.*"

Kerensky spoke to the same general effect, adding, "*I appeal to the people themselves to take into their hands the salvation of the country and fight for a full right to govern the state.*" The key-note of revolution was being sounded now. For the spirit of revolution breathed in the words, "The people wish to take affairs into their own hands," and in Kerensky's challenge, "I appeal to the people themselves to take into their hands the salvation of the country." The Duma was the logical center around which the democratic forces of the country could rally. Its moderate character determined this. Only its example was necessary to the development of a great national movement to overthrow the old régime with its manifold treachery, corruption, and incompetence. When, on August 22d, the Progressive Bloc was formed by a coalition of Constitutional Democrats, Progressives, Nationalists, and Octobrists—the last-named group having hitherto generally supported the government—there was a general chorus of approval throughout the country, If the program of the Bloc was not radical enough to satisfy the various Socialist groups, even the Laborites, led by Kerensky, it was, nevertheless, a program which they could support in the main, as far as it went.

All over the country there was approval of the demand for a responsible government. The municipal councils of the large cities passed resolutions in support of it. The great associations of manufacturers supported it. All over the nation the demand for a responsible government was echoed. It was generally believed that the Czar and his advisers would accept the situation and accede to the popular demand. But once more the influence of the reactionaries triumphed, and on September 3d came the defiant answer of the government to the people. It was an order suspending the Duma indefinitely. The gods make mad those whom they would destroy.

Things went from bad to worse. More and more oppressive grew the government; more and more stupidly brutal and reactionary in its dealings with the wide-spread popular unrest. Heavier and heavier grew the burden of unscientific and unjustly distributed taxation. Worse and worse became the condition of the soldiers at the front; ever more scandalous the neglect of the sick and wounded. Incompetence, corruption, and treason combined to hurry the nation onward to a disastrous collapse. The Germanophiles were still industriously at work in the most important and vital places, practising sabotage upon a scale never dreamed of before in the history of any nation. They played upon the fears of the miserable weakling who was the nominal ruler of the vast Russian Empire, and frightened him into sanctioning the most suicidal policy of devising new measures of oppression instead of making generous concessions.

Russia possessed food in abundance, being far better off in this respect than any other belligerent on either side, yet Russia was in the grip of famine. There was a vast surplus of food grains and cereals over and above the requirements of the army and the civilian population, yet there was wide-spread hunger. Prices rose to impossible levels. The most astonishing anarchy and disorganization characterized the administration of the food-supply. It was possible to get fresh butter within an hour's journey from Moscow for twenty-five cents a pound, but in Moscow the price was two and a half dollars a pound. Here, as throughout the nation, incompetence was reinforced by corruption and pro-German treachery. Many writers have called attention to the fact that even in normal times the enormous exportation of food grains in Russia went on side by side with per capita underconsumption by the peasants whose labor produced the great harvests, amounting to not less than 30 per cent. Now, of course, conditions were far worse.

When the government was urged to call a convention of national leaders to deal with the food situation it stubbornly refused. More than that, it made war upon the only organizations which were staving off famine and making it possible for the nation to endure. Every conceivable obstacle was placed in the way of the National Union of Zemstvos and the Union of Cities; the co-operative associations, which were rendering valuable service in meeting the distress of working-men's families, were obstructed and restricted in every possible way, their national offices being closed by the police. The officials of the labor-unions who were co-operating with employers in substituting arbitration in place of strikes, establishing soup-kitchens and relief funds, and doing other similar work to keep the nation alive, were singled out for arrest and imprisonment. The Black Hundreds were perniciously active in all this oppression and in the treacherous advocacy of a separate peace with Germany.

In October, 1916, a conference of chairmen of province zemstvos adopted and published a resolution which declared:

The tormenting and horrifying suspicion, the sinister rumors of perfidy and treason, of dark forces working in favor of Germany to destroy the unity of the nation, to sow discord and thus prepare conditions for an ignominious peace, have now reached the clear certainty that the hand of the enemy secretly influences the affairs of our state.

VI

An adequate comprehension of the things set forth in this terrible summary is of the highest importance to every one who would attempt the task of reaching an intelligent understanding of the mighty upheaval in Russia and its far-reaching consequences. The Russian Revolution of 1917 was not responsible for the disastrous separate peace with Germany. The foundations for that were laid by the reactionaries of the old régime. It was the logical outcome of their long-continued efforts. Lenine, Trotzky, and their Bolshevist associates were mere puppets, simple tools whose visions, ambitions, and schemes became the channels through which the conspiracy of the worst reactionaries in Russia realized one part of an iniquitous program.

The Revolution itself was a genuine and sincere effort on the part of the Russian people to avert the disaster and shame of a separate peace; to serve the Allied cause with all the fidelity of which they were capable. There would have been a separate peace if the old régime had remained in power a few weeks longer and the Revolution been averted. It is most likely that it would have been a more shameful peace than was concluded at Brest-Litovsk, and that it would have resulted in an actual and active alliance of the Romanov dynasty with the dynasties of the Hohenzollerns and the Habsburgs. The Russian Revolution of 1917 had this great merit: it so delayed the separate peace between Russia and Germany that the Allies were able to prepare for it. It had the merit, also, that it forced the attainment of the separate peace to come in such a manner as to reduce Germany's military gain on the western front to a minimum.

The manner in which the Bolsheviki in their wild, groping, and frenzied efforts to apply theoretical abstractions to the living world, torn as it was by the wolves of war, famine, treason, oppression, and despair, served the foes of freedom and progress must not be lost sight of. The Bolshevist, wherever he may present himself, is the foe of progress and the ally of reaction.

CHAPTER IV

THE SECOND REVOLUTION

I

When the Duma assembled On November 14, 1916—new style—the approaching doom of Czar Nicholas II was already manifest. Why the Revolution did not occur at that time is a puzzle not easy to solve. Perhaps the mere fact that the Duma was assembling served to postpone resort to drastic measures. The nation waited for the Duma to lead. It is probable, also, that fear lest revolution prove disastrous to the military forces exercised a restraining influence upon the people. Certain it is that it would have been easy enough to kindle the fires of revolution at that time. Never in the history of the nation, not even in 1905, were conditions riper for revolt, and never had there been a more solid array of the nation against the bureaucracy. Discontent and revolutionary temper were not confined to Socialists, nor to the lower classes. Landowners, capitalists, military officials, and Intellectuals were united with the peasants and artisans, to an even greater extent than in the early stages of the First Revolution. Conservatives and Moderates joined with Social Democrats and Socialist-Revolutionists in opposition to the corrupt and oppressive régime. Even the president of the Duma, Michael Rodzianko, a conservative landowner, assailed the government.

One of the principal reasons for this unexampled unity against the government was the wide-spread conviction, based, as we have seen, upon the most damning evidence, that Premier Sturmer and his Cabinet were not loyal to the Allies and that they contemplated making a separate peace with Germany. All factions in the Duma were bitterly opposed to a separate peace. Rodzianko was loudly cheered when he denounced the intrigues against the Allies and declared: "Russia gave her word to fight in common with the Allies till complete and final victory is won. Russia will not betray her friends, and with contempt refuses any consideration of a separate peace. Russia will not

93

be a traitor to those who are fighting side by side with her sons for a great and just cause." Notwithstanding the intensification of the class conflict naturally resulting from the great industrial development since 1906, patriotism temporarily overshadowed all class consciousness.

The cheers that greeted Rodzianko's declaration, and the remarkable ovation to the Allied ambassadors, who were present, amply demonstrated that, in spite of the frightful suffering and sacrifice which the nation had endured, all classes were united in their determination to win the war. Only a corrupt section of the bureaucracy, at one end of the social scale, and a small section of extreme left-wing Socialists, at the other end of the social scale, were at that time anti-war. There was this difference between the Socialist pacifists and the bureaucratic advocates of peace with Germany: the former were not pro-German nor anti-Ally, but sincere internationalists, honest and brave—however mistaken—advocates of peace. Outside of the bureaucracy there was no hostility to the Allies in Russia. Except for the insignificant Socialist minority referred to, the masses of the Russian people realized that the defeat of the Hohenzollern dynasty was necessary to a realization of the ideal of a free Russia. The new and greater revolution was already beginning, and determination to defeat the Hohenzollern bulwark of the Romanov despotism was almost universal. The whole nation was pervaded by this spirit.

Paul Miliukov, leader of the Constitutional Democrats, popularly known as the "Cadets," furiously lashed Premier Sturmer and quoted the irrefutable evidence of his pro-Germanism and of his corruption. Sturmer reeled under the smashing attack. In his rage he forbade the publication of Miliukov's speech, but hundreds of thousands of copies of it were secretly printed and distributed. Every one recognized that there was war between the Duma and the government, and notwithstanding the criticism of the Socialists, who naturally regarded it as a bourgeois body, the Duma represented Russia.

Sturmer proposed to his Cabinet the dissolution of the Duma, but failed to obtain the support of a majority. Then he determined to get the Czar's signature to a decree of dissolution. But the Czar was at the General Headquarters of the army at the time and therefore surrounded by army officers, practically all of whom were with the Duma and inspired by a bitter resentment of the pro-German intrigues, especially the neglect of the army organization. The weak will of Nicholas II was thus beyond the reach of Sturmer's influence for the time being. Meanwhile, the Ministers of the Army and Navy had appeared before the Duma and declared themselves to be on the side of the people and their parliament. On his way to visit the Czar at General Headquarters, Premier Sturmer was met by one of the Czar's messengers and handed his dismissal from office. The Duma had won.

The evil genius which inspired and controlled him led Nicholas II to appoint as Sturmer's successor the utterly reactionary bureaucrat, Alexander Trepov, and to retain in office as Minister of the Interior the infamous Protopopov, associate of the unsavory Rasputin. When Trepov made his first appearance as Premier in the Duma he was loudly hissed by the Socialists. Other factions, while not concealing their disappointment, were more tolerant and even became more hopeful when they realized that from the first Trepov was fighting to oust Protopopov. That meant, of course, a fight against Rasputin as well. Whatever Trepov's motives might be in fighting Protopopov and Rasputin he was helping the opposition. But Trepov was no match for such opponents. It soon became evident that as Premier he was a mere figurehead and that Rasputin and Protopopov held the government in their hands. Protopopov openly defied the Premier and the Duma.

In December it began to be rumored in political circles that Sturmer, who was now attached in some not clearly defined capacity to the Foreign Office, was about to be sent to a neutral country as ambassador. The rumor created the utmost consternation in liberal circles in Russia and in the Allied embassies. If true, it could only have one meaning, namely, that arrangements were being made to negotiate a separate peace with Germany—and that meant that Russia was to become Germany's economic vassal.

The Duma demanded a responsible Ministry, a Cabinet directly responsible to, and controlled by, the Duma as the people's representative. This demand had been constantly made since the First Revolution. Even the Imperial Council, upon which the Czar had always been able to rely for support against revolutionary movements, now joined forces with the Duma in making this demand. That traditionally reactionary, bureaucratic body, composed of former Premiers, Cabinet Ministers, and other high officials, formally demanded that the Czar take steps to make the government responsible to the popularly elected assemblage. This was a small revolution in itself. The fabric of Czarism had cracked.

II

There can be no doubt in the mind of any student of Russian affairs that the unity of the Imperial Council and the Duma, like the unity of classes, was due to the strong pro-Ally sentiment which at that time possessed practically the entire nation. On December 12th—new style—Germany offered Russia a separate peace, and three days later the Foreign Minister, Pokrovsky, visited the Duma and announced that Russia would reject the offer. The Duma immediately passed a resolution declaring that "the Duma unanimously favors a categorical refusal by the Allied governments to enter, under present conditions, into any peace negotiations whatever." On the 19th a similar resolution was adopted by the Imperial Council, which continued to follow the leadership of the Duma. Before adjourning for the Christmas holidays the Duma passed another resolution, aimed chiefly at Protopopov and Sturmer, protesting against the sinister activities which were undermining the war-making forces of the nation, and praising the work of the zemstvos and working-class organizations which had struggled bravely to sustain the army, feed the people, care for the sick and wounded, and avert utter chaos.

On December 30th, in the early hours of the morning, the monk Rasputin was murdered and his body thrown into the Neva. The strangest and most evil of all the actors in the Russian drama was dead, but the system which made him what he was lived. Rasputin dead exercised upon the diseased mind of the Czarina—and, through her, upon the Czar—even a greater influence than when he was alive. Nicholas II was as powerless to resist the insane Czarina's influence as he had proved himself to be when he banished the Grand-Duke Nicholas for pointing out that the Czarina was the tool of evil and crafty intriguers. Heedless of the warning implied in the murder of Rasputin, and of the ever-growing opposition to the government and the throne, the Czar inaugurated, or permitted to be inaugurated, new measures of reaction and repression.

Trepov was driven from the Premiership and replaced by Prince Golitizin, a bureaucrat of small brain and less conscience. The best Minister of Education Russia had ever had, Ignatyev, was replaced by one of the blackest of all reactionaries. The Czar celebrated the New-Year by issuing an edict retiring the progressive members of the Imperial Council, who had supported the Duma, and appointing in their stead the most reactionary men he could find in the Empire. At the head of the Council as president he placed the notorious Jew-hating Stcheglovitov. As always, hatred of the Jew sprang from fear of progress.

As one reads the history of January, 1917, in Russia, as it was reported in the press day by day, and the numerous accounts of competent and trustworthy observers, it is difficult to resist the conclusion that Protopopov deliberately sought to precipitate a revolution. Mad as this hypothesis seems to be, it is nevertheless the only one which affords a rational explanation of the policy of the government. No sooner was Golitizin made Premier than it was announced that the opening of the Duma would be postponed till the end of January, in order that the Cabinet might be reorganized. Later it was announced that the Duma opening would be again postponed—this time till the end of February. In the reorganization of the Cabinet, Shuvaviev, the War Minister, who had loyally co-operated with the zemstvos and had supported the Duma in November, was dismissed. Pokrovsky, the Foreign Minister, who had announced to the Duma in December the rejection of the German peace offer, was reported to be "sick" and given "leave of absence." Other changes were made in the Cabinet, in every case to the advantage of the reactionaries. It was practically impossible for anyone in Russia to find out who the Ministers of the government were.

Protopopov released Sukhomlinov, the former Minister of War who had been justly convicted of treason. This action, taken, it was said, at the direction of the Czarina, added to the already wide-spread belief that the government was animated by a desire to make peace with Germany. That the Czar himself was loyal to the Allies was generally believed, but there was no such belief in the loyalty of Protopopov, Sturmer, and their associates. The nation meantime was drifting into despair and anarchy. The railway system was deliberately permitted to become disorganized. Hunger reigned in the cities and the food reserves for the army were deliberately reduced to a two days' supply. The terror of hunger spread through the large cities and through the army at the front like prairie fire.

It became evident that Protopopov was carrying out the plans of the Germanophiles, deliberately trying to disorganize the life of the nation and make successful warfare impossible. Socialists and labor leaders charged that his agents were encouraging the pacifist minority and opposing the patriotic majority among the workers. The work of the War Industries Committee which controlled organizations engaged in the manufacture of war-supplies which employed hundreds of thousands of workers was hampered in every way. It is the testimony of the best-known and most-trusted working-class leaders in Russia that the vast majority of the workers, while anxious for a general democratic peace, were opposed to a separate peace with Germany and favored the continuation of the war against Prussianism and the co-operation of all classes to that end. The pacifists and "defeatist" Socialists represented a minority. To the minority every possible assistance was given, while the leaders of the working class who were loyal to the war, and who sought to sustain the morale of the workers in support of the war, were opposed and thwarted in their efforts and, in many cases, cast into prison. The Black Hundreds were still at work.

Socialist leaders of the working class issued numerous appeals to the workers, warning them that Protopopov's secret police agitators were trying to bring about strikes, and begging them not to lend themselves to such treacherous designs, which could only aid Germany at the expense of democracy in Russia and elsewhere. It became known, too, that large numbers of machine-guns were being distributed among the police in Petrograd and placed at strategic points throughout the city. It was said that Protopopov was mad, but it was the methodical madness of a desperate, reactionary, autocratic régime.

III

Protopopov and Sturmer and their associates recognized as clearly as the liberals did the natural kinship and interdependence of the three great autocracies, the Romanov, Habsburg, and Hohenzollern dynasties. They knew well that the crushing of autocracy in Austria-Hungary and Germany would make it impossible to maintain autocracy in Russia. They realized, furthermore, that while the nation was not willing to attempt revolution

98

during the war, the end of the war would inevitably bring with it revolution upon a scale far vaster than had ever been attempted before, unless, indeed, the revolutionary leaders could be goaded into making a premature attempt to overthrow the monarchy. In that case, it might be possible to crush them. Given a rebellion in the cities, which could be crushed by the police amply provided with machine-guns, and by "loyal" troops, with a vast army unprovided with food and no means of supplying it, there would be abundant justification for making a separate peace with Germany. Thus the Revolution would be crushed and the whole system of autocracy, Russian, Austrian, and German, preserved.

The morning of the 27th of February—new style—was tense with an ominous expectancy. In the Allied chancelleries anxious groups were gathered. They realized that the fate of the Allies hung in the balance. In Petrograd alone three hundred thousand workers went out on strike that day, and the police agents did their level best to provoke violence. The large bodies of troops massed at various points throughout the city, and the police with their machine-guns, testified to the thoroughness with which the government had prepared to crush any revolutionary manifestations. Thanks to the excellent discipline of the workers, and the fine wisdom of the leaders of the Social Democrats, the Socialist-Revolutionists, and the Labor Group, who constantly exhorted the workers not to fall into the trap set for them, there was no violence.

At the opening session of the Duma, Kerensky, leader of the Labor Group, made a characteristic address in which he denounced the arrest of the Labor Group members of the War Industries Committee. He directed his attack against the "system," not against individuals:

"We are living in a state of anarchy unprecedented in our history. In comparison with it the period of 1613 seems like child's play. Chaos has enveloped not only the political, but the economic life of the nation as well. It destroys the very foundations of the nation's social economic structure.

"Things have come to such a pass that recently one of the Ministries, shipping coal from Petrograd to a neighboring city, had armed the train with a special guard so that other authorities should not confiscate the coal on the way! We have arrived already at the primitive stage when each person defends with all the resources at his command the material in his possession, ready to enter into mortal combat for it with his neighbor. We are witnessing the same scenes which France went through at the time of the Revolution. Then also the products shipped to Paris were accompanied by special detachments of troops to prevent their being seized by the provincial authorities....

"Behold the Cabinet of Rittich-Protopopov-Golitizin dragging into the court the Labor Group of the War Industries Committee, charged with aiming at the creation of a Russian Social-Democratic republic! They did not even know that nobody aims at a 'Social-Democratic' republic. One aiming at a republic labors for popular government. But has the court anything to say about all these distinctions? We know beforehand what sentences are to be imposed upon the prisoners....

"I have no desire to criticize the individual members of the Cabinet. The greatest mistake of all is to seek traitors, German agents, separate Sturmers. *We have a still greater enemy than the German influence, than the treachery and treason of individuals. And that enemy is the system—the system of a medieval form of government.*"

How far the conspiracy of the government of Russia against the war of Russia and her Allies extended is shown by the revelations made in the Duma on March 3d by one of the members, A. Konovalov. He reported that two days previously, March 1st, the only two members of the Labor Group of the War Industries Committee who were not in prison issued an appeal to the workers not to strike. These two members of the Labor Group of the War Industries Committee, Anosovsky and Ostapenko, took their exhortation to the bureau of the War Industries Committee for its approval. But, although approved by this great and important organization, the appeal was not passed by the government censor. When Guchkov, president of the War Industries Committee, attempted to get the appeal printed in the newspapers he was prevented by action emanating from the office of Protopopov.

IV

Through all the early days of March there was labor unrest in Petrograd, as well as in some other cities. Petrograd was, naturally, the storm center. There were small strikes, but, fortunately, not much rioting. The extreme radicals were agitating for the release of the imprisoned leaders of the Labor Group and urging drastic action by the workers. Much of this agitation was sincere and honest, but no little of it was due to the provocative agents. These, disguised as workmen, seized every opportunity to urge revolt. Any pretext sufficed them; they stimulated the honest agitation to revolt as a protest against the imprisonment of the Labor Group, and the desperate threat that unless food was forthcoming revolution would be resorted to for sinister purposes. And all the time the police and the troops were massed to crush the first rising.

The next few days were destined to reveal the fact that the cunning and guile of Protopopov had overreached itself; that the soldiers could not be relied upon to crush any uprising of the people. There was some rioting in Petrograd on March 3d, and the next day the city was placed under martial law. On March 7th the textile workers went out on strike and were quickly followed by several thousand workers belonging to other trades. Next day there was a tremendous popular demonstration at which the workers demanded food. The strike spread during the next two or three days until there was a pretty general stoppage of industry. Students from the university joined with the striking workmen and there were numerous demonstrations, but little disposition to violence. When the Cossacks and mounted police were sent to break up the crowds, the Cossacks took great care not to hurt the people, fraternizing with them and being cheered by them. It was evident that the army would not let itself be used to crush the uprising of the people. The police remained "loyal," but they were not adequate in numbers. Protopopov had set in motion forces which no human agency could control. The Revolution was well under way.

The Duma remained in constant session. Meantime the situation in the capital was becoming serious in the extreme. Looting of stores began, and there were many victims of the police efforts to disperse the crowds. In the midst of the crisis the Duma repudiated the government and broke off all relations with it. The resolution of the Duma declared that "The government which covered its hands with the blood of the people should no longer be admitted to the Duma. With such a government the Duma breaks all relations forever." The answer of Czar Nicholas was an order to dissolve the Duma, which order the Duma voted to ignore, remaining in session as before.

On Sunday, March 11th, there was a great outpouring of people at a demonstration. Police established on the roofs of some public buildings attacked the closely packed throngs with machine-gun fire, killing and wounding hundreds. One of the famous regiments, the Volynski, revolted, killed its commander, and joined the people when ordered to fire into the crowds. Detachments of soldiers belonging to other regiments followed their example and refused to fire upon the people. One or two detachments of troops did obey orders and were immediately attacked by the revolutionary troops. There was civil war in Petrograd.

While the fighting was still going on, the president of the Duma sent the following telegram to the Czar:

The situation is grave. Anarchy reigns in the capital. The government is paralyzed. The transport of provisions and fuel is completely disorganized. General dissatisfaction is growing. Irregular rifle-firing is occurring in the streets. It is necessary to charge immediately some person enjoying the confidence of the people to form a new government. It is impossible to linger. Any delay means death. Let us pray to God that the responsibility in this hour will not fall upon a crowned head.

Rodzianko.

The Duma waited in vain that night for an answer from the Czar. The bourgeois elements in the Duma were terrified. Only the leaders of the different Socialist groups appeared to possess any idea of providing the revolutionary movement with proper direction. While the leaders of the bourgeois groups were proclaiming their conviction that the Revolution would be crushed in a few hours by the tens of thousands of troops in Petrograd who had not yet rebelled, the Socialist leaders were busy preparing plans to carry on the struggle. Even those Social Democrats who for various reasons had most earnestly tried to avert the Revolution gave themselves with whole-hearted enthusiasm to the task of organizing the revolutionary forces. Following the example set in the 1905 Revolution, there had been formed a central committee of the working-class organizations to direct the movement. This body, composed of elected representatives of the unions and Socialist societies, was later known as the Council of Workmen's Deputies. It was this body which undertook the organization of the Revolution. This Revolution, unlike that of 1905, was initiated by the bourgeoisie, but its originators manifested little desire and less capacity to lead it.

When Monday morning came there was no longer an unorganized, planless mass confusedly opposing a carefully organized force, but a compact, well-organized, and skilfully led movement. Processions were formed, each under responsible directors with very definite instructions. As on the previous day, the police stationed upon roofs of buildings, and at various strategic points, fired upon the people. As on the previous day, also, the soldiers joined the Revolution and refused to shoot the people. The famous Guards' Regiment, long the pet and pride of the Czar, was the first to rebel. The soldiers killed the officer who ordered them to fire, and then with cheers joined the rebels. When the military authorities sent out another regiment to suppress the rebel Guards' Regiment they saw the new force go over to the Revolution in a body. Other regiments deserted in the same manner. The flower of the Russian army had joined the people in revolting against the Czar and the system of Czarism.

On the side of the revolutionists were now many thousands of well-trained soldiers, fully armed. Soon they took possession of the Arsenal, after killing the commander. The soldiers made organized and systematic warfare upon the police. Every policeman seen was shot down, police stations were set on fire, and prisons were broken open and the prisoners released. The numerous political prisoners were triumphantly liberated and took their places in the revolutionary ranks. In rapid succession the great bastiles fell! Peter and Paul Fortress, scene of infinite martyrdom, fell into the hands of the revolutionary forces, and the prisoners, many of them heroes and martyrs of other uprisings, were set free amid frenzied cheering. The great Schlüsselburg Fortress was likewise seized and emptied. With twenty-five thousand armed troops on their side, the revolutionists were practically masters of the capital. They attacked the headquarters of the hated Secret Service and made a vast, significantly symbolical bonfire of its archives.

Once more Rodzianko appealed to the Czar. It is no reflection upon Rodzianko's honesty, or upon his loyalty to the people, to say that he was appalled by the development of the struggle. He sympathized with the people in their demand for political democracy and would wage war to the end upon Czarism, but he feared the effect of the Revolution upon the army and the Allied cause. Moreover, he was a landowner, and he feared Socialism. In 1906 he had joined forces with the government when the Socialists led the masses—and now the Socialist leaders were again at the head of the masses. Perhaps the result would have been otherwise if the Duma had followed up its repudiation of the government by openly and unreservedly placing itself at the head of the uprising. In any other country than Russia that would have been done, in all probability, but the Russian bourgeoisie was weak. This was due, like so much else in Russia, to the backwardness of the industrial system. There was not a strong middle class and, therefore, the bourgeoisie left the fighting to the working class. Rodzianko's new appeal to the Czar was pathetic. When hundreds of dead and dying lay in the streets and in churches, hospitals, and other public buildings, he could still imagine that the Czar could save the situation: "The situation is growing worse. It is necessary to take measures immediately, for to-morrow it will be too late," he telegraphed. "The last hour has struck to decide the fate of the country and of the dynasty." Poor, short-sighted bourgeois! It was already "too late" for "measures" by the weak-minded Nicholas II to avail. The "fate of the country and of the dynasty" was already determined! It was just as well that the Czar did not make any reply to the message.

The new ruler of Russia, King Demos, was speaking now. Workers and soldiers sent deputations to the Taurida Palace, where the Duma was sitting. Rodzianko read to them the message he had sent to the Czar, but that was small comfort. Thousands of revolutionists, civilian and military, stormed the Taurida Palace and clamored to hear what the Socialists in the Duma had to say. In response to this demand Tchcheidze, Kerensky, Skobelev, and other Socialists from various groups appeared and addressed the people. These men had a message to give; they understood the ferment and were part of it. They were of the Revolution—bone of its bone, flesh of its flesh, and so they were cheered again and again. And what a triumvirate they made, these leaders of the people! Tchcheidze, once a university professor, keen, cool, and as witty as George Bernard Shaw, listened to with the deference democracy always pays to intellect.

Kerensky, lawyer by profession, matchless as an orator, obviously the prophet and inspirer rather than the executive type; Skobelev, blunt, direct, and practical, a man little given to romantic illusions. It was Skobelev who made the announcement to the crowd outside the Taurida Palace that the old system was ended forever and that the Duma would create a Provisional Committee. He begged the workers and the soldiers to keep order, to refrain from violence against individuals, and to observe strict discipline. "Freedom demands discipline and order," he said.

That afternoon the Duma selected a temporary committee to restore order. The committee, called the Duma Committee of Safety, consisted of twelve members, representing all the parties and groups in the Duma. The hastily formed committee of the workers met and decided to call on the workmen to hold immediate elections for the Council of Workmen's Deputies—the first meeting of which was to be held that evening. That this was a perilous thing to do the history of the First Revolution clearly showed, but no other course seemed open to the workers, in view of the attitude of the bourgeoisie. On behalf of the Duma Committee, Rodzianko issued the following proclamation:

The Provisional Committee of the members of the Imperial Duma, aware of the grave conditions of internal disorder created by the measure of the old government, has found itself compelled to take into its hands the re-establishment of political and civil order. In full consciousness of the responsibility of its decision, the Provisional Committee expresses its trust that the population and the army will help it in the difficult task of creating a new government which will comply with the wishes of the population, and be able to enjoy its confidence.

Michail Rodzianko, *Speaker of the Imperial Duma.* February 27, 1917.[4]

That night the first formal session of the Council of Workmen's Deputies was held. Tchcheidze was elected president, Kerensky vice-president. The deputies had been elected by the working-men of many factories and by the members of Socialist organizations. It was not until the following day that soldiers' representatives were added and the words "and Soldiers" added to the title of the Council. At this first meeting the Council—a most moderate and capable body—called for a Constituent

Assembly on the basis of equal, direct, and secret universal suffrage. This demand was contained in an address to the people which read, in part:

To finish the struggle successfully in the interests of democracy, the people must create their own powerful organization.

The Council of the Workmen's Deputies, holding its session in the Imperial Duma, makes it its supreme task to organize the people's forces and their struggle for a final securing of political freedom and popular government in Russia.

We appeal to the entire population of the capital to rally around the Council, to form local committees in the various boroughs, and to take over the management of local affairs.

All together, with united forces, we will struggle for a final abolition of the old system and the calling of a Constituent Assembly on the basis of universal, equal, direct, and secret suffrage.

This document is of the highest historical importance and merits close study. As already noted, Tchcheidze, leader of the Mensheviki, was president of the Council, and this appeal to the people shows how fully the moderate views of his group prevailed. Indeed, the manner in which the moderate counsels of the Mensheviki dominated the Council at a time of great excitement and passion, when extremists might have been expected to obtain the lead, is one of the most remarkable features of the whole story of the Second Russian Revolution. It appeared at this time that the Russian proletariat had fully learned the tragic lessons of 1905-06.

It is evident from the text of the appeal that at the time the Council looked upon the Revolution as being primarily a political event, not as a movement to reconstruct the economic and social system. There is no reference to social democracy. Even the land question is not referred to. How limited their purpose was at the moment may be gathered from the statement, "The Council ... makes it its supreme task to organize the people's forces and their struggle for a final securing of political freedom and popular government." It is also clearly evident that, notwithstanding the fact that the Council itself was a working-class organization, a manifestation of the class consciousness of the workers, the leaders of the Council did not regard the Revolution as a proletarian event, nor doubt the necessity of co-operation on the part of all classes. Proletarian exclusiveness came later, but on March 13th the appeal of the Council was "to the entire population."

March 14th saw the arrest of many of the leading reactionaries, including Protopopov and the traitor Sukhomlinov, and an approach to order. All that day the representatives of the Duma and the representatives of the Council of Workmen's and Soldiers' Deputies, as it was now called, embryo of the first Soviet government, tried to reach an agreement concerning the future organization of Russia. The representatives of the Duma were pitifully lacking in comprehension of the situation. They wanted the Czar deposed, but the monarchy itself retained, subject to constitutional limitations analogous to those obtaining in England. They wanted the Romanov dynasty retained, their choice being the Czar's brother, Grand-Duke Michael. The representatives of the Soviet, on the other hand, would not tolerate the suggestion that the monarchy be continued. Standing, as yet, only for political democracy, they insisted that the monarchy must be abolished and that the new government be republican in form. The statesmanship and political skill of these representatives of the workers were immeasurably superior to those possessed by the bourgeois representatives of the Duma.

V

Thursday, March 15, 1917—new style—was one of the most fateful and momentous days in the history of mankind. It will always be remembered as the day on which Czarism ceased to exist in Russia. At three o'clock in the afternoon Miliukov, leader of the Constitutional Democrats, appeared in front of the Taurida Palace and announced to the waiting throngs that an agreement had been reached between the Duma and the Council of Workmen's and Soldiers' Deputies; that it had been decided to depose the Czar, to constitute immediately a Provisional Government composed of representatives of all parties and groups, and to proceed with arrangements for the holding of a Constituent Assembly at an early date to determine the form of a permanent democratic government for Russia.

At the head of the Provisional Government, as Premier, had been placed Prince George E. Lvov, who as president of the Union of Zemstvos had proved himself to be a democrat of the most liberal school as well as an extraordinarily capable organizer. The position of Minister of Foreign Affairs was given to Miliukov, whose strong sympathy with the Allies was well known. The position of Minister of Justice was given to Alexander Kerensky, one of the most extraordinary men in Russia, a leader of the Group of Toil, a party of peasant Socialists, vice-president of the Council of Workmen's and Soldiers' Deputies. At the head of the War Department was placed Alexander Guchkov, a soldier-politician, leader of the Octobrist party, who had turned against the First Revolution in 1905, when it became an economic war of the classes, evoking thereby the hatred of the Socialists, but who as head of the War Industries Committee had achieved truly wonderful results in the present war in face of the opposition of the government. The pressing food problem was placed in the hands of Andrei Shingarev. As Minister of Agriculture Shingarev belonged to the radical left wing of the Cadets.

It cannot be said that the composition of the Provisional Government was received with popular satisfaction. It was top-heavy with representatives of the bourgeoisie. There was only one Socialist, Kerensky. Miliukov's selection, inevitable though it was, and great as his gifts were, was condemned by the radical working-men because he was regarded as a dangerous "imperialist" on account of his advocacy of the annexation of Constantinople. Guchkov's inclusion was equally unpopular on account of his record at the time of the First Revolution. The most popular selection was undoubtedly Kerensky, because he represented more nearly than any of the others the aspirations of the masses. As a whole, it was the fact that the Provisional Government was too fully representative of the bourgeois parties and groups which gave the Bolsheviki and other radicals a chance to condemn it.

The absence of the name of Tchcheidze from the list was a surprise and a disappointment to most of the moderate Socialists, for he had come to be regarded as one of the most capable and trustworthy leaders of the masses. The fact that he was not included in the new government could hardly fail to cause uneasy suspicion. It was said later that efforts had been made to induce him to join the new government, but that he declined to do so. Tchcheidze's position was a very difficult one. Thoroughly in sympathy with the plan to form a coalition Provisional Government, and supporting Kerensky in his position, Tchcheidze nevertheless declined to enter the new

Cabinet himself. In this he was quite honest and not at all the tricky politician he has been represented as being.

Tchcheidze knew that the Duma had been elected upon a most undemocratic suffrage and that it did not and could not represent the masses of the peasants and wage-workers. These classes were represented in the Council of Workmen's and Soldiers' Deputies, which continued to exist as a separate body, independent of the Duma, but co-operating with it as an equal. From a Socialist point of view it would have been a mistake to disband the Council, Tchcheidze believed. He saw Soviet government as the need of the critical moment, rather than as the permanent, distinctive type of Russian Social democracy as the critics of Kerensky have alleged.

While the Provisional Government was being created, the Czar, at General Headquarters, was being forced to recognize the bitter fact that the Romanov dynasty could no longer live. When he could no more resist the pressure brought to bear upon him by the representatives of the Duma, he wrote and signed a formal instrument of abdication of the Russian throne, naming his brother, Grand-Duke Michael, as his successor. The latter dared not attempt to assume the imperial rôle. He recognized that the end of autocracy had been reached and declined to accept the throne unless chosen by a popular referendum vote. On March 16th, the day after the abdication of Nicholas II, Michael issued a statement in which he said:

This heavy responsibility has come to me at the voluntary request of my brother, who has transferred the Imperial throne to me during a time of warfare which is accompanied by unprecedented popular disturbances.

Moved by the thought, which is in the minds of the entire people, that the good of the country is paramount, I have adopted the firm resolution to accept the supreme power only if this be the will of our great people, who, by a plebiscite organized by their representatives in a Constituent Assembly, shall establish a form of government and new fundamental laws for the Russian state.

Consequently, invoking the benediction of our Lord, I urge all citizens of Russia to submit to the Provisional Government, established upon the initiative of the Duma and invested with full plenary powers, until such time which will follow with as little delay as possible, as the Constituent Assembly, on a basis of universal, direct, equal, and secret suffrage, shall, by its decision as to the new form of government, express the will of the people.

The hated Romanov dynasty was ended at last. It is not likely that Grand-Duke Michael entertained the faintest hope that he would ever be called to the throne, either by a Constituent Assembly or by a popular referendum. Not only was the Romanov dynasty ended, but equally so was monarchical Absolutism itself. No other dynasty would replace that of the Romanovs. Russia had thrown off the yoke of autocracy. The Second Revolution was an accomplished fact; its first phase was complete. Thoughtful men among the revolutionists recognized that the next phase would be far more perilous and difficult. "The bigger task is still before us," said Miliukov, in his address to the crowd that afternoon. A Constituent Assembly was to be held and that was bound to intensify the differences which had been temporarily composed during the struggle to overthrow the system of Absolutism. And the differences which existed between the capitalist class and the working class were not greater than those which existed within the latter.

CHAPTER V

FROM BOURGEOISIE TO BOLSHEVIKI

I

It required no great gift of prophecy to foretell the failure of the Provisional Government established by the revolutionary coalition headed by Prince Lvov. From the very first day it was evident that the Cabinet could never satisfy the Russian people. It was an anomaly in that the Revolution had been a popular revolution, while the Provisional Government was overwhelmingly representative of the landowners, manufacturers, bankers, and merchants—the despised and distrusted bourgeoisie. The very meager representation given to the working class, through Kerensky, was, in the circumstances, remarkable for its stupid effrontery and its disregard of the most obvious realities. Much has been said and written of the doctrinaire attitude which has characterized the Bolsheviki in the later phases of the struggle, but if by doctrinairism is meant subservience to preconceived theories and disregard of realities, it must be said that the statesmen of the bourgeoisie were as completely its victims as the Bolsheviki later proved to be. They were subservient to dogma and indifferent to fact.

The bourgeois leaders of Russia—and those Socialists who co-operated with them—attempted to ignore the biggest and most vital fact in the whole situation, namely, the fact that the Revolution was essentially a Socialist Revolution in the sense that the overwhelming mass of the people were bent upon the realization of a very comprehensive, though somewhat crudely conceived, program of socialization. It was not a mere political Revolution, and political changes which left the essential social structure unchanged, which did not tend to bring about equality of democratic opportunity, and which left the control of the nation in the hands of landowners and capitalists, could never satisfy the masses nor fail to invite their savage attack. Only the most hopeless and futile of doctrinaires could

111

have argued themselves into believing anything else. It was quite idle to argue from the experience of other countries that Russia must follow the universal rule and establish and maintain bourgeois rule for a period more or less prolonged. True, that had been the experience of most nations, but it was foolish in the extreme to suppose that it must be the experience of Russia, whose conditions were so utterly unlike those which had obtained in any nation which had by revolution established constitutional government upon a democratic basis.

To begin with, in every other country revolution by the bourgeoisie itself had been the main factor in the overthrow of autocracy. Feudalism and monarchical autocracy fell in western Europe before the might of a powerful rising class. That this class in every case drew to its side the masses and benefited by their co-operation must not be allowed to obscure the fact that in these other countries of all the classes in society the bourgeoisie was the most powerful. It was that fact which established its right to rule in place of the deposed rulers. The Russian middle class, however, lacked that historic right to rule. In consequence of the backwardness of the nation from the point of view of industrial development, the bourgeoisie was correspondingly backward and weak. Never in any country had a class so weak and uninfluential essayed the rôle of the ruling class. To believe that a class which at the most did not exceed six per cent. of the population could assert and maintain its rule over a nation of one hundred and eighty millions of people, when these had been stirred by years of revolutionary agitation, was at once pedantic and absurd.

The industrial proletariat was as backward and as relatively weak as the bourgeoisie. Except by armed force and tyranny of the worst kind, this class could not rule Russia. Its fitness and right to rule are not appreciably greater than the fitness and right of the bourgeoisie. It cannot even be said on its behalf that it had waged the revolutionary struggle of the working class, for in truth its share in the Russian revolutionary movement had been relatively small, far less than that of the peasant organizations. With more than one hundred and thirty-five millions of peasants, from whose discontent and struggle the revolutionary movement had drawn its main strength, neither the bourgeoisie nor the class-conscious section of the industrial proletariat could set up its rule without angry protest and attacks which, soon

112

or late, must overturn it. Every essential fact in the Russian situation, which was so unique, pointed to the need for a genuine and sincere co-operation by the intelligent leaders of all the opposition elements until stability was attained, together with freedom from the abnormal difficulties due to the war. In any event, the domination of the Provisional Government by a class so weak and so narrow in its outlook and aims was a disaster. As soon as time for reflection had been afforded the masses discontent and distrust were inevitable.

II

From the first days there were ominous murmurings. Yet it must be confessed that the Provisional Government manifested much greater enlightenment than might have been expected of it and hastened to enact a program—quite remarkable for its liberality and vision; a program which, had it come from a government more truly representative in its personnel of revolutionary Russia, might, with one important addition, have served as the foundation of an enduring structure. On March 18th the Provisional Government issued a statement of its program and an appeal to the citizens for support. This document, which is said to have been the joint work of P.I. Novgorodtzev, N.V. Nekrasov, and P.N. Miliukov, read as follows:

Citizens: The Executive Committee of the Duma, with the aid and support of the garrison of the capital and its inhabitants, has succeeded in triumphing over the obnoxious forces of the old régime so that we can proceed to a more stable organization of the executive power, with men whose past political activity assures them the country's confidence.

The new Cabinet will base its policy upon the following principles:

First.—An immediate and general amnesty for all political and religious offenses, including terrorist acts and military and agrarian offenses.

Second.—Liberty of speech and of the press; freedom for alliances, unions, and strikes, with the extension of these liberties to military officials, within the limits admitted by military requirements.

Third.—Abolition of all social, religious, and national restrictions.

Fourth.—To proceed forthwith to the preparation and convocation of

113

a Constituent Assembly, based on universal suffrage. This Assembly will establish a stable universal régime.

Fifth.—The substitution of the police by a national militia, with chiefs to be elected and responsible to the municipalities.

Sixth.—Communal elections to be based on universal, direct, equal, and secret suffrage.

Seventh.—The troops which participated in the revolutionary movement will not be disarmed, but will remain in Petrograd.

Eighth.—While maintaining strict military discipline for troops in active service, it is desirable to abrogate for soldiers all restrictions in the enjoyment of civil rights accorded other citizens.

The Provisional Government desires to add that it has no intention of taking advantage of war conditions to delay the realization of the measures of reform above mentioned.

This address is worthy of especial attention. The generous liberalism of the program it outlines cannot be denied, but it is political liberalism only. It is not directly and definitely concerned with the great fundamental economic issues which so profoundly affect the life and well-being of the working class, peasants, and factory-workers alike. It is the program of men who saw in the Revolution only a great epochal political advance. In this it reflects its bourgeois origin. With the exception of the right to organize unions and strikes—which is a political measure—not one of the important economic demands peculiar to the working class is met in the program. The land question, which was the economic basis of the Revolution, and without which there could have been no Revolution, was not even mentioned. And the Manifesto which the Provisional Government addressed to the nation on March 20th was equally silent with regard to the land question and the socialization of industry.

Evidently the Provisional Government desired to confine itself as closely as possible to political democracy, and to leave fundamental economic reform to be attended to by the Constituent Assembly. If that were its purpose, it would have helped matters to have had the purpose clearly stated and not merely left to inference. But whatever the shortcomings of its first official statements, the actual program of the Provisional Government during

114

the first weeks was far more satisfactory and afforded room for great hope. On March 21st the constitution of Finland was restored. On the following day amnesty was granted to all political and religious offenders. Within a few days freedom and self-government were granted to Poland, subject to the ratification of the Constituent Assembly. At the same time all laws discriminating against the Jews were repealed by the following decree:

All existing legal restrictions upon the rights of Russian citizens, based upon faith, religious teaching, or nationality, are revoked. In accordance with this, we hereby repeal all laws existing in Russia as a whole, as well as for separate localities, concerning:

1. Selection of place of residence and change of residence.

2. Acquiring rights of ownership and other material rights in all kinds of movable property and real estate, and likewise in the possession of, the use and managing of all property, or receiving such for security.

3. Engaging in all kinds of trades, commerce, and industry, not excepting mining; also equal participation in the bidding for government contracts, deliveries, and in public auctions.

4. Participation in joint-stock and other commercial or industrial companies and partnerships, and also employment in these companies and partnerships in all kinds of positions, either by elections or by employment.

5. Employment of servants, salesmen, foremen, laborers, and trade apprentices.

6. Entering the government service, civil as well as military, and the grade or condition of such service; participation in the elections for the institutions for local self-government, and all kinds of public institutions; serving in all kinds of positions of government and public establishments, as well as the prosecution of the duties connected with such positions.

7. Admission to all kinds of educational institutions, whether private, government, or public, and the pursuing of the courses of instruction of these institutions, and receiving scholarships. Also the pursuance of teaching and other educational professions.

8. Performing the duties of guardians, trustees, or jurors.

9. The use of language and dialects, other than Russian, in the proceedings of private societies, or in teaching in all kinds of private

educational institutions, and in commercial bookkeeping.

Thus all the humiliating restrictions which had been imposed upon the Jewish people were swept away. Had the Provisional Government done nothing else than this, it would have justified itself at the bar of history. But it accomplished much more than this: before it had been in office a month, in addition to its liberation of Finns, Poles, and Jews, the Provisional Government abolished the death penalty; removed all the provincial governors and substituted for them the elected heads of the provincial county councils; *confiscated the large land holdings of the Imperial family and of the monasteries*; levied an excess war-profits tax on all war industries; and fixed the price of food at rates greatly lower than had prevailed before. The Provisional Government had gone farther, and, while declaring that these matters must be left to the Constituent Assembly for settlement, had declared itself in favor of woman suffrage and of *the distribution of all land among the peasants, the terms and conditions of expropriation and distribution to be determined by the Constituent Assembly*.

The Provisional Government also established a War Cabinet which introduced various reforms into the army. All the old oppressive regulations were repealed and an attempt made to democratize the military system. Some of these reforms were of the utmost value; others were rather dangerous experiments. Much criticism has been leveled against the rules providing for the election of officers by the men in the ranks, for a conciliation board to act in disputes between men and officers over questions of discipline, and the abolition of the regulations requiring private soldiers to address officers by the title "Sir." It must be borne in mind, however, in discussing these things, that these rules represented a great, honest effort to restore the morale of an army that had been demoralized, and to infuse it with democratic faith and zeal in order that it might "carry on." It is not just to judge the rules without considering the conditions which called them forth.

Certainly the Provisional Government—which the government of the United States formally recognized on March 22d, being followed in this by the other Allied governments next day—could not be accused fairly of being either slothful or unfaithful. Its accomplishments during those first weeks were most remarkable. Nevertheless, as the days went by it became evident that it could not hope to satisfy the masses and that, therefore, it could not

116

last very long.

III

The Council of Workmen's and Soldiers' Delegates was pursuing its independent existence, under the leadership of Tchcheidze, Skobelev, Tseretelli, and other moderate Social Democrats. As yet the Bolsheviki were a very small and uninfluential faction, lacking capable leadership. There can be very little doubt that the Council represented the feelings of the great mass of the organized wage-earners far more satisfactorily than the Provisional Government did, or that it was trusted to a far greater degree, alike by the wage-earners of the cities and the peasants. A great psychological fact existed, a fact which the Provisional Government and the governments of the Allied nations might well have reckoned with: the Russian working-people, artisans and peasants alike, were aggressively class conscious and could trust fully only the leaders of their own class.

The majority of the Social Democratic party was, at the beginning, so far from anything like Bolshevism, so thoroughly constructive and opportunistic in its policies, that its official organ, *Pravda*—not yet captured by the Bolsheviki—put forward a program which might easily have been made the basis for an effective coalition. It was in some respects disappointingly moderate: like the program of the Provisional Government, it left the land question untouched, except in so far as the clause demanding the confiscation of the property of the royal family and the Church bore upon it. The Social Democratic party, reflecting the interests of the city proletariat, had never been enthusiastic about the peasants' claim for distribution of the land, and there had been much controversy between its leaders and the leaders of the Socialist-Revolutionary party, the party of the peasants. The program as printed in Pravda read:

1. A biennial one-house parliament.
2. Wide extension of the principle of self-government.
3. Inviolability of person and dwelling.
4. Unlimited freedom of the press, of speech, and of assembly.
5. Freedom of movement in business.
6. Equal rights for all irrespective of sex, religion, and nationality.

7. Abolition of class distinction.

8. Education in native language; native languages everywhere to have equal rights with official language.

9. Every nationality in the state to have the right of self-definition.

10. The right of all persons to prosecute officials before a jury.

11. Election of magistrates.

12. A citizen army instead of ordinary troops.

13. Separation of Church from state and school from Church.

14. Free compulsory education for both sexes to the age of sixteen.

15. State feeding of poor children.

16. Confiscation of Church property, also that of the royal family.

17. Progressive income tax.

18. An eight-hour day, with six hours for all under eighteen.

19. Prohibition of female labor where such is harmful to women.

20. A clear holiday once a week to consist of forty-two hours on end.

It would be a mistake to suppose that this very moderate program embraced all that the majority of the Social Democratic party aimed at. It was not intended to be more than an ameliorative program for immediate adoption by the Constituent Assembly, for the convocation of which the Social Democrats were most eager, and which they confidently believed would have a majority of Socialists of different factions.

In a brilliant and caustic criticism of conditions as they existed in the pre-Bolshevist period, Trotzky denounced what he called "the farce of dual authority." In a characteristically clever and biting phrase, he described it as "The epoch of Dual Impotence, the government not able, and the Soviet not daring," and predicted its culmination in a "crisis of unheard-of severity."[5] There was more than a little truth in the scornful phrase. On the one hand, there was the Provisional Government, to which the Soviet had given its consent and its allegiance, trying to discharge the functions of government. On the other hand, there was the Soviet itself, claiming the right to control the course of the Provisional Government and indulging in systematic criticism of the latter's actions. It was inevitable that the Soviet should have been driven irresistibly to the point where it must either renounce its own existence or oppose the Provisional Government.

The dominating spirit and thought of the Soviet was that of international social democracy. While most of the delegates believed that it was necessary to prosecute the war and to defeat the aggressions of the Central Empires, they were still Socialists, internationalists, fundamental democrats, and anti-imperialists. Not without good and sufficient reason, they mistrusted the bourgeois statesmen and believed that some of the most influential among them were imperialists, actuated by a desire for territorial expansion, especially the annexation of Constantinople, and that they were committed to various secret treaties entered into by the old régime with England, France, and Italy. In the meetings of the Soviet, and in other assemblages of workers, the ugly suspicion grew that the war was not simply a war for national defense, for which there was democratic sanction and justification, but a war of imperialism, and that the Provisional Government was pursuing the old ways of secret diplomacy.

Strength was given to this feeling when Miliukov, the Foreign Minister, in an interview championed the annexation of Constantinople as a necessary safeguard for the outlet to the Mediterranean which Russian economic development needed. Immediately there was an outcry of protest from the Soviet, in which, it should be observed, the Bolsheviki were already gaining strength and confidence, thanks to the leadership of Kamenev, Lenine's colleague, who had returned from Siberian exile. It was not only the Bolsheviki, however, who protested against imperialistic tendencies. Practically the whole body of Socialists, Mensheviki and Bolsheviki alike, agreed in opposing imperialism and secret diplomacy. Socialists loyal to the national defense and Socialists who repudiated that policy and deemed it treason to the cause of Socialism were united in this one thing.

The storm of protest which Miliukov's interview provoked was stilled temporarily when the Premier, Lvov, announced that the Foreign Minister's views concerning the annexation of Constantinople were purely personal and did not represent the policy of the Provisional Government. Assurances were given that the Provisional Government was in accord with the policy of the Soviet. On April 16th a national congress of the Councils of Workmen's and Soldiers' Delegates adopted a series of resolutions in which there was a distinct menace to the Provisional Government. An earlier proclamation by the Petrograd Soviet had taken the form of a letter addressed to "Proletarians and Working-people of all Countries," but being in fact an appeal to the German working class to rise and refuse to fight against democratic and free Russia.[6] It declared that the peoples must take the matter of deciding questions of war and peace into their own hands. The new declaration was addressed to the Russian people:

First.—The Provisional Government, which constituted itself during the Revolution, in agreement with the Council of Workmen's and Soldiers' Delegates of Petrograd, published a proclamation announcing its program. This Congress records that this program contains in principle political demands for Russian democracy, and *recognizes that so far the Provisional Government has faithfully carried out its promises.*

Second.—This Congress appeals to the whole revolutionary democracy of Russia to rally to the support of the Council of Workmen's and Soldiers' Delegates, which is the center of the organized democratic forces that are capable, in unison with other progressive forces, of counteracting any counter revolutionary attempt and of consolidating the conquests of the revolution.

Third.—The Congress recognizes the necessity of permanent political control, the necessity of exercising an influence over the Provisional Government which will keep it up to a more energetic struggle against anti-revolutionary forces, and the necessity of exercising an influence which will insure its democratizing the whole Russian life and paving the way for a common *peace without annexations or contributions*, but on a basis of free national development of all peoples.

Fourth.—The Congress appeals to the democracy, while declining responsibility for any of its acts, to support the Provisional Government as long as it continues to consolidate and develop the conquest of the Revolution, *and as long as the basis of its foreign policy does not rest upon aspirations for territorial expansion.*

Fifth.—The Congress calls upon the revolutionary democracy of Russia, rallying around the Council of Workmen's and Soldiers' Delegates, to be ready to *vigorously suppress any attempt by the government to elude the control of democracy or to renounce the carrying out of its pledges*.[7]

On April 27th, acting under pressure from the Soviet, the Provisional Government published a Manifesto to the Russian people in which it announced a foreign policy which conformed to that which the Congress of Councils of Workmen's and Soldiers' Delegates had adopted. On May 1st Miliukov, the Foreign Minister, transmitted this Manifesto to the Allied governments as a preliminary to an invitation to those governments to restate their war aims. Accompanying the Manifesto was a Note of explanation, which was interpreted by a great many of the Socialists as an intimation to the Allies that the Manifesto was intended merely for home consumption, and that the Provisional Government would be glad to have the Allies disregard it. It is difficult for any one outside of Russia, whose sympathies were with the Entente Allies, to gather such an impression from the text of the Note, which simply set forth that enemy attempts to spread the belief that Russia was about to make a separate peace with Germany made it necessary for the Provisional Government to state its "entire agreement" with the aims of the Allies as set forth by their statesmen, including President Wilson, and to affirm that "the Provisional Government, in safeguarding the right acquired for our country, will maintain a strict regard for its agreement with the allies of Russia."

Although it was explained that the Note had been sent with the knowledge and approval of the Provisional Government, the storm of fury it produced was directed against Miliukov and, in less degree, Guchkov. Tremendous demonstrations of protest against "imperialism" were held. In the Soviet a vigorous demand for the overthrow of the Provisional Government was made by the steadily growing Bolshevik faction and by many anti-Bolsheviki Socialists. To avert the disaster of a vote of the Soviet against it, the Provisional Government made the following explanation of the so-called Miliukov Note:

The Note was subjected to long and detailed examination by the Provisional Government, and was unanimously approved. This Note, in speaking of a "decisive victory," had in view a solution of the problems mentioned in the communication of April 9th, and which was thus specified:

"The government deems it to be its right and duty to declare now that free Russia does not aim at the domination of other nations, or at depriving them of their national patrimony, or at occupying by force foreign territories, but that its object is to establish a durable peace on the basis of the rights of nations to decide their own destiny.

"The Russian nation does not lust after the strengthening of its power abroad at the expense of other nations. Its aim is not to subjugate or humiliate any one. In the name of the higher principles of equity, the Russian people have broken the chains which fettered the Polish nation, but it will not suffer that its own country shall emerge from the great struggle humiliated or weakened in its vital forces.

"In referring to the 'penalties and guarantees' essential to a durable peace, the Provisional Government had in view the reduction of armaments, the establishment of international tribunals, etc.

"This explanation will be communicated by the Minister of Foreign Affairs to the Ambassadors of the Allied Powers."

This assurance satisfied a majority of the delegates to the Soviet meeting held on the evening of May 4th, and a resolution of confidence in the Provisional Government was carried, after a very stormy debate. The majority, however, was a very small one, thirty-five in a total vote of about twenty-five hundred. It was clearly evident that the political government and the Soviet, which was increasingly inclined to assume the functions of government, were nearing a serious breach. With each day the Council of Workmen's and Soldiers' Delegates, as the organized expression of the great mass of wage-workers in Petrograd, grew in power over the Provisional Government and its influence throughout the whole of Russia. On May 13th Guchkov resigned, and three days later Miliukov followed his example. The party of the Constitutional Democrats had come to be identified in the minds of the revolutionary proletariat with imperialism and secret diplomacy, and was utterly discredited. The crisis developed an intensification of the distrust of the bourgeoisie by the proletariat.

IV

The crisis was not due solely to the diplomacy of the Provisional Government. Indeed, that was a minor cause. Behind all the discussions and disputes over Miliukov's conduct of the affairs of the Foreign Office there was the far more serious issue created by the agitation of the Bolsheviki. Under the leadership of Kamenev, Lenine, and others less well known, who skillfully exploited the friction with the Provisional Government, the idea of overthrowing that bourgeois body and of asserting that the Councils of Workmen's and Soldiers' Delegates would rule Russia in the interests of the working class made steady if not rapid progress.

Late in April Lenine and several other active Bolshevik leaders returned to Petrograd from Switzerland, together with Martov and other Menshevik leaders, who, while differing from the Bolsheviki upon practically all other matters, agreed with them in their bitter and uncompromising opposition to the war and in demanding an immediate peace.[8] As is well known, they were granted special facilities by the German Government in order that they might reach Russia safely. Certain Swiss Socialist leaders, regarded as strongly pro-German, arranged with the German Government that the Russian revolutionists should be permitted to travel across Germany by rail, in closed carriages. Unusual courtesies were extended to the travelers by the German authorities, and it was quite natural that Lenine and his associates should have been suspected of being sympathizers with, if not the paid agents and tools of, the German Government. The manner in which their actions, when they arrived in Russia, served the ends sought by the German military authorities naturally strengthened the suspicion so that it became a strong conviction.

Suspicious as the circumstances undoubtedly were, there is a very simple explanation of the conduct of Lenine and his companions. It is not at all necessary to conclude that they were German agents. Let us look at the facts with full candor. Lenine had long openly advocated the view that the defeat of Russia, even by Germany, would be good for the Russian revolutionary movement. But that was in the days before the overthrow of the Czar. Since that time his position had naturally shifted somewhat; he had opposed the continuation of the war and urged the Russian workers to withhold support from it. He had influenced the Soviets to demand a restatement of war aims by the Allies, and to incessantly agitate for immediate negotiations looking toward a general and democratic peace. Of course, the preaching of such a policy in Russia at that time by a leader so powerful and influential as Lenine, bound as it was to divide Russia and sow dissension among the Allies, fitted admirably into the German plans. That Germany would have been glad to pay for the performance of service so valuable can hardly be doubted.

On his side, Lenine is far too astute a thinker to have failed to understand that the German Government had its own selfish interests in view when it arranged for his passage across Germany. But the fact that the Allies would suffer, and that the Central Empires would gain some advantage, was of no consequence to him. That was an unavoidable accident and was purely incidental. His own purpose, to lead the revolutionary movement into a new phase, in which he believed with fanatical thoroughness, was the only thing that mattered in the least. If the conditions had been reversed, and he could only have reached Russia by the co-operation of the Allies, whose cause would be served, however unintentionally, by his work, he would have felt exactly the same. On the other hand, it was of the essence of his faith that his policy would lead to the overthrow of all capitalist-imperialist governments, those of Germany and her allies no less than those ranged on the other side. Germany might reason that a revolutionary uprising led by Lenine would rid her of one of her enemies and enable her to hurl larger forces against the foe on the western front. At that reasoning Lenine would smile in derision, thoroughly believing that any uprising he might bring about in Russia would sweep westward and destroy the whole fabric of Austro-German capitalist-imperialism. Lenine knew that he was being used by Germany, but he believed that he, in turn, was using Germany. He was supremely confident that he could outplay the German statesmen and military leaders.

It was a dangerous game that Lenine was playing, and he knew it, but the stakes were high and worth the great risk involved. It was not necessary for Germany to buy the service he could render to her; that service would be an unavoidable accompaniment of his mission. He argued that his work could, at the worst, give only temporary advantage to Germany. So far as there is any evidence to show, Lenine has been personally incorruptible. Holding lightly what he scornfully derides as "bourgeois morality," unmoral rather than immoral, willing to use any and all means to achieve ends which he sincerely believes to be the very highest and noblest that ever inspired mankind, he would, doubtless, take German money if he saw that it would help him to achieve his purposes. He would do so, however, without any thought of self-aggrandizement. It is probably safe and just to believe that if

124

Lenine ever took money from the Germans, either at that time or subsequently, he did so in this spirit, believing that the net result of his efforts would be equally disastrous to all the capitalist governments concerned in the war. It must be remembered, moreover, that the distinctions drawn by most thoughtful men between autocratic governments like those which ruled Germany and Austria and the more democratic governments of France, England, and America, have very little meaning or value to men like Lenine. They regard the political form as relatively unimportant; what matters is the fundamental economic class interest represented by the governments. Capitalist governments are all equally undesirable.

What Lenine's program was when he left Switzerland is easily learned. A few days before he left Switzerland he delivered a lecture on "The Russian Revolution," in which he made a careful statement of his position. It gives a very good idea of Lenine's mental processes. It shows him as a Marxist of the most dogmatic type—the type which caused Marx himself to rejoice that he was not a "Marxist":

As to the revolutionary organization and its task, the conquest of the power of the state and militarism: From the praxis of the French Commune of 1871, Marx shows that "the working class cannot simply take over the governmental machinery as built by the bourgeoisie, and use this machinery for its own purposes." The proletariat must break down this machinery. And this has been either concealed or denied by the opportunists.[9] But it is the most valuable lesson of the Paris Commune of 1871 and the Revolution in Russia in 1905. The difference between us and the Anarchists is, that we admit the state is a necessity in the development of our Revolution. The difference with the opportunists and the Kautsky[10] disciples is that we claim that we do not need the bourgeois state machinery as completed in the "democratic" bourgeois republics, but *the direct power of armed and organized workers*. Such was the character of the Commune of 1871 and of the Council of Workmen and Soldiers of 1905 and 1917. On this basis we build.[11]

Lenine went on to outline his program of action, which was to begin a new phase of the Revolution; to carry the revolt against Czarism onward against the bourgeoisie. Notwithstanding his scorn for democracy, he declared at that time that his policy included the establishment of a "democratic republic," confiscation of the landed estates of the nobility in

125

favor of the peasants, and the opening up of immediate peace negotiations. But the latter he would take out of the hands of the government entirely. "Peace negotiations should not be carried on by and with bourgeois governments, but with the proletariat in each of the warring countries." In his criticism of Kerensky and Tchcheidze the Bolshevik leader was especially scornful and bitter.

In a letter which he addressed to the Socialists of Switzerland immediately after his departure for Russia, Lenine gave a careful statement of his own position and that of his friends. It shows an opportunistic attitude of mind which differs from the opportunistic attitude of the moderate Socialists *in direction only*, not in the *quality of being opportunistic*:

Historic conditions have made the Russians, *perhaps for a short period*, the leaders of the revolutionary world proletariat, *but Socialism cannot now prevail in Russia*. We can expect only an agrarian revolution, which will help to create more favorable conditions for further development of the proletarian forces and *may result in measures for the control of production and distribution*.

The main results of the present Revolution will have to be *the creation of more favorable conditions for further revolutionary development*, and to influence the more highly developed European countries into action.[12]

The Bolsheviki at this period had as their program the following:

(1) The Soviets of Workers, Soldiers, and Peasants to constitute themselves into the actual revolutionary government and establish the dictatorship of the proletariat; (2) immediate confiscation of landed estates without compensation, the seizure to be done by the peasants themselves, without waiting for legal forms or processes, the peasants to organize into Soviets; (3) measures for the control of production and distribution by the revolutionary government, nationalization of monopolies, repudiation of the national debt; (4) the workers to take possession of factories and operate them in co-operation with the technical staffs; (5) refusal by the Soviets to recognize any treaties made by the governments either of the Czar or the bourgeoisie, and the immediate publication of all such treaties; (6) the workers to propose at once and publicly an immediate truce and negotiations of peace, these to be carried on by the proletariat and not by and with the bourgeoisie; (7) bourgeois war debts to be paid exclusively by the capitalists.

According to Litvinov, who is certainly not an unfriendly authority, as soon as Lenine arrived in Russia he submitted a new program to his party which was so novel, and so far a departure from accepted Socialist principles, that "Lenine's own closest friends shrank from it and refused to accept it."[13]

This program involved the abandonment of the plans made for holding the Constituent Assembly, or, at any rate, such a radical change as to amount to the abandonment of the accepted plans. *He proposed that universal, equal, direct, and secret suffrage be frankly abandoned, and that only the industrial proletariat and the poorest section of the peasantry be permitted to vote at all!* Against the traditional Socialist view that class distinctions must be wiped out and the class war ended by the victorious proletariat, Lenine proposed to make the class division more rigid and enduring. He proposed to give the sole control of Russia into the hands of not more than two hundred thousand workers in a land of one hundred and eighty millions of people, more than one hundred and thirty-five millions of whom were peasants!

Of course, there could be no reconciliation between such views as these and the universally accepted Socialist principle of democratic government. Lenine did not hesitate to declare that democracy itself was a "bourgeois conception" which the revolutionary proletariat must overthrow, a declaration hard to reconcile with his demand for a "democratic republic." Russia must not become a democratic republic, he argued, for a democratic republic is a bourgeois republic. Again and again, during the time we are discussing and later, Lenine assailed the principle of democratic government. "Since March, 1917, the word 'democracy' is simply a shackle fastened upon the revolutionary nation," he declared in an article written after the Bolsheviki had overthrown Kerensky.[14]

When democracy is abolished, parliamentary government goes with it. From the first days after his return to Russia Lenine advocated, instead of a parliamentary republic similar to that of France or the United States, what he called a Soviet republic, which would be formed upon these lines: local government would be carried on by local Soviets composed of delegates elected by "the working class and the poorest peasantry," to use a common Bolshevik phrase which bothers a great many people whose minds insist upon classifying peasants as "working-people" and part of the working class.

127

What Lenine means when he uses the phrase, and what Litvinov means[15] is that the industrial wage-workers—to whom is applied the term "working class"—must be sharply distinguished from peasants and small farmers, though the very poorest peasants, not being conservative, as more prosperous peasants are, can be united with the wage-workers.

These local Soviets functioning in local government would, in Lenine's Soviet republic, elect delegates to a central committee of all the Soviets in the country, and that central committee would be the state. Except in details of organization, this is not materially different from the fundamental idea of the I.W.W. with which we are familiar.[16] According to the latter, the labor-unions, organized on industrial lines and federated through a central council, will take the place of parliamentary government elected on territorial lines. According to the Bolshevik plan, Soviets would take the place held by the unions in the plan of the I.W.W. It is not to be wondered at that, in the words of Litvinov, Lenine's own closest friends shrank from his scheme and Lenine "was compelled to drop it for a time."

V

Bolshevism was greatly strengthened in its leadership by the return of Leon Trotzky, who arrived in Petrograd on May 17th. Trotzky was born in Moscow about forty-five years ago. Like Lenine, he is of bourgeois origin, his father being a wealthy Moscow merchant. He is a Jew and his real name is Bronstein. To live under an assumed name has always been a common practice among Russian revolutionists, for very good and cogent reasons. Certainly all who knew anything at all of the personnel of the Russian revolutionary movement during the past twenty years knew that Trotzky was Bronstein, and that he was a Jew. The idea, assiduously disseminated by a section of the American press, that there must be something discreditable or mysterious connected with his adoption of an alias is extremely absurd, and can only be explained by monumental ignorance of Russian revolutionary history.

Trotzky has been a fighter in the ranks of the revolutionary army of Russia for twenty years. As early as 1900 his activities as a Socialist propagandist among students had landed him in prison in solitary confinement. In 1902 he was exiled to eastern Siberia, whence he managed to escape. During the next three years he lived abroad, except for brief intervals spent in Russia, devoting himself to Socialist journalism. His first pamphlet, published in Geneva in 1903, was an attempt to reconcile the two factions in the Social Democratic party, the Bolsheviki and the Mensheviki. He was an orthodox Marxist of the most extreme doctrinaire type, and naturally inclined to the Bolshevik view. Yet he never joined the Bolsheviki, preferring to remain aloof from both factions and steadfastly and earnestly striving to unite them.

When the Revolution of 1905 broke out Trotzky had already attained considerable influence among the Socialists. He was regarded as one of the ablest of the younger Marxians, and men spoke of him as destined to occupy the place of Plechanov. He became one of the most influential leaders of the St. Petersburg Soviet, and was elected its president. In that capacity he labored with titanic energy and manifested great versatility, as organizer, writer, speaker, and arbiter of disputes among warring individuals and groups. When the end came he was arrested and thrown into prison, where he remained for twelve months. After that he was tried and sentenced to life-exile in northern Siberia. From this he managed to escape, however, and from 1907 until the outbreak of the war in 1914 he lived in Vienna.

The first two years of the war he lived in France, doing editorial work for a radical Russian Socialist daily paper, the *Nashe Slovo*. His writing, together with his activity in the Zimmerwald movement of anti-war Socialists, caused his expulsion from France. The Swiss government having refused to permit him to enter Switzerland, he sought refuge in Spain, where he was once more arrested and imprisoned for a short time. Released through the intervention of Spanish Socialists, he set sail with his family for New York, where he arrived early in January, 1917. Soon after the news of the Russian Revolution thrilled the world Trotzky, like many other Russian exiles, made hasty preparations to return, sailing on March 27th on a Norwegian steamer. At Halifax he and his family, together with a number of other Russian revolutionists, were taken from the ship and interned in a camp for war prisoners, Trotzky resisting violently and having to be carried off the ship. The British authorities kept them interned for a month, but finally released them at the urgent demand of the Foreign Minister of the Russian

Provisional Government, Miliukov.

Such, in brief outline, is the history of the man Trotzky. It is a typical Russian history: the story of a persistent, courageous, and exceedingly able fighter for an ideal believed in with fanatical devotion. Lenine, in one of his many disputes with Trotzky, called him "a man who blinds himself with revolutionary phrases,"[17] and the description is very apt. He possesses all the usual characteristics of the revolutionary Jewish Socialists of Russia. To a high-strung, passionate, nervous temperament and an exceedingly active imagination he unites a keen intellect which finds its highest satisfaction in theoretical abstractions and subtleties, and which accepts, phrases as though they were realities.

Understanding of Trotzky's attitude during the recent revolutionary and counter-revolutionary struggles is made easier by understanding the development of his thought in the First Revolution, 1905-06. He began as an extremely orthodox Marxist, and believed that any attempt to establish a Socialist order in Russia until a more or less protracted intensive economic development, exhausting the possibilities of capitalism, made change inevitable, must fail. He accepted the view that a powerful capitalist class must be developed and perform its indispensable historical rôle, to be challenged and overthrown in its turn by the proletariat. That was the essence of his pure and unadulterated faith. To it he clung with all the tenacity of his nature, deriding as "Utopians" and "dreamers" the peasant Socialists who refused to accept the Marxian theory of Socialism as the product of historic necessity as applicable to Russia.

The great upheaval of 1905 changed his viewpoint. The manner in which revolutionary ideas spread among the masses created in Trotzky, as in many others, almost unbounded confidence and enthusiasm. In an essay written soon after the outbreak of the Revolution he wrote: "The Revolution has come. *One move of hers has lifted the people over scores of steps, up which in times of peace we would have had to drag ourselves with hardships and fatigue.*" The idea that the Revolution had "lifted the people over scores of steps" possessed him and changed his whole conception of the manner in which Socialism was to come. Still calling himself a Marxist, and believing as strongly as ever in the fundamental Marxian doctrines, as he understood them, he naturally devoted his keen mind with its peculiar aptitude for Talmudic hair-splitting to a new

130

interpretation of Marxism. He declared his belief that in Russia it was possible to change from Absolutism to Socialism immediately, without the necessity of a prolonged period of capitalist development. At the same time, he maintained a scornful attitude toward the "Utopianism" of the peasant Socialists, who had always made the same contention, because he believed they based their hopes and their policy upon a wrong conception of Socialism. He had small patience for their agrarian Socialism with its economic basis in peasant-proprietorship and voluntary co-operation.

He argued that the Russian bourgeoisie was so thoroughly infected with the ills of the bureaucratic system that it was itself decadent; not virile and progressive as a class aiming to possess the future must be. Since it was thus corrupted and weakened, and therefore incapable of fulfilling any revolutionary historical rôle, that became the *immediate* task of the proletariat. Here was an example of the manner in which lifting over revolutionary steps was accomplished. Of course, the peasantry was in a backward and even primitive state which unfitted it for the proletarian rôle. Nevertheless, it had a class consciousness of its own, and an irresistible hunger for land. Without this class supporting it, or, at least, acquiescing in its rule, the proletariat could never hope to seize and hold the power of government. It would be possible to solve the difficulty here presented, Trotzky contended, if the enactment of the peasant program were permitted during the Revolution and accepted by the proletariat as a *fait accompli*. This would satisfy the peasants and make them content to acquiesce in a proletarian dictatorship. Once firmly established in power, it would be possible for the proletariat to gradually apply the true Socialist solution to the agrarian problem and to convert the peasants. "Once in power, the proletariat will appear before the peasantry as its liberator," he wrote.

His imagination fired by the manner in which the Soviet of which he was president held the loyalty of the masses during the revolutionary uprising, and the representative character it developed, Trotzky conceived the idea that it lent itself admirably to the scheme of proletarian dictatorship. Parliamentary government cannot be used to impose and maintain a dictatorship, whether of autocracy or oligarchy, bourgeoisie or proletariat. In the Soviet, as a result of six weeks' experience in abnormal times, during which it was never for a moment subjected to the test of maintaining the economic life of the nation, Trotzky saw the ideal proletarian government. He once described the Soviet as "a true, unadulterated democracy," but, unless we are to dismiss the description as idle and vain rhetoric, we must assume that the word "democracy" was used in an entirely new sense, utterly incompatible with its etymological and historical meaning. Democracy has always meant absence of class rule; proletarian dictatorship is class rule.

In the foregoing analysis of the theoretical and tactical views which Trotzky held during and immediately after the First Revolution, it is easy to see the genesis of the policies of the Bolshevik government which came twelve years later. The intervening years served only to deepen his convictions. At the center of all his thinking during that period was his belief in the sufficiency of the Soviet, and in the need of proletarian dictatorship. Throwing aside the first cautious thought that these things arose from the peculiar conditions existing in Russia as a result of her retarded economic development, he had come to regard them as applicable to all nations and to all peoples, except, perhaps, the peoples still living in barbarism or savagery.

VI

After the crisis which resulted in the resignation of Miliukov and Guchkov, it was evident that the Lvov government could not long endure. The situation in the army, as well as in the country, was so bad that the complete reorganization of the Provisional Government, upon much more radical lines, was imperative. The question arose among the revolutionary working-class organizations whether they should consent to co-operation with the liberal bourgeoisie in a new coalition Cabinet or whether they should refuse such co-operation and fight exclusively on class lines. This, of course, opened the entire controversy between Bolsheviki and Mensheviki.

In the mean time the war-weary nation was clamoring for peace. The army was demoralized and saturated with the defeatism preached by the Porazhentsi. To deal with this grave situation two important conventions were arranged for, as follows: the Convention of Soldiers' Delegates from the Front, which opened on May 10th and lasted for about a week, and the First All-Russian Congress of Peasants' Delegates, which opened on May 17th and lasted for about twelve days. Between the two gatherings there was also an important meeting of the Petrograd Council of Workmen's and Soldiers' Deputies, which dealt with the same grave situation. The dates here are of the greatest significance: the first convention was opened three days before Miliukov's resignation and was in session when that event occurred; the second convention was opened four days after the resignation of Miliukov and one day after that of Guchkov. It was Guchkov's unique experience to address the convention of Soldiers' Delegates from the Front as Minister of War and Marine, explaining and defending his policy with great ability, and then, some days later, to address the same assembly as a private citizen.

Guchkov drew a terrible picture of the seriousness of the military situation. With truly amazing candor he described conditions and explained how they had been brought about. He begged the soldiers not to lay down their arms, but to fight with new courage. Kerensky followed with a long speech, noble and full of pathos. In some respects, it was the most powerful of all the appeals it fell to his lot to make to his people, who were staggering in the too strong sunlight of an unfamiliar freedom. He did not lack courage to speak plainly: "My heart and soul are uneasy. I am greatly worried and I must say so openly, no matter what ... the consequences will be. The process of resurrecting the country's creative forces for the purpose of establishing the new régime rests on the basis of liberty and personal responsibility.... A century of slavery has not only demoralized the government and transformed the old officials into a band of traitors, *but it has also destroyed in the people themselves the consciousness of their responsibility for their fate, their country's destiny.*" It was in this address that he cried out in his anguish: "I regret that I did not die two months ago. I would have died happy with the dream that the flame of a new life has been kindled in Russia, hopeful of a time when we could respect one another's right without resorting to the knout."

To the soldiers Kerensky brought this challenge: "You fired on the people when the government demanded. But now, when it comes to obeying your own revolutionary government, you can no longer endure further sacrifice! Does this mean that free Russia is a nation of rebellious slaves?" He closed with an eloquent peroration: "I came here because I believe in my right to tell the truth as I understand it. People who even under the old régime went about their work openly and without fear of death, those people, I say, will not be terrorized. The fate of our country is in our hands and the

133

country is in great danger. We have sipped of the cup of liberty and we are somewhat intoxicated; we are in need of the greatest possible sobriety and discipline. We must go down in history meriting the epitaph on our tombstones, 'They died, but they were never slaves.'"

From the Petrograd Council of Workmen's and Soldiers' Deputies came I.G. Tseretelli, who had just returned from ten years' Siberian exile. A native of Georgia, a prince, nearly half of his forty-two years had been spent either in Socialist service or in exile brought about by such service. A man of education, wise in leadership and a brilliant orator, his leadership of the Socialist Group in the Second Duma had marked him as one of the truly great men of Russia. To the Convention of Soldiers' Delegates from the Front Tseretelli brought the decisions of the Council of Workmen's and Soldiers' Deputies, in shaping which he had taken an important part with Tchcheidze, Skobelev, and others. The Council had decided "to send an appeal to the soldiers at the front, and to explain to them that *in order to bring about universal peace it is necessary to defend the Revolution and Russia by defending the front.*" This action had been taken despite the opposition of the Bolsheviki, and showed that the moderate Socialists were still in control of the Soviet. An Appeal to the Army, drawn up by Tseretelli, was adopted by the vote of every member except the Bolsheviki, who refrained from voting. This Appeal to the Army Tseretelli presented to the Soldiers' Delegates from the Front:

Comrades, soldiers at the front, in the name of the Revolutionary Democracy, we make a fervent appeal to you.

A hard task has fallen to your lot. You have paid a dear price, you have paid with your blood, a dear price indeed, for the crimes of the Czar who sent you to fight and left you without arms, without ammunition, without bread!

Why, the privation you now suffer is the work of the Czar and his coterie of self-seeking associates who brought the country to ruin. And the Revolution will need the efforts of many to overcome the disorganization left her as a heritage by these robbers and executioners.

The working class did not need the war. The workers did not begin it. It was started by the Czars and capitalists of all countries. Each day of war is for the people only a day of unnecessary suffering and misfortune. Having dethroned the Czar, the Russian people have selected for their first problem the ending of the war in the quickest possible manner.

The Council of Workmen's and Soldiers' Deputies has appealed to all nations to end the butchery. We have appealed to the French and the English, to the Germans and the Austrians.[18] Russia wants an answer to this appeal. Remember, however, comrades and soldiers, that our appeal will be of no value if the regiments of Wilhelm overpower Revolutionary Russia before our brothers, the workers and peasants of other countries, will be able to respond. Our appeal will become "a scrap of paper" if the whole strength of the revolutionary people does not stand behind it, if the triumph of Wilhelm Hohenzollern will be established on the ruins of Russian freedom. The ruin of free Russia will be a tremendous, irreparable misfortune, not only for us, but for the toilers of the whole world.

Comrades, soldiers, defend Revolutionary Russia with all your might!

The workers and peasants of Russia desire peace with all their soul. But this peace must be universal, a peace for all nations based on the agreement of all.

What would happen if we should agree to a separate peace—a peace for ourselves alone! What would happen if the Russian soldiers were to stick their bayonets into the ground to-day and say that they do not care to fight any longer, that it makes no difference to them what happens to the whole world!

Here is what would happen. Having destroyed our allies in the west, German Imperialism would rush in upon us with all the force of its arms. Germany's imperialists, her landowners and capitalists, would put an iron heel on our necks, would occupy our cities, our villages, and our land, and would force us to pay tribute to her. Was it to bow down at the feet of Wilhelm that we overthrew Nicholas?

Comrades—soldiers! The Council of Workmen's and Soldiers' Deputies leads you to peace by another route. We lead you to peace by calling upon the workers and peasants of Serbia and Austria to rise and revolt; we lead you to peace by calling an international conference of Socialists for a universal and determined revolt against war. There is a great necessity, comrades—soldiers, for the peoples of the world to awaken. Time is needed in order that they should rebel and with an iron hand force their Czars and capitalists to peace. Time is needed so that the toilers of all lands should join with us for a merciless war upon violators and robbers.

But remember, comrades—soldiers, this time will never come if you do not stop the advance of the enemy at the front, if your ranks are crushed and under the feet of Wilhelm falls the breathless corpse of the Russian Revolution.

Remember, comrades, that at the front, in the trenches, you are now standing in defense of Russia's freedom. You defend the Revolution, you defend your brothers, the workers and peasants. Let this defense be worthy of the great cause and the great sacrifices already made by you. *It is impossible to defend the front if, as has been decided, the soldiers are not to leave the trenches under any circumstances.*[19] At times only an attack can repulse and prevent the advance of the enemy. At times awaiting an attack means patiently waiting for death. Again, only the change to an advance may save you or your brothers, on other sections of the front, from destruction.

Remember this, comrades—soldiers! Having sworn to defend Russian freedom, do not refuse to start the offensive the military situation may require. The freedom and happiness of Russia are in your hands.

In defending this freedom be on the lookout for betrayal and trickery. The fraternization which is developing on the front can easily turn into such a trap.

Revolutionary armies may fraternize, but with whom? With an army also revolutionary, which has decided to die for peace and freedom. At present, however, not only in the German army, but even in the Austro-Hungarian army, in spite of the number of individuals politically conscious and honest, there is no revolution. In those countries the armies are still blindly following Wilhelm and Charles, the landowners and capitalists, and agree to annexation of foreign soil, to robberies and violence. There the General Staff will make use not only of your credulity, but also of the blind obedience of their soldiers. You go out to fraternize with open hearts. And to meet you an officer of the General Staff leaves the enemies' trenches, disguised as a common soldier. You speak with the enemy without any trickery. At that very time he photographs the surrounding territory. You stop the shooting to fraternize, but behind the enemies' trenches artillery is being moved, new positions built and troops transferred.

Comrades—soldiers, not by fraternization will you get peace, not by separate agreements made at the front by single companies, battalions, or regiments. Not in separate peace or in a separate truce lies the salvation of the Russian Revolution, the triumph of peace for the whole world.

The people who assure you that fraternizing is the road to peace lead you to destruction. Do not believe them. The road to peace is a different one. It has been pointed out to you already by the Council of Workmen's and Soldiers' Deputies: tread it. Sweep aside everything that weakens your fighting power, that brings into the army disorganization and loss of spirit.

Your fighting power serves the cause of peace. The Council of Workmen's and Soldiers' Deputies is able to continue its revolutionary work with all its might, to develop its struggle for peace, only by depending on you, knowing that you will not allow the military destruction of Russia.

Comrades—soldiers, the workers and peasants, not only of Russia, but of the whole world, look to you with confidence and hope.

Soldiers of the Revolution, you will prove worthy of this faith, for you know that your military tasks serve the cause of peace.

In the name of the happiness and freedom of Revolutionary Russia, in the name of the coming brotherhood of nations, you will fulfil your military duties with unconquerable strength.

Again and again Tseretelli was interrupted with cheers as he read this Appeal to the Army. He was cheered, too, when he explained that the Soviet had decided to support the reconstructed Provisional Government and called upon the soldiers to do likewise. There was a storm of applause when he said: "We well realize the necessity of having a strong power in Russia; however, the strength of this power must rely upon its progressive and revolutionary policy. Our government must adopt the revolutionary slogans of democracy. It must grant the demands of the revolutionary people. It must turn over all land to the laboring peasantry. It must safeguard the interests of the working class, enacting improved social legislation for the protection of labor. It must lead Russia to a speedy and lasting peace worthy of a great people."

When Plechanov was introduced to the convention as "the veteran of the Russian Revolution" he received an ovation such as few men have ever been accorded. The great Socialist theorist plunged into a keen and forceful attack upon the theories of the Bolsheviki. He was frequently interrupted by angry cries and by impatient questionings, which he answered with rapier-like sentences. He was asked what a "democratic" government should be, and replied:

"I am asked, 'What should a democratic government be? My answer is: It should be a government enjoying the people's full confidence and sufficiently strong to prevent any possibility of anarchy. Under what condition, then, can such a strong, democratic government be established? In my opinion it is necessary, for this purpose, *that the government be composed of representatives of all those parts of the population that are not interested in the restoration of the old order. What is called a coalition Ministry is necessary.* Our comrades, the Socialists, acknowledging the necessity of entering the government, can and should set forth definite conditions, definite demands. *But there should be no demands that would be unacceptable to the representatives of other classes, to the spokesmen of other parts of the population.*"

"Would you have us Russian proletarians fight in this war for England's colonial interests?" was one of the questions hurled at Plechanov, and greeted by the jubilant applause of the Bolsheviki. Plechanov replied with great spirit, his reply evoking a storm of cheers: "The answer is clear to every one who accepts the principle of self-determination of nations," he said. "The colonies are not deserts, but populated localities, and their populations should also be given the right to determine freely their own destinies. It is clear that Russia cannot fight for the sake of any one's predatory aspirations. *But I am surprised that the question of annexations is raised in Russia, whose sixteen*

138

provinces are under the Prussian heel! I do not understand this exclusive solicitude for Germany's interests."

To those who advocated fraternization, who were engaged in spreading the idea that the German working class would refuse to fight against the Russian revolutionists, the great Socialist teacher, possessing one of the ripest minds in the whole international Socialist movement, and an intimate knowledge of the history of that movement, made vigorous reply and recited a significant page of Socialist history:

"In the fall of 1906, when Wilhelm was planning to move his troops on the then revolutionary Russia, I asked my comrades, the German Social Democrats, 'What will you do in case Wilhelm declares war on Russia?' At the party convention in Mannheim, Bebel gave me an answer to this question. Bebel introduced a resolution in favor of the declaration of a general strike in the event of war being declared on Russia. But this resolution was not adopted; *members of the trade-unions voted against it.* This is a fact which you should not forget. Bebel had to beat a retreat and introduce another resolution. Kautsky and Rosa Luxemburg were dissatisfied with Bebel's conduct. I asked Kautsky whether there is a way to bring about a general strike against the workers' will. As there is no such way, there was nothing else that Bebel could do. *And if Wilhelm had sent his hordes to Russia in 1906, the German workers would not have done an earthly thing to prevent the butchery.* In September, 1914, the situation was still worse."

The opposition to Plechanov on the part of some of the delegates was an evidence of the extent to which disaffection, defeatism, and the readiness to make peace at any price almost—a general peace preferably, but, if not, then a separate peace—had permeated even the most intelligent part of the Russian army. Bolshevism and its ally, defeatism, were far more influential in the ranks of the soldiers than in those of the workers in the factories. Yet the majority was with Kerensky, Tseretelli, and Plechanov, as the following resolutions adopted by the convention prove:

The first convention of the Delegates from the Front, having heard reports on current problems from the representatives of the Provisional Government, members of the Executive Committee of the Council of Workmen's and Soldiers' Delegates, and from representatives of the Socialist parties, and having considered the situation, hereby resolves:

139

(1) That the disorganization of the food-supply system and the weakening of the army's fighting capacity, due to a distrust of a majority of the military authorities, to lack of inner organization, and to other temporary causes, have reached such a degree that the freedom won by the Revolution is seriously endangered.

(2) That the sole salvation lies in establishing a government enjoying the full confidence of the toiling masses, in the awakening of a creative revolutionary enthusiasm, and in concerted self-sacrificing work on the part of all the elements of the population.

The convention extends to the Council of Workmen's and Soldiers' Delegates its warmest appreciation of the latter's self-sacrificing and honest work for the strengthening of the new order in Russia, in the interests of the Russian Democracy and at the same time wishes to see, in the nearest possible future, the above Council transformed into an All-Russian Council of Workmen's and Soldiers' Delegates.

The convention is of the opinion that the war is at present conducted for purposes of conquest and against the interests of the masses, and it, therefore, urges the Council of Workmen's and Soldiers' Delegates to take the most energetic and effective measures for the purpose of ending this butchery, on the basis of free self-determination of nations and of renunciation by all belligerent countries of annexations and indemnities. Not a drop of Russian blood shall be given for aims foreign to us.

Considering that the earliest possible achievement of this purpose is contingent only upon a strong revolutionary army, which would defend freedom and government, and be fully supported by the organized Revolutionary Democracy, that is, by the Council of Workmen's and Soldiers' Delegates, responsible for its acts to the whole country, the convention welcomes the responsible decision of the Council of Workmen's and Soldiers' Delegates to take part in the new Provisional Government.

The convention demands that the representatives of the Church give up for the country's benefit the treasures and funds now in the possession of churches and monasteries. The convention makes an urgent appeal to all parts of the population.

1. To the comrade-soldiers in the rear: Comrades! Come to fill up our thinning ranks in the trenches and rise shoulder to shoulder with us for the

country's defense!

2. Comrade-workers! Work energetically and unite your efforts, and in this way help us in our last fight for universal peace for nations! By strengthening the front you will strengthen freedom!

3. Fellow-citizens of the capitalist class! Follow the historic example of Minin! Even as he, open your treasuries and quickly bring your money to the aid of Russia!

4. To the peasants: Fathers and Brothers! Bring your last mite to help the weakening front! Give us bread, and oats and hay to our horses. Remember that the future Russia will be yours!

5. Comrades-Intellectuals! Come to us and bring the light of knowledge into our dark trenches! Share with us the difficult work of advancing Russia's freedom and prepare us for the citizenship of new Russia!

6. To the Russian women: Support your husbands and sons in the performing of their civil duty to the country! Replace them where this is not beyond your strength! Let your scorn drive away all those who are slackers in these difficult times!

No one can read this declaration without a deep sense of the lofty and sincere citizenship of the brave men who adopted it as their expression. The fundamental loyalty of these leaders of the common soldiers, their spokesmen and delegates, is beyond question. Pardonably weary of a war in which they had been more shamefully betrayed and neglected than any other army in modern times, frankly suspicious of capitalist governments which had made covenants with the hated Romanov dynasty, they were still far from being ready to follow the leadership of Bolsheviki. They had, instead, adopted the sanely constructive policy of Tchcheidze, Tseretelli, Skobelev, Plechanov, and other Socialists who from the first had seen the great struggle in its true perspective. That they did not succeed in averting disaster is due in part to the fact that the Revolution itself had come too late to make military success possible, and in part to the failure of the governments allied with Russia to render intelligent aid.

VII

The Provisional Government was reorganized. Before we consider the actions of the All-Russian Congress of Peasants' Delegates, one of the most important gatherings of representatives of Russian workers ever held, the reorganization of the Provisional Government merits attention. On the 17th, at a special sitting of the Duma, Guchkov and Miliukov explained why they had resigned. Guchkov made it a matter of conscience. Anarchy had entered into the administration of the army and navy, he said: "In the way of reforms the new government has gone very far. Not even in the most democratic countries have the principles of self-government, freedom, and equality been so extensively applied in military life. We have gone somewhat farther than the danger limit, and the impetuous current drives us farther still.... I could not consent to this dangerous work; I could not sign my name to orders and laws which in my opinion would lead to a rapid deterioration of our military forces. A country, and especially an army, cannot be administered on the principles of meetings and conferences."

Miliukov told his colleagues of the Duma that he had not resigned of his own free will, but under pressure: "I had to resign, yielding not to force, but to the wish of a considerable majority of my colleagues. With a clear conscience I can say that I did not leave on my own account, but was compelled to leave." Nevertheless, he said, the foreign policy he had pursued was the correct one. "You could see for yourselves that my activity in foreign politics was in accord with your ideas," he declared amid applause which eloquently testified to the approval with which the bourgeoisie regarded policies and tendencies which the proletariat condemned. He pointed out that the pacifist policies of Zimmerwald and Keinthal had permeated a large part of the Socialist movement, and that the Soviet, the Councils of Workmen's and Soldiers' Delegates, claiming to exercise control over the Provisional Government, were divided. He feared that the proposal to establish a Coalition Government would not lead to success, because of "discord in the Council of Workmen's and Soldiers' Delegates itself." Not all the members of the latter body were agreed upon entering into a Coalition Government, and "it is evident that those who do not enter the government will continue to criticize those who have entered, and it is possible that the Socialists who enter the Cabinet will find themselves confronted with the same storm of criticism as the government did before." Still, because it meant the creation of a stronger government at once, which was the most vital need, he, like Guchkov, favored a coalition which would ally the Constitutional Democratic party with the majority of the Socialists.

The Soviet had decided at its meeting on May 14th to participate in a Coalition Ministry. The struggle upon that question between Bolsheviki and Mensheviki was long and bitter. The vote, which was forty-one in favor of participation to nineteen against, probably fairly represented the full strength of Bolshevism in its stronghold. After various conferences between Premier Lvov and the other Ministers, on the one side, and representatives of the Soviet, on the other side, a new Provisional Government was announced, with Prince Lvov again Prime Minister. In the new Cabinet there were seven Constitutional Democrats, six Socialists, and two Octobrists. As Minister of War and head of the army and navy Alexander Kerensky took the place of Guchkov, while P.N. Pereverzev, a clever member of the Socialist-Revolutionary party, succeeded Kerensky as Minister of Justice. In Miliukov's position at the head of the Ministry of Foreign Affairs was placed M.I. Terestchenko, a wealthy sugar-manufacturer, member of the Constitutional-Democratic party, who had held the post of Minister of Finance, which was now given to A.I. Shingariev, a brilliant member of the same party, who had proved his worth and capacity as Minister of Agriculture. To the latter post was appointed V.M. Chernov, the leader of the Socialist-Revolutionists, one of the most capable Socialists in Russia, or, for that matter, the world. Other Socialists of distinction in the new Provisional Government were I.G. Tseretelli, as Minister of Posts and Telegraphs, and M.I. Skobelev, as Minister of Labor. As Minister of Supply an independent Socialist, A.V. Peshekhonov, was chosen.

It was a remarkable Cabinet. So far as the Socialists were concerned, it would have been difficult to select worthier or abler representatives. As in the formation of the First Provisional Government, attempts had been made to induce Tchcheidze to accept a position in the Cabinet, but without success. He could not be induced to enter a Coalition Ministry, though he strongly and even enthusiastically supported in the Soviet the motion to participate in such a Ministry. Apart from the regret caused by Tchcheidze's decision, it was felt on every hand that the Socialists had sent into the Second Provisional Government their strongest and most capable representatives;

143

men who possessed the qualities of statesmen and who would fill their posts with honorable distinction and full loyalty. On the side of the Constitutional Democrats and the Octobrists, too, there were men of sterling character, distinguished ability, and very liberal minds. The selection of Terestchenko as Minister of Foreign Affairs was by many Socialists looked upon with distrust, but, upon the whole, the Coalition Ministry met with warm approbation. If any coalition of the sort could succeed, the Cabinet headed by Prince Lvov might be expected to do so.

On the 18th, the Petrograd Council of Workmen's and Soldiers' Delegates adopted a resolution, introduced by Tchcheidze, president of the Council, warmly approving the entrance of the Socialist Ministers into the Cabinet and accepting the declaration of the new Provisional Government as satisfactory. This resolution was bitterly opposed by the Bolsheviki, who were led in the fight by Trotzky. This was Trotzky's first speech in Petrograd since his arrival the previous day from America. His speech was a demagogic appeal against co-operation with any bourgeois elements. Participation in the Coalition Ministry by the Socialists was a dangerous policy, he argued, since it sacrificed the fundamental principle of class struggle. Elaborating his views further, he said: "I never believed that the emancipation of the working class will come from above. Division of power will not cease with the entrance of the Socialists into the Ministry. A strong revolutionary power is necessary. The Russian Revolution will not perish. But I believe only in a miracle from below. There are three commandments for the proletariat. They are: First, transmission of power to the revolutionary people; second, control over their own leaders; and third, confidence in their own revolutionary powers."

This was the beginning of Trotzky's warfare upon the Coalition Government, a warfare which he afterward systematically waged with all his might. Tchcheidze and others effectively replied to the Bolshevik leader's criticisms and after long and strenuous debate the resolution of the Executive Committee presented by Tchcheidze was carried by a large majority, the opposition only mustering seven votes. The resolution read as follows:

Acknowledging that the declaration of the Provisional Government, which has been reconstructed and fortified by the entrance of representatives of the Revolutionary Democracy, conforms to the idea and purpose of strengthening the achievements of the Revolution and its further development, the Council of Workmen's and Soldiers' Delegates has determined:

I. Representatives of the Council of Workmen's and Soldiers' Delegates must enter into the Provisional Government.

II. Those representatives of the Council of Workmen's and Soldiers' Delegates who join the government must, until the creation of an All-Russian organ of the Council of Workmen's and Soldiers' Delegates, consider themselves responsible to the Petrograd Council of Workmen's and Soldiers' Delegates, and must pledge themselves to give accounts of all their activities to that Council.

III. The Council of Workmen's and Soldiers' Delegates expresses its full confidence in the new Provisional Government, and urges all friends of democracy to give this government active assistance, which will insure it the full measure of power necessary for the safety of the Revolution's gains and for its further development.

If there is any one thing which may be said with certainty concerning the state of working-class opinion in Russia at that time, two months after the overthrow of the old régime, it is that the overwhelming majority of the working-people, both city workers and peasants, supported the policy of the Mensheviki and the Socialist-Revolutionists—the policy of co-operating with liberal bourgeois elements to win the war and create a stable government—as against the policy of the Bolsheviki. The two votes of the Petrograd Soviet told where the city workers stood. That very section of the proletariat upon which the Bolsheviki leaders based their hopes had repudiated them in the most emphatic manner. The Delegates of the Soldiers at the Front had shown that they would not follow the advice of the leaders of the Bolsheviki. And at the first opportunity which presented itself the peasants placed themselves in definite opposition to Bolshevism.

On the afternoon preceding the action of the Soviet in giving its indorsement to the new Provisional Government and instructing its representatives to enter the Coalition Cabinet, there assembled in the People's House, Petrograd, more than one thousand peasant delegates to the first All-Russian Congress of Peasants. Never before had so many peasant delegates been gathered together in Russia to consider their special problems. There were present delegates from every part of Russia, even from the

145

extreme border provinces, and many from the front. On the platform were the members of the Organizing Committee, the Executive Committee of the Council of Workmen's and Soldiers' Delegates, the Socialist-Revolutionary party, the Social Democratic party, and a number of prominent Socialist leaders. As might be expected in a peasants' Congress, members of the Socialist-Revolutionary party were in the majority, numbering 537. The next largest group was the Social Democratic party, including Bolsheviki and Mensheviki, numbering 103. There were 136 delegates described as non-partizan; 4 belonged to the group called the "People's Socialists" and 6 to the Labor Group. It was the most representative body of peasant workers ever brought together.

Among the first speakers to address the Congress was the venerable "Grandmother" of the Russian Revolution, Catherine Breshkovskaya, who spoke with the freedom accorded to her and to her alone. "Tell me," she demanded, "is there advantage to us in keeping our front on a war footing and in allowing the people to sit in trenches with their hands folded and to die from fever, scurvy, and all sorts of contagious diseases? If our army had a real desire to help the Allies, the war would be finished in one or two months, *but we are prolonging it by sitting with our hands folded*." V.M. Chernov, leader of the Socialist-Revolutionary party, the new Minister of Agriculture, made a notable address in which he traversed with great skill and courage the arguments of the Bolsheviki, making a superb defense of the policy of participation in the government.

Kerensky, idol of the peasants, appearing for the first time as Minister of War and head of the army and navy, made a vigorous plea for unity, for self-discipline, and for enthusiastic support of the new Provisional Government. He did not mince matters: "I intend to establish an iron discipline in the army. I am certain that I shall succeed in my undertaking, because it will be a discipline based upon duty toward the country, the duty of honor.... By all means, we must see that the country becomes free and strong enough to elect the Constituent Assembly, the Assembly which, through its sovereign, absolute power, will give to the toiling Russian peasants that for which they have been yearning for centuries, the land.... We are afraid of no demagogues, whether they come from the right or from the left. We shall attend to our business, quietly and firmly." Kerensky begged the

146

peasants to assert their will that there should be "no repetition of the sad events of 1905-06, when the entire country seemed already in our hands, but slipped out because it became involved in anarchy." The speech created a profound impression and it was voted to have it printed in millions of copies, at the expense of the Congress, and have them distributed throughout the army.

A similar honor was accorded the speech of I.I. Bunakov, one of the best known and most popular of the leaders of the Socialist-Revolutionary party. With remorseless logic he traversed the arguments of the Bolsheviki and the Porazhentsi. Taking the cry that there must be "no annexations," for example, he declared that the peasants of Russia could only accept that in the sense that Poland be reunited and her independence be restored; that the people of Alsace and Lorraine be permitted to be reunited to France; that Armenia be taken from Turkey and made independent. The peasants could not accept the *status quo ante* as a basis for peace. He assailed the treacherous propaganda for a separate peace with terrific scorn: "But such peace is unacceptable to us peasants. A separate peace would kill not only our Revolution, but the cause of social revolution the world over. A separate peace is dishonor for Russia and treason toward the Allies.... We must start an offensive. To remain in the trenches without moving is a separate truce, more shameful even than a separate peace. A separate truce demoralizes the army and ruins the people. This spring, according to our agreement with the Allies, we should have begun a general offensive, but instead of that we have concluded a separate truce. *The Allies saved the Russian Revolution, but they are becoming exhausted....* When our Minister of War, Kerensky, speaks of starting an offensive, the Russian army must support him with all its strength, with all the means available.... From here we should send our delegates to the front and urge our army to wage an offensive. Let the army know that it must fight and die for Russia's freedom, for the peace of the whole world, and for the coming Socialist commonwealth."

In the resolutions which were adopted the Congress confined itself to outlining a program for the Constituent Assembly, urging the abolition of private property in land, forests, water-power, mines, and mineral resources. It urged the Provisional Government to "issue an absolutely clear and unequivocal statement which would show that on this question the

147

Provisional Government will allow nobody to oppose the people's will." It also issued a special appeal "to the peasants and the whole wage-earning population of Russia" to vote at the forthcoming elections for the Constituent Assembly, "only for those candidates who pledge themselves to advocate the nationalization of the land without reimbursement on principles of equality." In the election for an Executive Committee to carry on the work of the Congress and maintain the organization the delegates with Bolshevist tendencies were "snowed under." Those who were elected were, practically without exception, stalwart supporters of the policy of participation in and responsibility for the Provisional Government, and known to be ardent believers in the Constituent Assembly. Chernov, with 810 votes, led the poll; Breshkovskaya came next with 809; Kerensky came third with 804; Avksentiev had 799; Bunakov 790; Vera Finger 776, and so on. Nineteenth on the list of thirty elected came the venerable Nicholas Tchaykovsky, well known in America. Once more a great representative body of Russian working-people had spoken and rejected the teachings and the advice of the Bolsheviki.

VIII

As we have seen, it was with the authority and mandate of the overwhelming majority of the organized workers that the Socialists entered the Coalition Ministry. It was with that mandate that Kerensky undertook the Herculean task of restoring the discipline and morale of the Russian army. In that work he was the agent and representative of the organized working class. For this reason, if for no other, Kerensky and his associates were entitled to expect and to receive the loyal support of all who professed loyalty to the working class. Instead of giving that support, however, the Bolsheviki devoted themselves to the task of defeating every effort of the Provisional Government to carry out its program, which, it must be borne in mind, had been approved by the great mass of the organized workers. They availed themselves of every means in their power to hamper Kerensky in his work and to hinder the organization of the economic resources of the nation to sustain the military forces.

Kerensky had promised to organize preparations for a vigorous

148

offensive against the Austro-German forces. That such offensive was needed was obvious and was denied by none except the ultra-pacifists and the Bolsheviki. The Congress of Soldiers' Delegates from the Front and the Petrograd Soviet had specifically urged the need of such an offensive, as had most of the well-known peasants' leaders. It was a working-class policy. But that fact did not prevent the Bolsheviki from throwing obstacles in the way of its fulfilment. They carried on an active propaganda among the men in the army and the navy, urging insubordination, fraternization, and refusal to fight. They encouraged sabotage as a means of insuring the failure of the efforts of the Provisional Government. So thoroughly did they play into the hands of the German military authorities, whether intentionally or otherwise, that the charge of being in the pay of Germany was made against them—not by prejudiced bourgeois politicians and journalists, but by the most responsible Socialists in Russia.

The epic story of Kerensky's magnificently heroic fight to recreate the Russian army is too well known to need retelling here. Though it was vain and ended in failure, as it was foredoomed to do, it must forever be remembered with gratitude and admiration by all friends of freedom. The audacity and the courage with which Kerensky and a few loyal associates strove to maintain Russia in the struggle made the Allied nations, and all the civilized world, their debtors. Many mistakes were made, it is true, yet it is very doubtful if human beings could have achieved more or succeeded where they failed. It must be confessed, furthermore, that the governments of the nations with which they were allied made many grievous mistakes on their part.

Perhaps the greatest blunder that a discriminating posterity will charge to Kerensky's account was the signing of the famous Declaration of Soldiers' Rights. This document, which was signed on May 27th, can only be regarded in the light of a surrender to overpowering forces. In his address to the All-Russian Congress of Peasants' Delegates, on May 18th, speaking for the first time in his capacity as Minister of War, Kerensky had declared, "I intend to establish an iron discipline in the army," yet the Declaration of Soldiers' Rights which he signed nine days later was certain to make any real discipline impossible. Was it because he was inconsistent, vacillating, and weak that Kerensky attached his name to such a document?

Such a judgment would be gravely unjust to a great man. The fact is that Kerensky's responsibility was very small indeed. He and his Socialist associates in the Cabinet held their positions by authority of the Council of Workmen's and Soldiers' Delegates, and they had agreed to be subject to its guidance and instruction. The Soviet was responsible for the Declaration of Soldiers' Rights. Kerensky was acting under its orders. The Soviet had already struck a fatal blow at military discipline by its famous Order Number One, which called on the soldiers not to execute the orders of their officers unless the orders were first approved by the revolutionary authorities—that is, by the Soviet or its accredited agents. That the order was prompted by an intense love for revolutionary ideals, or that it was justified by the amount of treachery which had been discovered among the officers of the army, may explain and even excuse it, but the fact remains that it was a deadly blow at military discipline. The fact that Kerensky's predecessor, Guchkov, had to appear at a convention of soldiers' delegates and explain and defend his policies showed that discipline was at a low ebb. It brought the army into the arena of politics and made questions of military strategy subject to political maneuvering.

The Declaration of Soldiers' Rights was a further step along a road which inevitably led to disaster. That remarkable document provided that soldiers and officers of all ranks should enjoy full civic and political rights; that they should be free to speak or write upon any subject; that their correspondence should be uncensored; that while on duty they should be free to receive any printed matter, books, papers, and so on, which they desired. It provided for the abolition of the compulsory salute to officers; gave the private soldier the right to discard his uniform when not actually on service and to leave barracks freely during "off-duty" hours. Finally, it placed all matters pertaining to the management in the hands of elective committees in the composition of which the men were to have four-fifths of the elective power and the officers one-fifth.

Of course, the Declaration of Soldiers' Rights represented a violent reaction. Under the old régime the army was a monstrously cruel machine; the soldiers were slaves. At the first opportunity they had revolted and, as invariably happens, the pendulum had swung too far. On May 28th the Council of Workmen's and Soldiers' Delegates issued a declaration in which it was said: "From now on the soldier-citizen is free from the slavery of saluting, and as an equal, free person will greet whomsoever he chooses.... Discipline in the Revolutionary Army will exist, prompted by popular enthusiasm and the sense of duty toward the free country rather than by a slavish salute." If we are tempted to laugh at this naïve idealism, we Americans will do well to remember that it was an American statesman-idealist who believed that we could raise an army of a million men overnight, and that a shrewd American capitalist-idealist sent forth a "peace ship" with a motley crew of dreamers and disputers to end the greatest war in history.

IX

Throughout the first half of June, while arrangements for a big military offensive were being made, and were causing Kerensky and the other Socialist Ministers to strain every nerve, Lenine, Trotzky, Kamenev, Zinoviev, and other leaders of the Bolsheviki were as strenuously engaged in denouncing the offensive and trying to make it impossible. Whatever gift or genius these men possessed was devoted wholly to destruction and obstruction. The student will search in vain among the multitude of records of meetings, conventions, debates, votes, and resolutions for a single instance of participation in any constructive act, one positive service to the soldiers at the front or the workers' families in need, by any Bolshevik leader. But they never missed an opportunity to embarrass those who were engaged in such work, and by so doing add to the burden that was already too heavy.

Lenine denounced the offensive against Germany as "an act of treason against the Socialist International" and poured out the vials of his wrath against Kerensky, who was, as we know, simply carrying out the decisions of the Soviet and other working-class organizations. Thus we had the astonishing and tragic spectacle of one Socialist leader working with titanic energy among the troops who had been betrayed and demoralized by the old régime, seeking to stir them into action against the greatest militarist system in the world, while another Socialist leader worked with might and main to defeat that attempt and to prevent the rehabilitation of the demoralized army. And all the while the German General Staff gloated at every success of the Bolsheviki. There was a regular system of communications between the irreconcilable revolutionists and the German General Staff. In proof of this statement only one illustration need be offered, though many such could be cited: At the All-Russian Congress of Workmen's and Soldiers' Delegates, on June 22d, Kerensky read, in the presence of Lenine, a long message, signed by the commander-in-chief of the German eastern front, sent by wireless in response to a declaration of certain delegates of the Council of Workmen's and Soldiers' Delegates.

At this session Lenine bitterly assailed the proposed offensive. He said that it was impossible for either side to win a military victory, revamping all the defeatist arguments that were familiar in every country. He minimized the loss which Russia had suffered at Germany's hands, and the gains Germany had made in Belgium and northern France, pointing out that she had, on the other hand, lost her colonies, which England would be very unlikely to give back unless compelled to do so by other nations. Taunted with being in favor of a separate peace with Germany, Lenine indignantly denied the accusation. "It is a lie," he cried. "Down with a separate peace! *We Russian revolutionists will never consent to it.*" He argued that there could be only one policy for Socialists in any country—namely, to seize the occasion of war to overthrow the capitalist-class rule in that country. No war entered into by a capitalist ruling class, regardless what its motives, should be supported by Socialists. He argued that the adoption of his policy by the Russian working class would stand ten times the chance of succeeding that the military policy would have. The German working class would compel their government and the General Staff to follow the example of Russia and make peace.

Kerensky was called upon to reply to Lenine. At the time when the restoration of the army required all his attention and all his strength, it was necessary for Kerensky to attend innumerable and well-nigh interminable debates and discussions to maintain stout resistance to the Bolshevik offensive always being waged in the rear. That, of course, was part of the Bolshevist plan of campaign. So Kerensky, wearied by his tremendous efforts to perform the task assigned him by the workers, answered Lenine. His reply was a forensic masterpiece. He took the message of the commander-in-chief of the German eastern front and hurled it at Lenine's head, figuratively speaking, showing how Lenine's reasoning was paralleled in the German propaganda. With merciless logic and incisive phrase he showed how the Bolsheviki were using the formula, "the self-determination of nationalities," as the basis of a propaganda to bring about the dismemberment of Russia and its reduction to a chaotic medley of small, helpless states. To Lenine's statements about the readiness of the German working class to rebel, Kerensky made retort that Lenine should have remained in Germany while on his way to Russia and preached his ideas there.

A few days earlier, at a session of the same Congress, Trotzky and Kamenev had made vigorous assault upon the Coalition Government and upon the Socialist policy with reference thereto. In view of what subsequently transpired, it is important to note that Trotzky made much of the delay in calling together the Constituent Assembly: "The policy of continual postponement *and the detailed preparations* for calling the Constituent Assembly is a false policy. It may destroy even the very realization of the Constituent Assembly." This profession of concern for the Constituent Assembly was hypocritical, dishonest, and insincere. He did not in the least care about or believe in the Constituent Assembly, and had not done so at any time since the First Revolution of 1905-06. His whole thought rejected such a democratic instrument. However, he and his associates knew that the demand for a Constituent Assembly was almost universal, and that to resist that demand was impossible. Their very obvious policy in the circumstances was to try and force the holding of the Assembly prematurely, without adequate preparation, and without affording an opportunity for a nation-wide electoral campaign. A hastily gathered, badly organized Constituent Assembly would be a mob-gathering which could be easily stampeded or controlled by a determined minority.

Trotzky assailed the Coalition Government with vitriolic passion. At the moment when it was obvious to everybody that unity of effort was the only possible condition for the survival of the Revolution, and that any division in the ranks of the revolutionists, no matter upon what it might be based, must imperil the whole movement, he and all his Bolshevik colleagues deliberately stirred up dissension. Even if their opposition to political union with non-proletarian parties was right as the basis of a sound policy, to insist upon it at the moment of dire peril was either treachery or madness. When a house is already on fire the only thing in order, the only thing that can have

153

the sanction of wisdom and honor, is to work to extinguish the fire. It is obviously not the time to debate whether the house was properly built or whether mistakes were made. Russia was a house on fire; the Bolsheviki insisted upon endless debating.

Kamenev followed Trotzky's lead in attacking the Coalition Government. In a subtle speech he supported the idea of splitting Russia up into a large number of petty states, insisting that the formula, "self-determination of peoples," applied to the separatist movement in the Ukraine. He insisted that for the Russian working-people it was a matter of indifference whether the Central Empires or the Entente nations won in the war. He argued that the only hope for the Russian Revolution must be the support of the revolutionary proletariat in the other European countries, particularly those adjacent to Russia: "If the revolutionary proletariat of Europe fails to support the Russian Revolution the latter will be ruined. As that support is the only guaranty of the safety of the Revolution, we cannot change our policy by discussing the question of how much fraternizing will stimulate the awakening of the proletariat of Europe." In other words, Kamenev was in the position of a desperate gambler who stakes his life and his all upon one throw of the dice or one spin of the wheel.

It was in this manner that the Bolshevist leaders conspired to Russia's destruction. They were absorbing the time and energies of the men who were really trying to do something, compelling them to engage in numerous futile debates, to the neglect of their vitally important work, debates, moreover, which could have no other effect than to weaken the nation. Further, they were actively obstructing the work of the government. Thus Tseretelli, Kerensky, Skobelev, and many others whose efforts might have saved the Revolution, were thwarted by men wholly without a sense of responsibility. Lenine was shrieking for the arrest of capitalists because they were capitalists, when it was obvious that the services of those same capitalists were needed if the nation was to live. Later on, when confronted by the realities and responsibilities of government, he availed himself of the special powers and training of the despised capitalists. At this earlier period he was, as Tseretelli repeatedly reminded the workers, without any sense of responsibility for the practical results of his propaganda. And that was equally true of the Bolsheviki as a whole. They talked about sending "ultimatums" to the Allies, while the whole system of national defense was falling to pieces. Tseretelli made the only reply it was possible for a sane man to make:

"It is proposed that we speak to the Allies with ultimatums, but did those who made this silly proposal think that this road might lead to the breaking of diplomatic relations with the Allies, and to that very separate peace which is condemned by all factions among us? Did Lenine think of the actual consequences of his proposal to arrest several dozen capitalists at this time? Can the Bolsheviki guarantee that their road will lead us to the correct solution of the crisis? No. If they guarantee this they do not know what they are doing and their guaranty is worthless. The Bolshevik road can lead us only to one end, civil war."

Once more the good sense of the working class prevailed. By an overwhelming majority of votes the Congress decided to uphold the Coalition Government and rejected the Bolshevik proposals. The resolution adopted declared that "the passing over of all power to the bourgeoisie elements would deal a blow at the revolutionary cause," but that equally the transfer of all power to the Soviets would be disastrous to the Revolution, and "would greatly weaken her powers by prematurely driving away from her elements which are still capable of serving her, and would threaten the ruin of the Revolution." Therefore, having heard the explanations of the Socialist Ministers and having full confidence in them, the Congress insisted that the Socialist Ministers be solely responsible to the "plenipotentiary and representative organ of the whole organized Revolutionary Democracy of Russia, which organ must be composed of the representatives of the All-Russian Congress of Councils of Workmen's and Soldiers' Delegates, as well as of representatives of the All-Russian Congress of Peasants' Delegates."

But in spite of the fact that the workers upon every opportunity repudiated their policies, the Bolsheviki continued their tactics. Lenine, Trotzky, Tshitsherin, Zinoviev, and others called upon the workers to stop working and to go out into the streets to demonstrate for peace. The All-Russian Congress of Workmen's and Soldiers' Delegates issued an appeal to the workers warning them not to heed the call of the Bolsheviki, which had been made at the "moment of supreme danger." The appeal said:

Comrades, in the name of millions of workers, peasants, and soldiers, we tell you, "Do not do that which you are called upon to do." At this dangerous moment you are called out into the streets to demand the overthrow of the Provisional Government, to whom the All-Russian Congress has just found it necessary to give its support. And those who are calling you cannot but know that out of your peaceful demonstrations bloodshed and chaos may result.... You are being called to a demonstration in favor of the Revolution, *but we know that counter-revolutionists want to take advantage of your demonstration ... the counter-revolutionists are eagerly awaiting the moment when strife will develop in the ranks of the Revolutionary Democracy and enable them to crush the Revolution.*

X

Not only in this way were the Bolsheviki recklessly attempting to thwart the efforts of the Socialist Ministers to carry out the mandates of the majority of the working class of Russia, but they were equally active in trying to secure the failure of the attempt to restore the army. All through June the Bolshevik papers denounced the military offensive. In the ranks of the army itself a persistent campaign against further fighting was carried on. The Duma had voted, on June 17th, for an immediate offensive, and it was approved by the Petrograd Soviet. The Provisional Government on that date published a Note to the Allied governments, requesting a conference with a view to making a restatement of their war aims. These actions were approved by the All-Russian Congress of Workmen's and Soldiers' Delegates, as was also the expulsion from Russia of the Swiss Socialist, Robert Grimm, who was a notorious agent of the German Government. Grimm, as is now well known, was acting under the orders of Hoffman, the Swiss Minister of Foreign Affairs, and was trying to bring about a separate peace between Russia and Germany. He was also intimately connected with the infamous "Parvus," the trusted Social Democrat who was a spy and tool of the German Government. As always, the great majority of the representatives of the actual working class of Russia took the sane course.

But the Bolsheviki were meanwhile holding mass meetings among the troops, preaching defeatism and surrender and urging the soldiers not to obey the orders of "bourgeois" officers. The Provisional Government was not blind to the peril of this propaganda, but it dared not attempt to end it by force, conscious that any attempt to do so would provoke revolt which could not be stayed. The Bolsheviki, unable to control the Workmen's and Soldiers' Council, sought in every possible manner to weaken its influence and to discredit it. They conspired to overthrow the Provisional Government. Their plot was to bring about an armed revolt on the 24th of June, when the All-Russian Congress of Soviets would be in session. They planned to arrest the members of the Provisional Government and assume full power. *At the same time, all the soldiers at the front were to be called on to leave the trenches.* On the eve of the date when it was to be executed this plot was divulged. There was treachery within their own ranks. The Bolshevik leaders humbly apologized and promised to abandon their plans. Under other conditions the Provisional Government might have refused to be satisfied with apologies, might have adopted far sterner measures, but it was face to face with the bitter fact that the nation was drunk with the strong wine of freedom. The time had not yet arrived when the masses could be expected to recognize the distinction between liberty within the law and the license that leads always to tyranny. It takes time and experience of freedom to teach the stern lesson that, as Rousseau has it, freedom comes by way of self-imposed compulsions to be free.

The offensive which Kerensky had urged and planned began on July 1st and its initial success was encouraging. It seemed as though the miracle of the restoration of the Russian army had been achieved, despite everything. Here was an army whose killed and dead already amounted to more than three million men,[20] an army which had suffered incredible hardships, again going into battle with songs. On the 1st of July more than thirty-six thousand prisoners were taken by the Russians on the southwestern front. Then came the tragic harvest of the Bolshevist propaganda. In northeastern Galicia the 607th Russian Regiment left the trenches and forced other units to do the same thing, opening a clear way for the German advance. Regiment after regiment refused to obey orders. Officers were brutally murdered by their men. Along a front of more than one hundred and fifty miles the Russians, greatly superior in numbers, retreated without attempting to fight, while the enemy steadily advanced. This was made possible by the agitation of the Bolsheviki, especially by the mutiny which they provoked among the troops in the garrison at Petrograd. On the 17th of July, at the very time when the separatist movement in the Ukraine, the resignation of the Constitutional Democrats from the government, and the revolt and treachery among the troops had produced a grave crisis, seizing the opportunity afforded by the general chaos, the Bolsheviki attempted to realize their aim of establishing what they called a "dictatorship of the proletariat," but which was in reality the dictatorship of a small part of the proletariat. There was no pretense that they represented a majority of the proletariat, even. It was a desperate effort to impose the dictatorship of a small minority of the proletariat upon the whole nation. For two days the revolt lasted, more than five hundred men, women, and children being killed in the streets of Petrograd.

On the 20th Prince Lvov resigned as Premier. In the mean time the Bolshevist uprising had been put down by Cossack troops and the leaders were in hiding. Kerensky stepped into Lvov's position as Premier and continued to address himself to the task of bringing order out of the chaos. There could not have been any selfish ambition in this; no place-hunter would have attempted to bear the heavy burden Kerensky then assumed, especially with his knowledge of the seriousness of the situation. He knew that the undertaking was practically hopeless, yet he determined never to give up the struggle so long as there was a single thing to be done and his comrades desired him to do it.[21]

There had been created a revolutionary body representing all the organized workers, called the United Executive Committee of the All-Russian Councils of Workmen's, Soldiers' and Peasants' Delegates, a body of more than three hundred elected representatives of the various Soviets. They represented the views of many millions. This body vigorously denounced the Bolsheviki and rallied to the support of Kerensky and his colleagues. In a Manifesto to the people the Bolsheviki were charged with responsibility for the blood of all who had been slain in the uprising. On July 21st a second Manifesto was issued by the Committee calling upon the workers to uphold the government so long as the authorized representatives of the working class determined that to be the proper course to follow. The charge that Lenine, Zinoviev, Trotzky, and others were acting under German instructions and receiving German money spread until it was upon almost every tongue in Petrograd. On July 24th Gregory Alexinsky, a well-known Socialist, in his paper, *Bez Lisnih Slov*, published a circumstantial story of German intrigue in the Ukraine, revealed by one Yermolenko, an ensign in the 16th Siberian Regiment, who had been sent to Russia by the German Government. This Yermolenko charged that Lenine had been instructed by the authorities in Berlin, just as he himself had been, and that Lenine had been furnished with almost unlimited funds by the German Government, the arrangement being that it was to be forwarded through one Svendson, at Stockholm.[22] By a vote of 300 to 11 the United Executive Committee of the All-Russian Councils of Workmen's, Soldiers' and Peasants' Delegates adopted the following resolution:

The whole Revolutionary Democracy desires that the Bolsheviki group accused of having organized disorders, or inciting revolt, or of having received money from German sources be tried publicly. In consequence, the Executive Committee considers it absolutely inadmissible that Lenine and Zinoviev should escape justice, and demands that the Bolsheviki faction immediately and categorically express its censure of the conduct of its leaders.

Later on, under the "terror," there was some pretense of an "investigation" of the charge that Lenine and others had received German money, but there has never been a genuine investigation so far as is known. Groups of Russian Socialists belonging to various parties and groups have asked that a commission of well-known Socialists from the leading countries of Europe and from the United States, furnished with reliable interpreters, be sent to Russia to make a thorough investigation of the charge.

The United Executive Committee of the workers' organizations adopted a resolution demanding that all members and all factions, and the members of all affiliated bodies, obey the mandate of the majority, and that all majority decisions be absolutely obeyed. They took the position—too late, alas!—that the will of the majority must be observed, since the only alternative was the rule of the majority by the aggressive minority. Repressive measures against the Bolsheviki were adopted by the Kerensky Cabinet with the full approval of the Committee. Some of the Bolshevik papers were suppressed and the death penalty, which had been abolished at the very beginning of the Revolution, was partially restored in that it was ordered that it should be applied to traitors and deserters at the front. Lenine and

Zinoviev were in hiding, but Trotzky, Kamenev, Alexandra Kollontay, and many other noted Bolsheviki were imprisoned for a few days.

It was Kerensky's hope that by arranging for an early conference by the Allies, at which the war aims would be restated in terms similar to those which President Wilson had employed, and by definitely fixing the date for the Constituent Assembly elections, September 30th, while sternly repressing the Bolsheviki, it might be possible to save Russia. But it was too late. Despite his almost superhuman efforts, and the loyal support of the great majority of the Soviets, he was defeated. Day after day conditions at the front grew worse. By the beginning of August practically the whole of Galicia was in the hands of the Germans. Russian soldiers in large numbers retreated before inferior numbers of Germans, refusing to strike a blow. Germans furnished them with immense quantities of spirits, and an orgy of drunkenness took place. The red flag was borne by debauched and drunken mobs. What a fate for the symbol of universal freedom and human brotherhood!

It was a time of terrible strain and upheaval. Crisis followed upon crisis. Chernov resigned his position as Minister of Agriculture. Kerensky resigned as Premier, but the members of the Provisional Government by unanimous vote declined to accept the resignation. They called a joint meeting of all the Cabinet, of leaders of all political parties, of the Duma, of the Soviets of workers, peasants, and soldiers. At this meeting the whole critical situation was discussed and all present joined in demanding that Kerensky continue in office. The political parties represented were the Social Democrats, the Socialist-Revolutionists, the Democratic Radicals, the Labor Union party, the Popular Socialists, and the Constitutional Democrats. From these groups came an appeal which Kerensky could not deny. He said:

"In view of the evident impossibility of establishing, by means of a compromise between the various political groups, Socialist as well as non-Socialist, a strong revolutionary government ... I was obliged to resign. Friday's conference, ... after a prolonged discussion, resulted in the parties represented at the conference deciding to intrust me with the task of reconstructing the government. Considering it impossible for me in the present circumstances, when defeat without and disintegration within are threatening the country, to withdraw from the heavy task which is now intrusted to me, I regard this task as an express order of the country to construct a strong revolutionary government in the shortest possible time and in spite of all the obstacles which might arise."

For the second time Kerensky was Premier at the head of a Coalition Ministry. No other government was possible for Russia except a strong despotism. Theorists might debate the advisability of such coalition, but the stern reality was that nothing else was possible. The leader of the peasants, Chernov, returned to his old post as Minister of Agriculture and the Constitutional Democrats took their share of the burden. There were six parties and groups in the new Cabinet, four of them of various shades of Socialism and two of them liberal bourgeoisie. Never before, perhaps, and certainly only rarely, if ever, have men essayed a heavier or more difficult task than that which this new Provisional Government undertook.

Heroically Kerensky sought to make successful the efforts of General Kornilov, as commander-in-chief, to restore order and discipline in the army, but it was too late. The disintegration had gone too far. The measures which the Revolutionary Democracy had introduced into the army, in the hope of realizing freedom, had reduced it to a wild mob. Officers were butchered by their men; regiment after regiment deserted its post and, in some instances, attempted to make a separate peace with the enemy, even offering to pay indemnities. Moreover, the industrial organization of the country had been utterly demoralized. The manufacture of army supplies had fallen off more than 60 per cent., with the result that the state of affairs was worse than in the most corrupt period of the old régime.

XI

It became evident to the Provisional Government that something big and dramatic must be done, without waiting for the results of the Constituent Assembly elections. Accordingly, it was decided to call together a great extraordinary council, representing all classes and all parties, to consider the situation and the best means of meeting it. The Extraordinary National Conference, as it was called, was opened in Moscow, on August 26th, with more than fourteen hundred members in attendance. Some of these members—principally those from the Soviets—had been elected as delegates, but the others had been invited by the government and could not be said to speak as authorized representatives. There were about one hundred and ninety men who had been members of one or other of the Dumas; one hundred representatives of the peasants' Soviets and other peasant organizations; about two hundred and thirty representatives of the Soviets of industrial workers and of soldiers; more than three hundred from co-operatives; about one hundred and eighty from the trade-unions; about one hundred and fifty from municipalities; one hundred and fifty representatives of banks and industrial concerns, and about one hundred and twenty from the Union of Zemstvos and Towns. It was a Conference more thoroughly representative of Russia than any that had ever been held. There were, indeed, no representatives of the old régime, and there were few representatives of the Bolsheviki. The former had no place in the new Russia that was struggling for its existence; the repressive measures that had been found necessary accounted for the scant representation of the latter.

It was to this Conference that President Wilson sent his famous message giving the assurance of "every material and moral assistance" to the people and government of Russia. For three days the great assembly debated and listened to speeches from men representing every section of the country, every class, and every party. Kerensky, Tseretelli, Tchcheidze, Boublikov, Plechanov, Kropotkin, Breshkovskaya, and others, spoke for the workers; General Kornilov and General Kaledine spoke for the military command; Miliukov, Nekrasov, Guchkov, Maklakov, and others spoke for the bourgeoisie. At times feeling ran high, as might have been expected, but throughout the great gathering there was displayed a remarkable unanimity of feeling and immediate purpose; a common resolve to support the Provisional Government, to re-establish discipline in the army and navy, to remain loyal to the Allies, and reject with scorn all offers of a separate peace, and to work for the success of the Constituent Assembly.

But, notwithstanding the unity upon these immediately vital points, the Moscow Conference showed that there was still a great gulf between the classes, and that no matter how they might co-operate to meet and overcome the peril that hung over the nation like the sword of Damocles, there could be no unity in working out the great economic and social program which must be the basis for the Social Democratic commonwealth which the workers sought to establish, and which the bourgeois elements feared almost as much as they feared the triumph of Germany. In some respects the Conference intensified class feeling and added to, instead of lessening, the civil strife. The Bolsheviki were not slow to exploit this fact. They pointed to the Conference as evidence of a desire on the part of the Socialist Ministers, and of the officials of the Soviets, to compromise with the bourgeoisie. This propaganda had its effect and Bolshevism grew in consequence, especially in Petrograd.

Then followed the disastrous military and political events which made it practically impossible for the Kerensky government to stand. At the front the soldiers were still revolting, deserting, and retreating. Kornilov was quite helpless. Germany began a new offensive, and on September 2d German armies crossed the Dvina near Riga. On September 3d Riga was surrendered to the Germans in the most shameful manner and panic reigned in Petrograd. Then on the 9th came the revolt of Kornilov against the Provisional Government and the vulgar quarrel between him and Kerensky. Kornilov charged that the Provisional Government, under pressure from the Bolsheviki, was playing into the hands of the German General Staff. Kerensky, backed by the rest of the Cabinet, ordered Kornilov's removal, while Kornilov despatched a division of troops, drawn from the front, against Petrograd.

It was a most disastrous conflict for which no adequate explanation can be found except in the strained mental condition of all the principal parties concerned. In less strenuous times, and in a calmer atmosphere, the two leaders, equally patriotic, would have found no difficulty in removing misunderstandings. As things were, a mischievous intermediary, and two men suffering the effects of a prolonged and intense nervous strain, provided all the elements of a disaster. Kornilov's revolt was crushed without great trouble and with very little bloodshed, Kornilov himself being arrested. The Soviets stood by the Provisional Government, for they saw in the revolt the attempt to set up a personal dictatorship. Even the Bolsheviki were temporarily sobered by the sudden appearance of the "man on horseback." Kerensky, by direction of his colleagues, became commander-in-chief of the Russian armies. Always, it seemed, through every calamity, all parties except the Bolsheviki agreed that he was the one man strong enough to undertake the heaviest and hardest tasks.

Toward the end of September what may be termed the Kerensky régime entered upon its last phase. For reasons which have been already set forth, the Bolsheviki kept up a bitter attack upon the Provisional Government, and upon the official leaders of the Soviets, on account of the Moscow Conference. They demanded that the United Executive Committee of the Soviets convoke a new Conference. They contended that the Moscow Conference had been convoked by the government, not by the Soviets, and that the United Executive Committee must act for the latter. The United Executive Committee complied and summoned a new National Democratic Conference, which assembled on September 27th. By this time, as a result of the exhaustion of the patience of many workers, many of the Soviets had ceased to exist, while others existed on paper only. According to the *Izvestya Soveta*, there had been more than eight hundred region organizations at one time, many scores of which had disappeared. According to the same authority, the peasants were drawing away from the Workers' and Soldiers' Soviets. The United Executive Committee, which had been elected in June, was, of course, dominated by anti-Bolsheviki—that is, by Menshevik Social Democrats and by Socialist-Revolutionists.

The Democratic Conference was not confined to the Soviets. It embraced delegates from Soviets of peasants, soldiers, and industrial workers; from municipalities, from zemstvos, co-operatives, and other organizations. It differed from the Moscow Conference principally in that the delegates were elected and that it did not include so many representatives of the capitalist class. The petty bourgeoisie was represented, but not the great capitalists. There were more than a thousand members in attendance at this Democratic Conference, which was dominated by the most moderate section of the Social Democrats. The Socialist-Revolutionists were not very numerous.

This Conference created another Coalition Cabinet, the last of the Kerensky régime. Kerensky continued as Premier and as commander-in-chief of the army. There were in the Cabinet five Social Democrats, two Socialist-Revolutionists, eight Constitutional Democrats, and two non-partisans. It was therefore as far as its predecessors from meeting the standards insisted upon by many radical Socialists, who, while not Bolsheviki, still believed that there should be at least an absolute Socialist predominance in the Provisional Government. Of course, the new Coalition Ministry infuriated the Bolsheviki. From his hiding-place Lenine issued a series of "Letters to the Comrades," which were published in the *Rabochiy Put*, in which he urged the necessity of an armed uprising like that of July, only upon a larger scale. In these letters he scoffed at the Constituent Assembly as a poor thing to satisfy hungry men. Meanwhile, Trotzky, out of prison again, and other Bolshevik leaders were agitating by speeches, proclamations, and newspaper articles for an uprising. The Provisional Government dared not try to suppress them. Its hold upon the people was now too weak.

The Democratic Conference introduced one innovation. It created a Preliminary Parliament, as the new body came to be known, though its first official title was the Provisional Council of the Republic. This new body was to function as a parliament until the Constituent Assembly convened, when it would give place to whatever form of parliamentary body the Constituent Assembly might create. This Preliminary Parliament and its functions were thus described:

This Council, in which all classes of the population will be represented, and in which the delegates elected to the Democratic Conference will also participate, will be given the right of addressing questions to the government and of securing replies to them in a definite period of time, of working out legislative acts and discussing all those questions which will be presented for consideration by the Provisional Government, as well as those which will arise on its own initiative. Resting on the co-operation of such a Council, the government, preserving, in accordance with its pledge, the unity of the governmental power created by the Revolution, will regard it its duty to consider the great public significance of such a Council in all its acts up to the time when the Constituent Assembly gives full and complete representation to all classes of the population of Russia.

This Preliminary Parliament was really another Duma—that is, it was a very limited parliamentary body. Its life was short and quite uneventful. It assembled for the first time on October 8th and was dispersed by the Bolsheviki on November 7th. When it assembled there were 555

165

members—the number fixed by the decree of the Provisional Government. Of these, 53 were Bolsheviki, but these withdrew almost at the opening with three others, thus reducing the actual membership of the body to less than five hundred. Even with the Bolsheviki withdrawn, when Kerensky appeared before the Preliminary Parliament on November 6th and made his last appeal, a resolution expressing confidence in his government was carried only by a small majority. Only about three hundred members were in attendance on this occasion, and of these 123 voted the expression of confidence, while 102 voted against it, and 26 declined to vote at all.

The Bolsheviki had forced the United Executive Committee to convene a new All-Russian Congress of Soviets, and the date of its meeting had been fixed at November 7th. While the elections and arrangements for this Congress were proceeding, the Bolsheviki were actively and openly organizing an uprising. In their papers and at their meetings they announced that on November 7th there would be an armed uprising against the government. Their intentions were, therefore, thoroughly well known, and it was believed that the government had taken every necessary step to repress any attempt to carry those intentions into practice. It was said that of the delegates to the All-Russian Congress of Soviets-numbering 676 as against more than one thousand at the former Congress of peasant Soviets alone—a majority were Bolsheviki. It was charged that the Bolsheviki had intimidated many workers into voting for their candidates; that they had, in some instances, put forward their men as anti-Bolsheviki and secured their election by false pretenses; that they had practised fraud in many instances. It was quite certain that a great many Soviets had refused to send delegates, and that many thousands of workers, and these all anti-Bolsheviki, had simply grown weary and disgusted with the whole struggle. Whatever the explanation might be, the fact remained that of the 676 delegates 390 were generally rated as Bolsheviki, while 230 were Socialist-Revolutionists and Mensheviki. Not all of the Socialist-Revolutionists could be counted as anti-Bolsheviki, moreover. There were fifty-six delegates whose position was not quite clearly defined, but who were regarded as being, if not Bolsheviki, at least anti-government. For the first time in the whole struggle the Bolsheviki apparently had a majority of delegates in a working-class convention.

On the night of the 6th, a few hours before the opening of the

Congress of Soviets, the Bolsheviki struck the blow they had been so carefully planning. They were not met with the resistance they had expected—for reasons which have never been satisfactorily explained. Kerensky recognized that it was useless for him to attempt to carry on the fight. The Bolsheviki had organized their Red Guards, and these, directed by military leaders, occupied the principal government buildings, such as the central telephone and telegraph offices, the military-staff barracks, and so on. Part of the Petrograd garrison joined with the Bolsheviki, the other part simply refusing to do anything. On the morning of November 7th the members of the Provisional Government were arrested in the Winter Palace, but Kerensky managed to escape. The Bolshevik *coup d'état* was thus accomplished practically without bloodshed. A new government was formed, called the Council of People's Commissaries, of which Nikolai Lenine was President and Leon Trotzky Commissioner for Foreign Affairs. The "dictatorship of the proletariat" was thus begun. Kerensky's attempt to rally forces enough to put an end to this dictatorship was a pathetic failure, as it was bound to be. It was like the last fitful flicker with which a great flame dies. The masses wanted peace—for that they would tolerate even a dictatorship.

CHAPTER VI

THE BOLSHEVIK WAR AGAINST DEMOCRACY

I

The defenders and supporters of the Bolsheviki have made much of the fact that there was very little bloodshed connected with the successful Bolshevik uprising in Petrograd. That ought not to be permitted, however, to obscure the fundamental fact that it was a military *coup d'état*, the triumph of brute force over the will of the vast majority of the people. It was a crime against democracy. That the people were passive, worn out, and distracted, content to wait for the Constituent Assembly, only makes the Bolshevik crime appear the greater. Let us consider the facts very briefly. Less than three weeks away was the date set for the Constituent Assembly elections. Campaigns for the election of representatives to that great democratic convention were already in progress. It was to be the most democratic constitutional convention that ever existed in any country, its members being elected by the entire population, every man and woman in Russia being entitled to vote. The suffrage was equal, direct, universal, and secret.

Moreover, there was a great democratic reconstruction of the nation actually in progress at the time. The building up of autonomous democratic local governing bodies, in the shape of a new type of zemstvos, was rapidly progressing. The old-time zemstvos had been undemocratic and did not represent the working-people, but the new zemstvos were composed of representatives nominated and elected by universal suffrage, equal, secret, and direct. Instead of being very limited in their powers as the old zemstvos were, the new zemstvos were charged with all the ordinary functions of local government. The elections to these bodies served as an admirable practical education in democracy, making it more certain than would otherwise have been the case that the Russian people would know how to use their new political instrument so as to secure a Constituent Assembly fully representing

168

their will and their desire.

At the same time active preparations for holding the election of members to the Constituent Assembly were actually under way. The Socialist parties were making special efforts to educate the illiterate voters how to use their ballots correctly. The Provisional Government, on its part, was pushing the preparations for the elections as rapidly as possible. All over the country special courts were established, in central places, to train the necessary workers so that the elections might be properly conducted. Above all, the great problem of the socialization of the land which had been agitated for so many years had now reached the stage at which its solution might almost have been said to be complete. The National Soviet of Peasants, together with the Socialist Revolutionary party, had formulated a law on the subject which represented the aspiration and the best thought of the leaders of the peasants' movement. That law had been approved in the Council of Ministers and was ready for immediate promulgation. Peasant leaders like Chernov, Rakitnikov, Vikhiliaev, and Maslov had put an immense amount of work into the formulation of this law, which aimed to avoid anarchy, to see to it that instead of an individualistic scramble by the peasants for the land, in small and unorganized holdings, the problem should be scientifically dealt with, lands being justly distributed among the peasant communes, and among the peasants who had been despoiled, and large estates co-operatively organized and managed.

All this the Bolsheviki knew, for it was common knowledge. There is no truth whatever in the claim set up by many of the apologists for the Bolsheviki that they became enraged and resorted to desperate tactics because nothing effective was being done to realize the aims of the Revolution, to translate its ideals into fact. Quite the contrary is true. *The Bolshevik insurrection was precipitated by its leaders precisely because they saw that the Provisional Government was loyally and intelligently carrying out the program of the Revolution, in co-operation with the majority of the working-class organizations and their leaders.*

The Bolsheviki did not want the ideals of the Revolution to be realized, for the very simple reason that they were opposed to those ideals. In all the long struggle from Herzen to Kerensky the revolutionary movement of Russia had stood for political democracy first of all. Now, at the moment

169

when political democracy was being realized, the Bolsheviki sought to kill it and to set up something else—namely, a dictatorship of a small party of less than two hundred thousand over a nation of one hundred and eighty millions. There can be no dispute as to this aim; it has been stated by Lenine with great frankness. "*Just as one hundred and fifty thousand lordly landowners under Czarism dominated the one hundred and thirty millions of Russian peasants, so two hundred thousand members of the Bolshevik party are imposing their proletarian will on the mass, but this time in the interest of the latter.*"[23]

Lenine's figures probably exaggerate the Bolshevik numbers, but, assuming them to be accurate, can anybody in his right mind, knowing anything of the history of the Russian revolutionary movement, believe that the substitution of a ruling class of one hundred and fifty thousand by one of two hundred thousand, to govern a nation of one hundred and eighty millions, was the end to which so many lives were sacrificed? Can any sane and sincere person believe that the class domination described by the great arch-Bolshevik himself comes within measurable distance of being as much of a realization of the ideals of the Revolution as did the Constituent Assembly plan with its basis of political democracy, universal, equal, direct, secret, all-determining suffrage? We do not forget Lenine's statement that this new domination of the people by a ruling minority differs from the old régime in that the Bolsheviki are imposing their will upon the mass "*in the interest of the latter.*" What ruling class ever failed to make that claim? Was it not the habit of the Czars, all of them, during the whole revolutionary epoch, to indulge in the pious cant of proclaiming that they were motived only by their solicitude for the interests and well-being of the peasants?

It is a curious illustration of the superficial character of the Bolshevist mentality that a man so gifted intellectually as Lenine undoubtedly is should advance in justification of his policy a plea so repugnant to morality and intelligence, and that it should be quietly accepted by men and women calling themselves radical revolutionists. Some years ago a well-known American capitalist announced with great solemnity that he and men like himself were the agents of Providence, charged with managing industry "for the good of the people." Naturally, his naïve claim provoked the scornful laughter of every radical in the land. Yet, strange as it may seem, whenever I have pointed out to popular audiences that Lenine asserted the right of two hundred thousand proletarians to impose their rule upon Russia, always, without a single exception, some defender of the Bolsheviki—generally a Socialist or a member of the I.W.W.—has entered the plea, "Yes, but it is for the good of the people!"

If the Bolsheviki had wanted to see the realization of the ideals of the Revolution, they would have found in the conditions existing immediately prior to their insurrection a challenge calling them to the service of the nation, in support of the Provisional Government and the Preliminary Parliament. They would have permitted nothing to imperil the success of the program that was so well advanced. As it was, determination to defeat that program was their impelling motive. Not only did they fear and oppose *political* democracy; they were equally opposed to democracy in *industry*, to that democracy in the economic life of the nation which every Socialist movement in the world had at all times acknowledged to be its goal. As we shall see, they united to political dictatorship industrial dictatorship. They did not want democracy, but power; they did not want peace, even, as they wanted power.

The most painstaking and sympathetic study of the Russian Revolution will not disclose any great ideal or principle, moral or political, underlying the distinctive Bolshevik agitation and program. Nothing could well be farther from the truth than the view taken by many amiable people who, while disavowing the actions of the Bolsheviki, seek to mitigate the judgment which mankind pronounces against them by the plea that, after all, they are extreme idealists, misguided, of course, but, nevertheless, inspired by a noble ideal; that they are trying, as John Brown and many others have tried, to realize a great ideal, but have been made incapable of seeing their ideal in its proper perspective, and, therefore, of making the compromises and adjustments which the transmutation of ideals to reality always requires.

No sympathizer with Russia—certainly no Socialist—can fail to wish that this indulgent criticism were true. Its acceptance would lighten the darkest chapter in Russian history, and, at the same time, remove from the great international Socialist movement a shameful reproach. But the facts are incompatible with such a theory. Instead of being fanatical idealists, incapable of compromises and adjustments, the Bolsheviki have, from the very beginning, been loudly scornful of rigid and unbending idealism; have made

171

numerous compromises, alliances, and "political deals," and have repeatedly shifted their ground in accordance with political expediency. They have been consistently loyal to no aim save one—the control of power. They have been opportunists of the most extreme type. There is not a single Socialist or democratic principle which they have not abandoned when it served, their political ends; not a single instrument, principle, or device of autocratic despotism which they have not used when by so doing they could gain power. For the motto of Bolshevism we might well paraphrase the well-known line of Horace, and make it read, "Get power, honestly, if you can, if not—somehow or other."

Of course, this judgment applies only to Bolshevism as such: to the special and peculiar methods and ideas which distinguish the Bolsheviki from their fellow-Socialists. It is not to be questioned that as Socialists and revolutionists they have been inspired by some of the great ideals common to all Socialists everywhere. But they differed from the great mass of Russian Socialists so fundamentally that they separated themselves from them and became a separate and distinct party. *That which caused this separation is the essence of Bolshevism—not the ideals held in common.* No understanding of Bolshevism is possible unless this fundamental fact is first fully understood. Power, to be gained at any cost, and ruthlessly applied, by the proletarian minority, is the basic principle of Bolshevism as a distinct form of revolutionary movement. Of course, the Bolshevik leaders sought this power for no sordid, self-aggrandizing ends; they are not self-seeking adventurers, as many would have us believe. They are sincerely and profoundly convinced that the goal of social and economic freedom and justice can be more easily attained by their method than by the method of democratic Socialism. Still, the fact remains that what social ideals they hold are no part of Bolshevism. They are Socialist ideals. Bolshevism is a distinctive method and a program, and its essence is the relentless use of power by the proletariat against the rest of society in the same manner that the bourgeois and military rulers of nations have commonly used it against the proletariat. Bolshevism has simply inverted the old Czarist régime.

The fairness and justice of this judgment are demonstrated by the Bolsheviki themselves. They denounced Kerensky's government for not holding the elections for the Constituent Assembly sooner, posing as the champions of the Constituante. When they had themselves assumed control of the government they delayed the meeting of the Constituent Assembly and then suppressed it by force of arms! They denounced Kerensky for having restored the death penalty in the army in cases of gross treachery, professing an intense horror of capital punishment as a form of "bourgeois savagery." When they came into power they instituted capital punishment for *civil* and *political offenses*, establishing public hangings and floggings as a means of impressing the population![24] They had bitterly assailed Kerensky for his "militarism," for trying to build up the army and for urging men to fight. In less critical circumstances they themselves resorted to forced conscription. They condemned Kerensky and his colleagues for "interfering with freedom of speech and press." When they came into power they suppressed all non-Bolshevist papers and meetings in a manner differing not at all from that of the Czar's régime, forcing the other Socialist parties and groups to resort to the old pre-Revolution "underground" methods.

The evidence of all these things, and things even worse than these, is conclusive and unimpeachable. It is contained in the records of the Bolshevik government, in its publications, and in the reports of the great Socialist parties of Russia, officially made to the International Socialist Bureau. Surely the evidence sustains the charge that, whatever else they may or may not be, the Bolsheviki are not unbending and uncompromising idealists of the type of John Brown and William Lloyd Garrison, as they are so often represented as being by well-meaning sentimentalists whose indulgence of the Bolsheviki is as unlimited as their ignorance concerning them.

Some day, perhaps, a competent psychologist will attempt the task of explaining the psychology of our fellow-citizens who are so ready to defend the Bolsheviki for doing the very things they themselves hate and condemn. In any list of men and women in this country friendly to the Bolsheviki it will be found that they are practically all pacifists and anti-conscriptionists, while a great many are non-resistants and conscientious objectors to military service. Practically all of them are vigorous defenders of the freedom of the press, of the right of public assemblage and of free speech. With the exception of a few Anarchists, they are almost universally strong advocates of radical political democracy. How can high-minded and intelligent men and women—as many of them are—holding such beliefs as these give countenance to the Bolsheviki, who bitterly and resolutely oppose all of them? How can they denounce America's adoption of conscription and say that it means that "Democracy is dead in America" while, at the same time, hailing the birth of democracy in Russia, where conscription is enforced by the Bolsheviki? How, again, can they at one and the same time condemn American democracy for its imperfections, as in the matter of suffrage, while upholding and defending the very men who, in Russia, deliberately set out to destroy the universal equal suffrage already achieved? How can they demand freedom of the press and of assemblage, even in war-time, and denounce such restrictions as we have had to endure here in America, and at the same time uphold the men responsible for suppressing the press and public assemblages in Russia in a manner worse than was attempted by the Czar? Is there no logical sense in the average radical's mind? Or can it be that, after all, the people who make up the Bolshevist following, and who are so much given to engaging in protest demonstrations of various kinds, are simply restless, unanchored spirits, for whom the stimulant and excitation of revolt is a necessity? How many are simply victims of subtle neuroses occasioned by sex derangements, by religious chaos, and similar causes?

II

The Bolshevik rule began as a reign of terror. We must not make the mistake of supposing that it was imposed upon the rest of Russia as easily as it was imposed upon Petrograd, where conditions were exceptional. In the latter city, with the assistance of the Preobrajenski and Seminovsky regiments from the garrison, and of detachments of sailors from the Baltic fleet, to all of whom most extravagant promises were made, the *coup d'état* was easily managed with little bloodshed. But in a great many other places the Bolshevist rule was effected in no such peaceful fashion, but by means of a bloody terror. Here, for example, is the account of the manner in which the counter-revolution of the Bolsheviki was accomplished at Saratov, as given by a competent eye-witness, a well-known Russian Socialist whose long and honorable service in the revolutionary movement entitles her to the honor of every friend of Free Russia—Inna Rakitnikov:[25]

Here ... is how the Bolshevist *coup d'état* took place at Saratov. I was

174

witness to these facts myself. Saratov is a big university and intellectual center, possessing a great number of schools, libraries, and divers associations designed to elevate the intellectual standard of the population. The Zemstvo of Saratov was one of the best in Russia. The peasant population of this province, among whom the revolutionary Socialist propaganda was carried on for several years, by the Revolutionary Socialist party, is wide awake and well organized. The Municipality and the Agricultural Committees were composed of Socialists. The population was actively preparing for the elections to the Constituent Assembly; the people discussed the list of candidates, studied the candidates' biographies, as well as the programs of the different parties. On the night of October 28th [November 10th, European calendar], by reason of an order that had come from Petrograd, the Bolshevik *coup d'état* broke out at Saratov. The following forces were its instruments: the garrison, which was a stranger to the mass of the population, a weak party of workers, and, in the capacity of leaders, some Intellectuals, who, up to that time, had played no rôle in the public life of the town.

It was indeed a military *coup d'état. The city hall, where sat the Socialists, who were elected by equal, direct, and secret universal suffrage, was surrounded by soldiers; machine-guns were placed in front and the bombardment began. This lasted a whole night; some were wounded, some killed.* The municipal judges were arrested. Soon after a Manifesto solemnly announced to the population that the "enemies of the people," the "counter-revolutionaries," were overthrown; that the power of Saratov was going to pass into the hands of the Soviet (Bolshevist) of the Workmen's and Soldiers' Delegates.

As soon as the overthrow of the existing authorities was effected and the Bolsheviki, through their Red Guards and other means, were in a position to exert their authority, they resorted to every method of oppression and repression known to the old autocratic régime. They suppressed the papers of the Socialist parties and groups opposed to them, and in some instances confiscated the plants, turned out the editors, and used the papers themselves. In one of his "Letters to the Comrades," published in the *Rabochiy Put*, a few days before the insurrection, Lenine had confessed that Kerensky had maintained freedom of the press and of assemblage. The passage is worth quoting, not only for the information it contains concerning the Kerensky régime, but also because it affords a standard by which to judge

175

the Bolsheviki. Lenine wrote:

The Germans have only one Liebknecht, no newspapers, no freedom of assemblage, no councils; they are working against the intense hostility of all classes of the population, including the wealthy peasants—with the imperialist bourgeoisie splendidly organized—and yet the Germans are making some attempt at agitation; *while we, with tens of papers, with freedom of assemblage, with the majority of the Council with us, we, the best situated of all the proletarian internationalists, can we refuse to support the German revolutionists in organizing a revolt?*

That it was not the "German revolutionists" who in November, 1917, wanted the Russians to revolt against the Kerensky government, but the Majority Socialists, upon whom Lenine had poured his contempt, on the one hand, and the German General Staff, on the other hand, is a mere detail. The important thing is that Lenine admitted that under the Kerensky government the Russian workers, including the Bolsheviki, were "the best situated of all the proletarian internationalists," and that they had "tens of papers, with freedom of assemblage." In the face of such statements by Lenine himself, written a few days before the Bolshevik counter-revolution, what becomes of the charge that the suppression of popular liberties under Kerensky was one of the main causes of the revolt of the Bolsheviki?

Against the tolerance of Kerensky, the arbitrary and despotic methods of the Bolsheviki stand out in strong contrast. Many non-Bolshevist Socialist organs were suppressed; papers containing matter displeasing to the Bolshevik authorities were suspended, whole issues were confiscated, and editors were imprisoned, precisely as in the days of the Czar. It became necessary for the Socialist-Revolutionists to issue their paper with a different title, and from a different place, every day. Here is the testimony of Inna Rakitnikov again, contained in an official report to the International Socialist Bureau:

All the non-Bolshevik newspapers were confiscated or prosecuted and deprived of every means of reaching the provinces; their editors' offices and printing-establishments were looted. After the creation of the "Revolutionary Tribunal" the authors of articles that were not pleasing to the

Bolsheviki, as well as the directors of newspapers, were brought to judgment and condemned to make amends or go to prison, etc.

The premises of numerous organizations were being constantly pillaged. The Red Guard came there to search, destroying different documents; frequently objects which were found on the premises disappeared. Thus were looted the premises of the Central Committee of the Revolutionary Socialist party (27 Galernaia Street) and—several times—the office of the paper *Dielo Naroda* (22 Liteinia Street) ... the office of the paper Volya Naroda, etc.... But the Central Committee ... continued to issue a daily paper, only changing its title, as in the time of Czarism, and thus continued its propaganda....

The *Yolya Naroda*, referred to by Inna Rakitnikov, was the official organ of the Socialist-Revolutionary party. It was raided on several occasions. For example, in January, 1918, the leaders of the party reported that a detachment of Bolshevik Red Guards had broken into the office of the paper, committed various depredations, and made several arrests.[26] Here is another Socialist witness: One of the ablest of the leaders of the Bohemian Socialists in the United States is Joseph Martinek, the brilliant and scholarly editor of the Bohemian Socialist weekly, the *Delnicke Listy*. He has always been identified with the radical section of the movement. A student of Russian history, speaking the language fluently, it was his good fortune to spend several weeks in Petrograd immediately before and after the Bolshevik counter-revolution. He testifies that the "freedom of the press established by Kerensky" was "terminated by the Bolsheviki."[27] This is not the testimony of "capitalist newspapers," but of Socialists of unquestionable authority and standing. The *Dielo Naroda* was a Socialist paper, and the volunteer venders of it, who were brutally beaten and shot down by Red Guards, were Socialist working-men.[28] When Oskar Tokoi, the well-known revolutionary Finnish Socialist leader, former Prime Minister of Finland, declares that "freedom of assemblage, association, free speech, and free press is altogether destroyed,"[29] the Bolsheviki and their sympathizers cannot plead that they are the victims of "capitalist misrepresentation." The attitude of the Bolshevik leaders toward the freedom of the press has been frankly stated editorially in Pravda, their official organ, in the following words:

The press is a most dangerous weapon in the hands of our enemies.

We will tear it from them, we will reduce it to impotence. It is the moment for us to prepare battle. We will be inflexible in our defense of the rights of the exploited. The struggle will be decisive. We are going to smite the journals with fines, to shut them up, to arrest the editors, and hold them as hostages.[30]

Is it any wonder that Paul Axelrod, who was one of the representatives of Russia on the International Socialist Bureau prior to the outbreak of the war, has been forced to declare that the Bolsheviki have "introduced into Russia a system worse than Czarism, suppressing the Constituent Assembly and the liberty of the press"?[31] Or that the beloved veteran of the Russian Revolution, Nicholas Tchaykovsky, should lament that "the Bolshevik usurpation is the continuation of the government by which Czarism held the country in an iron grip"?[32]

III

Lenine, Trotzky, Zinoviev, and other Bolshevik leaders early found themselves so much at variance with the accepted Socialist position that they decided to change their party name. They had been Social Democrats, a part of the Social Democratic party of Russia. Now ever since Bronterre O'Brien first used the terms "Social Democrat" and "Social Democracy," in 1839, their meaning has been pretty well established. A Social Democrat is one who aims to base government and industry upon democracy. Certainly, this cannot be said to be an accurate description of the position of men who believe in the rule of a nation of one hundred and eighty millions by a small party of two hundred thousand or less—or even by an entire class representing not more than six per cent. of the population—and Lenine and his friends, recognizing the fact, decided to change the name of their group to the *Communist party*, by which name they are now known in Russia. Lenine frankly admits that it would be a mistake to speak of this party as a party of democracy. He says:

The word "democracy" cannot be scientifically applied to the Communist party. Since March, 1917, the word democracy is simply a shackle fastened upon the revolutionary nation and preventing it from establishing boldly, freely, and regardless of all obstacles a new form of power; the Council of Workmen's, Soldiers' and Peasants' Deputies, harbinger of the abolition of every form of authority.[33]

The phrase "harbinger of the abolition of every form of authority" would seem to indicate that Lenine's ideal is that of the old Nihilists—or of Anarchists of the Bakuninist school. That is very far from the truth. The phrase in question is merely a rhetorical flourish. No man has more caustically criticized and ridiculed the Anarchists for their dream of organization without authority than Nikolai Lenine. Moreover, his conception of Soviet government provides for a very strong central authority. It is a new kind of state, but a state, nevertheless, and, as we shall discover, far more powerful than the political state with which we are familiar, exercising far greater control over the life of the individual. It is not to be a democratic state, but a very despotic one, a dictatorship by a small but powerful ruling class. It was not the word "democracy" which Lenine felt to be a "shackle upon the revolutionary nation," but democracy itself.

The manner in which they betrayed the Constituent Assembly will prove the complete hostility of the Bolsheviki to democratic government. In order to excuse and justify the Bolsheviki's actions in this regard, their supporters in this country have assiduously circulated two statements. They are, first, that the Provisional Government purposely and with malicious intent delayed the convocation of the Constituent Assembly, hoping to stave it off altogether; second, that such a long time had elapsed between the elections and the convocation that when the latter date was reached the delegates no longer represented the true feeling of the electorate.

With regard to the first of these statements, which is a repetition of a charge made by Trotzky before the Bolshevik revolt, it is to be noted that it is offered in justification of the Bolshevik *coup d'état*. If the charge made were true, instead of false, as it can easily be shown to be, it would only justify the counter-revolution if the counter-revolution itself were made the instrument for insuring the safety of the Constituent Assembly. But the Bolsheviki *suppressed the Constituent Assembly*. By what process of reasoning do we reach the result that because the Provisional Government delayed the convocation of the Constituent Assembly, which the people desired, a counter-revolutionary movement to *suppress it altogether*, by force of arms, was

179

right and proper?

With regard to the second statement, which is a repetition of an argument advanced in Russia, it should be sufficient to emphasize a few dates. The Bolsheviki seized the power of government on November 7th and the elections for the Constituent Assembly took place on November 25th—nearly three weeks later. The date set by the Kerensky government for the opening of the Constituent Assembly was December 12th and on that date some forty-odd members put in an appearance. Recognizing that they could not begin business until a quorum appeared, these decided to wait until at least a quorum should be present. They did not attempt to do any work. What happened is told in the following passages from a signed statement by 109 members—all Socialist-Revolutionists.[34]

On the appointed day and hour of the opening of the session of the Constituent Assembly ... the delegates to the Constituent Assembly who had arrived in Petrograd gathered at the Tavrichesky Palace. The elected representatives of the people beheld innumerable banners and large crowds surrounding the palace. This was Petrograd greeting the representatives of the people. At the doors of the palace the picture changed. There stood armed guards and at the orders of the usurpers, the Bolsheviki, they refused to let the delegates pass into the Tavrichesky Palace. It appeared that, in order to enter the building, the *delegates had first to pay respects to the Commissaire, a satellite of Lenine and Trotzky, and there receive special permission.* The delegates would not submit to that; elected by the people and equipped with formal authorization, they had the right to freely enter any public building assigned for their meeting. The delegates decided to enter the Tavrichesky Palace without asking the new authorities, and they succeeded in doing so. On the first day the guards did not dare to lift their arms against the people's elected representatives and allowed them to enter the building without molestation.

There was no struggle, no violence, no sacrifices; the delegates demanded that the guards respect their rights; they demanded to be admitted, and the guards yielded.

In the Tavrichesky Palace the delegates opened their meeting; V.M. Chernov was elected chairman. There were, altogether, about forty delegates present. They realized that there were not enough present to start the work of the Constituent Assembly. *It was decided that it would be advisable to await the arrival of the other delegates and start the work of the Constituent Assembly only when a sufficient number were present.* Those already there decided to meet daily at the Tavrichesky Palace in order to count all the delegates as they arrived, and on an appointed day to publicly announce the day and hour of the beginning of the activities of the Constituent Assembly.

When the delegates finished their session and adjourned, the old guards had been dismissed for their submissive attitude toward the delegates and replaced by armed civilian followers of Lenine and Trotzky. The latter issued an order to disband the delegates, but there were none to be disbanded.

The following day the government of the Bolsheviki dishonestly and basely slandered the people's representatives in their official announcement which appeared in Pravda. That lying newspaper wrote that the representatives of the people had forced their way into the palace, accompanied by Junkers and the White Guards of the bourgeoisie, that the representatives wanted to take advantage of their small numbers and had begun the work of the Constituent Assembly. Every one knows that this is slanderous as regards the representatives of the people. Such lies and slanders were resorted to by the old régime.

The aim of the slanders and the lies is clear. *The usurpers do not want the people's representatives to have the supreme power and therefore are preparing to disband the Constituent Assembly.* On the 28th of November, in the evening, *having begun to arrest members of the Constitutional-Democratic party, the Bolsheviki violated the inviolability of the Constituent Assembly. On December 3d a delegate to the Constituent Assembly, the Socialist-Revolutionist, Filippovsky, who was elected by the army on the southwestern front, was arrested.*

In accordance with their decision reached on November 28th, the delegates gathered at the Tavrichesky Palace on November 29th and 30th. As on the first day, armed soldiers stood guard at the entrance of the palace and would not let any one pass. The delegates, however, insisted and were finally allowed to enter.

On the third day, scenes of brutal violence toward the people's representatives took place at the palace. Peasants were the unfortunate victims of this violence.

When the delegates had ended their session and all that remained was the affixing of the signatures to the minutes, sailors forced their way into the hall; these were headed by a Bolshevik officer, *a former commander of the Fortress of St. Peter and St. Paul.* The commander demanded that the delegates disband. In reply it was stated that the delegates would disband after they had finished their business. Then at the order of the commander the sailors took the delegate Ilyan, elected by the peasants of the Province of Tambov, by the arm and dragged him to the exit. After Ilyan, the sailors dragged out the peasant delegate from the Province of Moscow, Bikov; then the sailors approached Maltzev, a peasant delegate from the Province of Kostroma. He, however, shouted out that he would rather be shot than to submit to such violence. His courage appealed to the sailors and they stopped.

Now all the halls in the Tavrichesky Palace are locked and it is impossible to meet there. The delegates who come to the Tavrichesky Palace cannot even gather in the lobby, for as soon as a group gathers, the armed hirelings of Lenine and Trotzky disperse them. Thus, in former times, behaved the servants of the Czar and the enemies of the people, policemen and gendarmes.

This is not the testimony of correspondents of bourgeois journals; it is from a statement prepared at the time and signed by more than a hundred Socialists, members of the oldest and largest Socialist party in Russia, many of them men whose long and honorable service has endeared them to their comrades in all lands. It is not testimony that can be impeached or controverted. It forms part of the report of these well-known and trusted Socialists to their comrades in Russia and elsewhere. The claim that the elections to the Constituent Assembly were held on the basis of an obsolete register, before the people had a chance to become acquainted with the Bolshevist program, and that so long a time had elapsed since the elections that the delegates could not be regarded as true representatives of the people, was first put forward by the Bolsheviki when the Constituent Assembly was finally convened, on January 18th. It was an absurd claim for the Bolsheviki to make, for one of the very earliest acts of the Bolshevik government, after the overthrow of Kerensky, was to issue a decree ordering that the elections be held as arranged. By that act they assumed responsibility for the elections, and could not fairly and honorably enter the plea, later on, that the elections were not valid.

Here is the story of the struggle for the Constituent Assembly, briefly summarized. The first Provisional Government issued a Manifesto on March 20, 1917, promising to convoke the Constituent Assembly "as soon as possible." This promise was repeated by the Provisional Government when it was reorganized after the resignation of Miliukov and Guchkov in the middle of May. That the promise was sincere there can be no reasonable doubt, for the Provisional Government at once set about creating a commission to work out the necessary machinery and was for the election by popular vote of delegates to the Constituent Assembly. Russia was not like a country which had ample electoral machinery already existing; new machinery had to be devised for the purpose. This commission was opened on June 7, 1917; its work was undertaken with great earnestness, and completed in a remarkably short time, with the result that on July 22d the Provisional Government—Kerensky at its head—announced that the elections to the Constituent Assembly would be held on September 30th, and the convocation of the Assembly itself on the 12th of December. It was soon found, however, that it would be physically impossible for the local authorities all to be prepared to hold the election on the date set—it was necessary, among other things, to first elect the local authorities which were to arrange for the election of the delegates to the Constituent Assembly—and so, on August 22d, Kerensky signed the following decree, making *the one and only postponement* of the Constituent Assembly, so far as the Provisional Government was concerned:

Desiring to assure the convocation of the Constituent Assembly as soon as possible, the Provisional Government designated the 30th of September as election-day, in which case the whole burden of making up the election lists must fall on the municipalities and the newly elected zemstvos. *The enormous labor of holding the elections for the local institution has taken time.* At present, in view of the date of establishment of the local institutions, on the basis decreed by the government—direct, general, equal, and secret suffrage—the Provisional Government has decided:

To set aside as the day for the elections to the Constituent Assembly the 25th of November, of the year 1917, and as the date for the convocation of the Constituent Assembly the 12th of December, of the year 1917.

Notwithstanding this clear and honorable record, we find Trotzky, at a Conference of Northern Councils of Workmen's and Soldiers' Delegates, on October 25th, when he well knew that arrangements for holding the Constituent Assembly elections were in full swing, charging that Kerensky was engaged in preventing the convocation of the Constituent Assembly! He demanded at that time that all power should be taken from the Provisional Government and transferred to the Soviets. These, he said, would convoke the Assembly on the date that had been assigned, December 12th.

The Bolshevik *coup d'état* took place, as already noted, less than three weeks before the date set for the elections, for which every preparation had been made by the government and the local authorities. It was at the beginning of the campaign, and the Bolsheviki had their own candidates in the field in many places. It was a foregone conclusion that the Constituent Assembly brought into being by the universal suffrage would be dominated by Socialists. There was never the slightest fear that it would be dominated by the bourgeois parties. What followed is best told in the exact language of a protest to the International Socialist Bureau by Inna Rakitnikov, representative of the Revolutionary Socialist party, which was, be it remembered, the largest and the oldest of the Russian Socialist parties:

The *coup d'état* was followed by various other manifestations of Bolshevist activity—arrests, searches, confiscation of newspapers, ban on meetings. Bands of soldiers looted the country houses in the suburbs of the city; a school for the children of the people and the buildings of the Children's Holiday Settlement were also pillaged. Bands of soldiers were forthwith sent into the country to cause trouble there.... The bands of soldiers who were sent into the country used not only persuasion, but also violence, *trying to force the peasants to give their votes for the Bolshevik candidates at the time of the elections to the Constituent Assembly; they tore up the bulletins of the Socialist-Revolutionists, overturned the ballot-boxes, etc....* The inhabitants of the country proved themselves in all that concerned the elections wide awake to the highest degree. There were hardly any abstentions; *90 per cent. of the population took part in the voting.* The day of the voting was kept as a solemn feast; the priest said mass; the peasants dressed in their best clothes; they believed that the Constituent Assembly would give them order, laws, the land. In the Government of Saratov, out of fourteen deputies elected, there were twelve Socialist-Revolutionists. There were others (such as the Government of Pensa, for example) that elected only Socialist-Revolutionists. The Bolsheviki had the majority only in Petrograd and Moscow and in certain units of the army. To violence and conquest of power by force of arms the population answered by the elections to the Constituent Assembly, the people sent to this Assembly, not the Bolsheviki, but, by an overwhelming majority, Socialist-Revolutionists.

Of course, this is the testimony of one who is confessedly anti-Bolshevist, one who has suffered deep injury at the hands of the Bolsheviki of whom she writes. For all that, her testimony cannot be ignored or laughed aside. It has been indorsed by E. Roubanovitch, a member of the International Socialist Bureau, and a man of the highest integrity, in the following words: "I affirm that her sincere and matured testimony cannot be suspected of partizanship or of dogmatic partiality against the Bolsheviki." What is more important, however, is that the subsequent conduct of the Bolsheviki in all matters relating to the Constituent Assembly was such as to confirm belief in her statements.

No Bolshevik spokesman has ever yet challenged the accuracy of the statement that an overwhelming majority of the deputies elected to the Constituent Assembly were representatives of the Revolutionary Socialist party. As a matter of fact, the Bolsheviki elected less than one-third of the deputies. In the announcement of their withdrawal from the Constituent Assembly when it assembled in January the Bolshevik members admitted that the Socialist-Revolutionists had "obtained a majority of the Constituent Assembly."

The attitude of the Bolsheviki toward the Constituent Assembly changed as their electoral prospects changed. At first, believing that, as a result of their successful *coup*, they would have the support of the great mass of the peasants and city workers, they were vigorous in their support of the Assembly. In the first of their "decrees" after the overthrow of the Kerensky Cabinet, the Bolshevik "Commissaries of the People" announced that they were to exercise complete power "until the meeting of the Constituent Assembly," which was nothing less than a pledge that they would regard the latter body as the supreme, ultimate authority. Three days after the revolt Lenine, as president of the People's Commissaries, published this decree:

185

In the name of the Government of the Republic, elected by the All-Russian Congress of Councils of Workmen's and Soldiers' Delegates, with the participation of the Peasants' Delegates, the Council of the People's Commissaries decrees:

1. That the elections to the Constituent Assembly shall be held on November 25th, the day set aside for this purpose.

2. All electoral committees, all local organizations, the Councils of Workmen's, Soldiers' and Peasants' Delegates and the soldiers' organizations at the front are to bend every effort toward safeguarding the freedom of the voters and fair play at the elections to the Constituent Assembly, which will be held on the appointed date.

If this attitude had been maintained throughout, and had the Bolsheviki loyally accepted the verdict of the electorate when it was given, there could have been no complaint. But the evidence shows that their early attitude was not maintained. Later on, as reports received from the interior of the country showed that the masses were not flocking to their banners, they began to assume a critical attitude toward the Constituent Assembly. The leaders of the Socialist-Revolutionary party were warning their followers that the Bolsheviki would try to wreck the Constituent Assembly, for which they were bitterly denounced in organs like *Pravda* and *Izvestya*. Very soon, however, these Bolshevist organs began to discuss the Constituent Assembly in a very critical spirit. It was possible, they pointed out, that it would have a bourgeois majority, treating the Socialist-Revolutionists and the Cadets as being on the same level, equally servants of the bourgeoisie. Then appeared editorials to show that it would not be possible to place the destinies of Russia in the hands of such people, even though they were elected by the "unthinking masses." Finally, when it was clear that the Socialist-Revolutionary party had elected a majority of the members, *Pravda* and *Izvestya* took the position that *the victorious people did not need a Constituent Assembly*; that a new instrument had been created which made the old democratic method obsolete.[35] The "new instrument" was, of course, the Bolshevist Soviet.

IV

For the moment we are not concerned with the merits or the failings of the Soviet considered as an instrument of government. We are concerned only with democracy and the relation of the Bolshevist method to democracy. From this point of view, then, let us consider the facts. The Soviet was not something new, as so many of our American drawing-room champions of Bolshevism seem to think. The Soviet was the type of organization common to Russia. There were Soviets of peasants, of soldiers, of teachers, of industrial workers, of officers, of professional men, and so on. Every class and every group in the classes had its own Soviet. The Soviet in its simplest form is a delegate body consisting of representatives of a particular group—a peasants' Soviet, for example. Another type, more important, roughly corresponds to the Central Labor Union in an American city, in that it is composed of representatives of workers of all kinds. These delegates are, in the main, chosen by the workers in the shops and factories and in the meetings of the unions. The anti-Bolshevist Socialists, such as the Mensheviki and the Socialist-Revolutionists, were not opposed to Soviets as working-class organizations. On the contrary, they approved of them, supported them, and, generally, belonged to them.

They were opposed only to the theory that these Soviets, recruited in a more or less haphazard manner, as such organizations must necessarily be, were better adapted to the governing of a great country like Russia than a legal body which received its mandate in elections based upon universal, equal, direct, and secret suffrage. No one ever pretended that the Soviets represented all the workers of Russia—including peasants in that term—or even a majority of them. No one ever pretended that the Soviet, as such, was a stable and constant factor. New Soviets were always springing up and others dying out. Many existed only in name, on paper. *There never has been an accurate list of the Soviets existing in Russia.* Many lists have been made, but always by the time they could be tabulated and published there have been many changes. For these and other reasons which will suggest themselves to the mind of any thoughtful reader, many of the leaders of the revolutionary movement in Russia have doubted the value of the Soviet as a *unit of government, while highly valuing it as a unit of working-class organization and struggle.*

Back of all the strife between the Bolsheviki centered around the

Soviets and the Socialist-Revolutionists and Mensheviki, centered around the Constituent Assembly, was a greater fact than any we have been discussing, however. The Bolsheviki with their doctrinaire Marxism had carried the doctrine of the class struggle to such extreme lengths that they virtually placed the great mass of the peasants with the bourgeoisie. The Revolution must be controlled by the proletariat, they argued. The control of the government and of industry by the people, which was the slogan of the old democracy, will not do, for the term "the people" includes bourgeois elements. Even if it is narrowed by excluding the great capitalists and landowners, still it embraces the lesser capitalists, small landowners, shopkeepers, and the petty bourgeoisie in general. These elements weaken the militancy of the proletariat. What is needed is the dictatorship of the proletariat. Now, only a very small part of the peasantry, the very poor peasants, can be safely linked to the proletariat—and even these must be carefully watched. It was a phase of the old and familiar conflict between agrarian and industrial groups in the Socialist movement. It is not very many years since the Socialist party of America was convulsed by a similar discussion. Could the farmer ever be a genuine and sincere and trustworthy Socialist? The question was asked in the party papers in all seriousness, and in one or two state organizations measures were taken to limit the number of farmers entering the party, so that at all times there might be the certainty of a preponderance of proletarian over farmer votes.

Similar distrust, only upon a much bigger scale, explains the fight for and against the Constituent Assembly. Lenine and his followers distrusted the peasants as a class whose interests were akin to the class of small property-owners. He would only unite with the poor, propertyless peasants. The leaders of the peasantry, on the other hand, supported by the more liberal Marxians, would expand the meaning of the term "working class" and embrace within its meaning all the peasants as well as all city workers, most of the professional classes, and so on. We can get some idea of this strife from a criticism which Lenine directs against the Mensheviki:

In its class composition this party is not Socialist at all. It does not represent the toiling masses. It represents fairly prosperous peasants and working-men, petty traders, many small and some even fairly large capitalists, and a certain number of real but gullible proletarians who have been caught in the bourgeois net.[36]

It is clear from this criticism that Lenine does not believe that a genuine Socialist party—and, presumably, therefore, the same must apply to a Socialist government—can represent "fairly prosperous peasants and working-men." We now know how to appraise the Soviet government. The constitution of Russia under the rule of the Bolsheviki is required by law to be posted in all public places in Russia. In Article II, Chapter V, paragraph 9, of this document it is set forth that "the Constitution of the Russian Socialist Federated Soviet Republic involves, in view of the present transition period, the establishment of a dictatorship of the urban and rural proletariat and the poorest peasantry in the form of a powerful All-Russian Soviet authority." Attention is called to this passage here, not for the sake of pointing out the obvious need for some exact definition of the loose expression, "the poorest peasantry," nor for the sake of any captious criticism, but solely to point out the important fact that Lenine only admits a part of the peasantry—the poorest—to share in the dictatorship of the proletariat.

Turning to another part of the same important document—Article III, Chapter VI, Section A, paragraph 25—we find the basis of representation in the All-Russian Congress of Soviets stated. There are representatives of town Soviets and representatives of provincial congresses of Soviets. The former represent the industrial workers; the latter represent the peasants almost exclusively. It is important, therefore, to note that there is one delegate for every twenty-five thousand city voters and one for every one hundred and twenty-five thousand peasant voters! In Section B of the same Article, Chapter X, paragraph 53, we find the same discrimination: it takes five peasants' votes to equal the vote of one city voter; it was this general attitude of the Bolsheviki toward the peasants, dividing them into classes and treating the great majority of them as petty, rural bourgeoisie, which roused the resentment of the peasants' leaders. They naturally insisted that the peasants constituted a distinct class, co-operating with the proletariat, not to be ruled by it. Even Marie Spiridonova, who at first joined with the Bolsheviki, was compelled, later on, to assert this point of view.

It is easy to understand the distrust of the Bolsheviki by the Socialist parties and groups which represented the peasants. The latter class constituted more than 85 per cent. of the population. Moreover, it had furnished the great majority of the fighters in the revolutionary movement. Its leaders and spokesmen resented the idea that they were to be dictated to and controlled by a minority, which was, as Lenine himself admitted, not materially more numerous than the old ruling class of landowners had been. They wanted a democratic governmental system, free from class rule, while the Bolsheviki wanted class rule. Generalizations are proverbially perilous, and should be very cautiously made and applied to great currents of thought and of life. But in a broad sense we may fairly say that the Socialism of the Socialist-Revolutionists and the Mensheviki, the Socialism of Kerensky and the men who were the majority of the Constituent Assembly, was the product of Russian life and Russian economic development, while the Socialism that the Bolsheviki tried by force of arms to impose upon Russia was as un-Russian as it could be. The Bolshevist conception of Socialism had its origin in Marxian theory. Both Marx and Engels freely predicted the setting up of "a dictatorship of the proletariat"—the phrase which the Bolsheviki have made their own.

Yet, the Bolsheviki are not Marxians. Their Socialism is as little Marxian as Russian. When Marx and Engels forecasted the establishment of proletarian dictatorship it was part of their theorem that economic evolution would have reduced practically all the masses to a proletarian state; that industrial and commercial concentration would have reached such a stage of development that there would be on the one side a small class of owners, and, on the other side, the proletariat. There would be, they believed, no middle class. The disappearance of the middle class was, for them and for their followers, a development absolutely certain to take place. They saw the same process going on with the same result in agriculture. It might be less rapid in its progress, but not one whit less certain. It was only as the inevitable climax to this evolution that they believed the "dictatorship of the proletariat" would be achieved. In other words, the proletariat would be composed of the overwhelming majority of the body politic and social. That is very different from the Bolshevist attempt to set up the dictatorship of the proletariat in a land where more than 85 per cent, of the people are peasants; where industrial development is behind the rest of the world, and where dictatorship of the proletariat means the domination of more than one hundred and eighty millions of people by two hundred thousand "proletarians and the poorest peasants," according to Lenine's statement, or by six per cent. of the population *if we assume the entire proletariat to be united in the dictatorship!*

V

At the time of the disturbances which took place in Petrograd in December, over the delay in holding the Constituent Assembly, the Bolshevik government announced that the Constituante would be permitted to convene on January 18th, provided that not less than four hundred delegates were in attendance. Accordingly, the defenders of the Constituent Assembly arranged for a great demonstration to take place on that day in honor of the event. It was also intended to be a warning to the Bolsheviki not to try to further interfere with the Constituante. An earnest but entirely peaceful mass of people paraded with flags and banners and signs containing such inscriptions as "Proletarians of All Countries, Unite!" "Land and Liberty," "Long Live the Constituent Assembly," and many others. They set out from different parts of the city to unite at the Field of Mars and march to the Taurida Palace to protest against any interference with the Constituent Assembly. As they neared the Taurida Palace they were confronted by Red Guards, who, without any preliminary warning or any effort at persuasion, fired into the crowd. Among the first victims was a member of the Executive Committee of the Soviet of Peasants' Delegates, the Siberian peasant Logvinov, part of whose head was shot away by an explosive bullet. Another victim was the militant Socialist-Revolutionist Gorbatchevskaia. Several students and a number of workmen were also killed. Similar massacres occurred at the same time in other parts of the city. Other processions wending their way toward the meeting-place were fired into. Altogether one hundred persons were either killed or very seriously wounded by the Red Guards, who said that they had received orders "not to spare the cartridges." Similar demonstrations were held in Moscow and other cities and were similarly treated by the Red Guards. In Moscow especially the loss of life was great. Yet the Bolshevist organs passed these tragic events over in complete silence. They did not mention the massacres, nor did they mention the great demonstration at the funeral of the victims, four days later.

191

When the Constituent Assembly was formally opened, on January 18th, it was well known on every hand that the Bolshevik government would use force to destroy it if the deputies refused to do exactly as they were told. The corridors were filled with armed soldiers and sailors, ready for action.

The Lenine-Trotzky Ministry had summoned an extraordinary Congress of Soviets to meet in Petrograd at the same time, and it was well understood that they were determined to erect this Soviet Congress into the supreme legislative power. If the Constituent Assembly would consent to this, so much the better, of course. In that case there would be a valuable legal sanction, the sanction of a democratically elected body expressly charged with the task of determining the form and manner of government for Free Russia. Should the Constituent Assembly not be willing, there was an opportunity for another *coup d'état*.

In precisely the same way as the Ministry during the last years of Czarism would lay before the Duma certain documents and demand that they be approved, so the Central Executive Committee of the Soviets—the Bolshevik power—demanded that the Constituent Assembly meekly assent to a document prepared for it in advance. It was at once a test and a challenge; if the Assembly was willing to accept orders from the Soviet authority and content itself with rubber-stamping the decrees of the latter, as ordered, it could be permitted to go on—at least for a time. At the head of the Constituent Assembly, as president, the deputies elected Victor Chernov, who had been Minister of Agriculture under Kerensky. At the head of the Bolshevik faction was Sverdlov, chairman of the Executive Committee of the Soviets. He it was who opened the fight, demanding that the following declaration be adopted by the Constituante as the basis of a Constitution for Russia:

Declaration Of The Right's Of The Toiling And Exploited People

I

1. Russia is to be declared a republic of the workers', soldiers' and peasants' Soviets. All power in the cities and in the country belongs to the Soviets.

192

2. The Russian Soviet Republic is based on the free federation of free peoples, on the federation of national Soviet republics.

II

Assuming as its duty the destruction of all exploitation of the workers, the complete abolition of the class system of society, and the placing of society upon a socialistic basis, and the ultimate bringing about of victory for Socialism in every country, the Constituent Assembly further decides:

1. That the socialization of land be realized, private ownership of land be abolished, all the land be proclaimed common property of the people and turned over to the toiling masses without compensation on the basis of equal right to the use of land.

All forests, mines, and waters which are of social importance, as well as all living and other forms of property, and all agricultural enterprises, are declared national property.

2. To confirm the decree of the Soviets concerning the inspection of working conditions, the highest department of national economy, which is the first step in achieving the ownership by the Soviets of the factories, mines, railroads, and means of production and transportation.

3. To confirm the decree of the Soviets transferring all banks to the ownership of the Soviet Republic, as one of the steps in the freeing of the toiling masses from the yoke of capitalism.

4. To enforce general compulsory labor, in order to destroy the class of parasites, and to reorganize the economic life. In order to make the power of the toiling masses secure and to prevent the restoration of the rule of the exploiters, the toiling masses will be armed and a Red Guard composed of workers and peasants formed, and the exploiting classes shall be disarmed.

III

1. Declaring its firm determination to make society free from the chaos of capitalism and imperialism, which has drenched the country in blood in this most criminal war of all wars, the Constituent Assembly accepts completely the policy of the Soviets, whose duty it is to publish all secret treaties, to organize the most extensive fraternization between the workers and peasants of warring armies, and by revolutionary methods to bring about a democratic peace among the belligerent nations without annexations and

indemnities, on the basis of the free self-determination of nations—at any price.

2. For this purpose the Constituent Assembly declares its complete separation from the brutal policy of the bourgeoisie, which furthers the well-being of the exploiters in a few selected nations by enslaving hundreds of millions of the toiling peoples of the colonies and the small nations generally.

The Constituent Assembly accepts the policy of the Council of People's Commissars in giving complete independence to Finland, in beginning the withdrawal of troops from Persia, and in declaring for Armenia the right of self-determination.

A blow at international financial capital is the Soviet decree which annuls foreign loans made by the governments of the Czar, the landowners and the bourgeoisie. The Soviet government is to continue firmly on this road until the final victory from the yoke of capitalism is won through international workers' revolt.

As the Constituent Assembly was elected on the basis of lists of candidates nominated before the November Revolution, when the people as a whole could not yet rise against their exploiters, and did not know how powerful would be the strength of the exploiters in defending their privileges, and had not yet begun to create a Socialist society, the Constituent Assembly considers it, even from a formal point of view, unjust to oppose the Soviet power. The Constituent Assembly is of the opinion that at this moment, in the decisive hour of the struggle of the people against their exploiters, the exploiters must not have a seat in any government organization or institution. The power completely and without exception belongs to the people and its authorized representatives—the workers', soldiers' and peasants' Soviets.

Supporting the Soviet rule and accepting the orders of the Council of People's Commissars, the Constituent Assembly acknowledges its duty to outline a form for the reorganization of society.

Striving at the same time to organize a free and voluntary, and thereby also a complete and strong, union among the toiling classes of all the Russian nations, the Constituent Assembly limits itself to outlining the basis of the federation of Russian Soviet Republics, leaving to the people, to the

194

workers and soldiers, to decide for themselves, in their own Soviet meetings, if they are willing, and on what conditions they prefer, to join the federated government and other federations of Soviet enterprise. These general principles are to be published without delay, and the official representatives of the Soviets are required to read them at the opening of the Constituent Assembly.

The demand for the adoption of this declaration gave rise to a long and stormy debate. The leaders of the Socialist-Revolutionists and the Mensheviki stoutly contended that the adoption of the declaration would be virtually an abdication of the task for which the Constituent Assembly had been elected by the people, and, therefore, a betrayal of trust. They could not admit the impudent claim that an election held in November, based upon universal suffrage, on lists made up as recently as September, could in January be set aside as being "obsolete" and "unrepresentative." That a majority of the Bolshevik candidates put forward had been defeated, nullified, they argued, the claim of the Bolsheviki that the fact that the candidates had all been nominated before the November insurrection should be regarded as reason for acknowledging the Bolshevik Soviet as superior to the Constituent Assembly. They insisted upon the point, which the Bolshevik spokesmen did not attempt to controvert, that the Constituent Assembly represented the votes of many millions of men and women,[37] while the total actual membership represented by the Soviet power did not at the time number one hundred thousand!

As might have been expected, the proposal to adopt the declaration submitted to the Constituent Assembly in this arrogant fashion was rejected by an enormous majority. The Bolshevik members, who had tried to make the session a farce, thereupon withdrew after submitting a statement in which they charged the Constituent Assembly with being a counter-revolutionary body, and the Revolutionary-Socialist party with being a traitorous party "directing the fight of the bourgeoisie against the workers' revolution." The statement said that the Bolshevik members withdrew "in order to permit the Soviet power to determine what relations it would hold with the counter-revolutionary section of the Constituent Assembly"—a threat which needed no interpretation.

After the withdrawal of the Bolshevik members, the majority very

195

quickly adopted a declaration which had been carefully prepared by the Socialist-Revolutionists during the weeks which had elapsed since the elections in the preliminary conferences which had been held for that purpose. The declaration read as follows:

Russia's Form Of Government

In the name of the peoples who compose the Russian state, the All-Russian Constituent Assembly proclaims the Russian State to be the Russian Democratic Federated Republic, uniting indissolubly into one whole the peoples and territories which are sovereign within the limits prescribed by the Federal Constitution.

Laws Regarding Land Ownership

1. *The right to privately own land within the boundaries of the Russian Republic is hereby abolished forever.*

2. All land within the boundaries of the Russian Republic, with all mines, forests, and waters, is hereby declared the property of the nation.

3. The republic has the right to control all land, with all the mines, forests, and waters thereof, through the central and local administration, in accordance with the regulation provided by the present law.

4. The autonomous provinces of the Russian Republic have title to land on the basis of the present law and in accordance with the Federal Constitution.

5. The tasks of the central and local governments as regards the use of lands, mines, forests, and waters are:

a. The creation of conditions conducive to the best possible utilization of the country's natural resources and the highest possible development of its productive forces.

b. The fair distribution of all natural wealth among the people.

6. The rights of individuals and institutions to land, mines, forests, and waters are restricted merely to utilization by said individuals and institutions.

7. The use of all mines, forests, land, and waters is free to all citizens of the Russian Republic, regardless of nationality or creed. This includes all unions of citizens, also governmental and public institutions.

8. The right to use the land is to be acquired and discontinued on the basis prescribed by this fundamental law.

9. *All titles to land at present held by the individuals, associations, and*

197

institutions are abolished in so far as they contradict this law.

10. All land, mines, forests, waters, at present owned by and otherwise in the possession of individuals, associations, and institutions, *are confiscated without compensation for the loss incurred.*

Democratic Peace

In the name of the peoples of the Russian Republic, the All-Russian Constituent Assembly expresses the firm will of the people to *immediately discontinue the war* and conclude a just and general peace, appeals to the Allied countries proposing to define jointly the exact terms of the democratic peace acceptable to all the belligerent nations, in order to present these terms, in behalf of the Allies, to the governments fighting against the Russian Republic and her allies.

The Constituent Assembly firmly believes that the attempts of the peoples of Russia to end the disastrous war will meet with a unanimous response on the part of the peoples and the governments of the Allied countries, and that by common efforts a speedy peace will be attained, which will safeguard the well-being and dignity of all the belligerent countries.

The Constituent Assembly resolves to elect from its midst an authorized delegation which will carry on negotiations with the representatives of the Allied countries and which will present the appeal to jointly formulate terms upon which a speedy termination of the war will be possible, as well as for the purpose of carrying out the decisions of the Constituent Assembly regarding the question of peace negotiations with the countries fighting against us.

This delegation, which is to be under the guidance of the Constituent Assembly, is to immediately start fulfilling the duties imposed upon it.

Expressing, in the name of the peoples of Russia, its regret that the negotiations with Germany, which were started without preliminary agreement with the Allied countries, have assumed the character of negotiations for a separate peace, the Constituent Assembly, in the name of the peoples of the Federated Republic, *while continuing the armistice, accepts the further carrying on of the negotiations with the countries warring against us* in order to work toward a general democratic peace which shall be in accordance "with the people's will and protect Russia's interests."

VI

Immediately following the dissolution of the Constituent Assembly a body of Red Guards shot the two Constitutional Democrats, Kokoshkin and Shingariev, who were at the time confined as prisoners who were ill in the Naval Hospital. The reason for the brutal murder of these men was that they were bourgeoisie and, therefore, enemies of the working class! It is only just to add that the foul deed was immediately condemned by the Bolshevik government and by the Soviet of Petrograd. "The working class will never approve of any outrages upon our prisoners, whatever may have been their political offense against the people and their Revolution," the latter body declared, in a resolution on the subject of the assassinations. Two days after the dissolution of the Constituent Assembly twenty-three Socialist-Revolutionist members of that body, assembled at the office of their party, were arrested, and the premises occupied by Red Guards, the procedure being exactly as it used to be in the old days under the Czar.

There is a relentless logic of life and action from which there can be no escape. Czarism was a product of that inexorable process. All its oppression and brutality proceeded by an inevitable and irresistible sequence from the first determination and effort to realize the principle of autocracy. Any dictatorship, whether of a single man, a group or class, must rest ultimately upon oppressive and coercive force. Believing that the means would be justified by the end, Lenine and Trotzky and their associates had suppressed the Constituent Assembly, claiming that parliamentary government, based upon the equal and free suffrage of all classes, was, during the transition period, dangerous to the proletariat; that in its stead a new type of government must be established—government by associations of wage-earners, soldiers, and peasants, called Soviets.

But what if among these there should develop a purpose contrary to the purpose of the Bolsheviki? Would men who, starting out with a belief in the Constituante, and as its champions, used force to destroy and suppress it the moment it became evident that its purpose was not their purpose, hesitate to suppress and destroy any Soviet movement which adopted policies contrary to their own? What assurance could there be, once their point of view, their initial principle, was granted, that the freedom denied to the Constituante would be assured to the Soviets? In the very nature of the case there could be no such assurance. However honest and sincere the Bolsheviki themselves might be in their belief that there would be such assurance, there could in fact be none, for the logic of life is stronger than any human will.

As was inevitable, the Bolsheviki soon found themselves in the position of suppressing Soviets which they could not control as freely and in the same manner as they had suppressed the Constituent Assembly. When, for example, the soldiers of the Preobrajenski Regiment—the very men who helped the Bolsheviki into power—became dissatisfied and organized, publishing their own organ, *The Soldier's Cloak*, the paper was confiscated and the organization suppressed.[38] The forcible suppression of Soviets was common. The Central Executive Committee of the National Soviet of Peasants' Delegates, together with the old Central Executive Committee of the Soviets of Workmen's and Soldiers' Delegates (who had never acknowledged the October elections), convoked an extraordinary assembly of Soviets on January 8th, the same date as that on which the Bolshevik Congress of Soviets was convoked. Circumstances compelled the opening to be deferred until two days later, the 10th. This conference, called the Third All-Russian Congress of Peasants' Soviets, was suppressed by force, many of the 359 delegates and all the members of the Executive Committee being arrested. The following extract from a declaration of protest addressed by the outraged peasants to the Congress of Soviets of Workmen, Soldiers, and Peasants convoked by the Bolshevik government tells the story:

As soon as the Congress was opened, sailors and Red Guards, armed with guns and hand-grenades, broke into the premises (11 Kirillovskaia Street), surrounded the house, poured into the corridors and the session hall, and ordered all persons to leave.

"In whose name do you order us, who are Delegates to the Peasants' Congress of All-Russia, to disperse?" asked the peasants.

"In the name of the Baltic fleet," the sailor's replied.

The peasants refused; cries of protest were raised. One by one the peasants ascended the tribune to stigmatize the Bolsheviki in speeches full of indignation, and to express the hopes that they placed in the Constituent

Assembly....

This session of the Congress presented a strange spectacle: disturbed by men who confessed that they did not know why they were there, the peasants sang revolutionary songs; the sailors, armed with guns and grenades, joined them. Then the peasants knelt down to sing a funeral hymn to the memory of Logvinov, whose coffin was even yesterday within the room. The soldiers, lowering their guns, knelt down also.

The Bolshevik authorities became excited; they did not expect such a turn of events. "Enough said," declared the chiefs; "we have come not to speak, but to act. If they do not want to go to Smolny, let them get out of here." And they set themselves to the task.

In groups of five the peasants were conducted down-stairs, trampled upon, and, on their refusal to go to Smolny, pushed out of doors during the night in the midst of the enormous city of which they knew nothing.

Members of the Executive Committee were arrested,[39] the premises occupied by sailors and Red Guards, the objects found therein stolen.

The peasants found shelter in the homes of the inhabitants of Petrograd, who, indignant, offered them hospitality. A certain number were lodged in the barracks of the Preobrajenski Regiment. The sailors, who but a few minutes before had sung a funeral hymn to Logvinov, and wept when they saw that they had understood nothing, now became the docile executioners of the orders of the Bolsheviki. And when they were asked, "Why do you do this?" they answered, as in the time, still recent, of Czarism: "It is the order. No need to talk."[40]

We do not need to rely upon the testimony of witnesses belonging to the Revolutionary Socialist party, the Mensheviki, or other factions unfriendly to the Bolsheviki. However trustworthy such testimony may be, and however well corroborated, we cannot expect it to be convincing to those who pin their faith to the Bolsheviki. Such people will believe only what the Bolsheviki themselves say about Bolshevism. It is well, therefore, that we can supplement the testimony already given by equally definite and direct testimony from official Bolshevist sources to the same effect. From the official organs of the Bolsheviki it can be shown that the Bolshevik authorities suppressed Soviet after Soviet; that when they found that Soviets were controlled by Socialists who belonged to other factions they dissolved

201

them and ordered new elections, refusing to permit the free choice of the members to be expressed in selecting their officers.

The Bolsheviki did this, it should be remembered, not merely in cases where Mensheviki or Socialist-Revolutionists were in the majority, but also in cases where the majority consisted of members of the Socialist-Revolutionary party of the Left—the faction which had united with the Bolsheviki in suppressing the Constituante. Their union with the Bolsheviki was from the first a compromise, based upon the political opportunism of both sides. The Socialist-Revolutionists of the Left did not believe in the Bolshevik theories or program, but they wanted the political assistance of the Bolsheviki. The latter did not believe in the theories or program of the Socialist-Revolutionists of the Left, but they wanted their political support. The union could not long endure; the differences were too deeply rooted. Before very long the Bolsheviki were fighting their former allies and the Socialist-Revolutionists of the Left, like Marie Spiridonova, for example, were fighting the Bolsheviki. At Kazan, where Lenine went to school, the Soviet was dissolved because it was controlled by Socialist-Revolutionists of the Left, former allies, now hostile to the Bolsheviki. Here are two paragraphs from *Izvestya*, one of the Bolshevist official organs:

Kazan, July 26th. As the important offices in the Soviet were occupied by Socialist-Revolutionists of the Left, the Extraordinary Commission has dissolved the Provisional Soviet. The governmental power is now represented by a Revolutionary Committee. (Izvestya, July 28, 1918.)

Kazan, *August 1.* The state of mind of the workmen is revolutionary. *If the Mensheviki dare to carry on their propaganda, death menaces them. (Idem, August 3.)*

And here is confirmation from another official organ of the Bolsheviki, *Pravda:*

Kazan, *August 4th.* The Provisional Congress of the Soviets of the Peasants has been dissolved because of the absence from it of poor peasants and *because its state of mind is obviously counter-revolutionary. (Pravda, August 6, 1918.)*

As early as April, 1918, the Soviet at Jaroslav was dissolved by the Bolshevik authorities and new elections ordered.[41] In these elections the Mensheviki and the Socialist-Revolutionists everywhere gained an absolute

202

majority.[42] The population here wanted the Constituent Assembly and they wanted Russia to fight on with the Allies. Attempts to suppress this majority led to insurrection, which the Bolsheviki crushed in the most brutal manner, and when the people, overpowered and helpless, sought to make peace, the Bolsheviki only *increased the artillery fire*! Here is an "Official Bulletin," published in *Izvestya*, July 21, 1918:

At Jaroslav the adversary, gripped in the iron ring of our troops, has tried to enter into negotiations. *The reply has been given under the form of redoubled artillery fire.*

Izvestya published, on July 25th, a Bolshevist military proclamation addressed to the inhabitants of Jaroslav concerning the insurrection which originally arose from the suppression of the Soviet and other popular assemblages:

The General Staff notifies to the population of Jaroslav that all those who desire to live are invited to abandon the town in the course of twenty-four hours and to meet near the America Bridge. Those who remain will be treated as insurgents, *and no quarter will be given to any one.* Heavy artillery fire and gas-bombs will be used against them. *All those who remain will perish In the ruins of the town with the insurrectionists, the traitors, and the enemies of the Workers' and Peasants' Revolution.*

Next day, July 26th, *Izvestya* published the information that "after minute questionings and full inquiry" a special commission appointed to inquire into the events relating to the insurrection at Jaroslav had listed 350 persons as having "taken an active part in the insurrection and had relations with the Czecho-Slovaks," and that by order of the commissioners the whole band of 350 had been shot!

It is needless to multiply the illustrations of brutal oppression—of men and women arrested and imprisoned for no other crime than that of engaging in propaganda in favor of government by universal suffrage; of newspapers confiscated and suppressed; of meetings banned and Soviets dissolved because the members' "state of mind" did not please the Bolsheviki. Maxim Gorky declared in his *Novya Zhizn* that there had been "ten thousand lynchings." Upon what authority Gorky—who was inclined to sympathize with the Bolsheviki, and who even accepted office under them—based that statement is not known. Probably it is an exaggeration.

203

One thing, however, is quite certain, namely, that a reign of terror surpassing the worst days of the old régime was inflicted upon unhappy Russia by the Bolsheviki. At the very beginning of the Bolshevik régime Trotzky laughed to scorn all the protests against violence, threatening that resort would be had to the guillotine. Speaking to the opponents of the Bolshevik policy in the Petrograd Soviet, he said:

"You are perturbed by the mild terror we are applying against our class enemies, but know that not later than a month hence this terror will take a more terrible form on the model of the terror of the great revolutionaries of France. Not a fortress, but the guillotine will be for our enemies."

That threat was not literally carried out, but there was a near approach to it when public hangings for civil offenses were established. For reintroducing the death penalty into the army as a means of putting an end to treason and the brutal murder of officers by rebellious soldiers, the Bolsheviki excoriated Kerensky. *Yet they themselves introduced hanging and flogging in public for petty civil crimes!* The death penalty was never inflicted for civil crimes under the late Czar. It was never inflicted for political offenses. Only rarely was it inflicted for murder. It remained for a so-called "Socialist" government to resort to such savagery as we find described in the following extract from the recognized official organ of the Bolshevik government:

Two village robbers were condemned to death. All the people of Semenovskaia and the surrounding communes were invited to the ceremony. On July 6th, at midday, a great crowd of interested spectators arrived at the village of Loupia. The organizers of the execution gave to each of the bystanders the opportunity of flogging the condemned to obtain from them supplementary confessions. The number of blows was unlimited. Then a vote of the spectators was taken as to the method of execution. The majority was for hanging. In order that the spectacle could be easily seen, the spectators were ranged in three ranks—the first row sat down, the second rested on the knee, and the third stood up.[43]

The Bolshevik government created an All-Russian Extraordinary Commission, which in turn created Provincial and District Extraordinary Commissions. These bodies—the local not less than the national—were empowered to make arrests and even decree and carry out capital sentences.

There was no appeal from their decisions; they were simply required to *report afterward.* Only members of the Bolshevik party were immune from this terror. Alminsky, a Bolshevist writer of note, felt called upon to protest against this hideous travesty of democratic justice, and wrote in *Pravda:*

The absence of the necessary restraint makes one feel appalled at the "instruction" issued by the All-Russian Extraordinary Commission to "All Provincial Extraordinary Commissions," which says: "The All-Russian Extraordinary Commission is perfectly independent in its work, carrying out house searches, arrests, executions, of which it *afterward* reports to the Council of the People's Commissaries and to the Central Executive Council." Further, the Provincial and District Extraordinary Commissions "are independent in their activities, and when called upon by the local Executive Council present a report of their work." In so far as house searches and arrests are concerned, a report made *afterward* may result in putting right irregularities committed owing to lack of restraint. The same cannot be said of executions.... It can also be seen from the "instruction" that personal safety is to a certain extent guaranteed only to members of the government, of the Central Council, and of the local Executive Committees. With the exception of these few persons all members of the local committees of the [Bolshevik] Party, of the Control Committees, and of the Executive Committee of the party may be shot at any time by the decision of any Extraordinary Commission of a small district town if they happen to be on its territory, and a report of that made *afterward.*[44]

VII

While in some respects, such as this terrible savagery, Bolshevism has out-Heroded Herod and surpassed the régime of the Romanovs in cruel oppression, upon the whole its methods have been very like that of the latter. There is really not much to choose between the ways of Stolypin and Von Plehve and those of the Lenine-Trotzky rule. The methods employed have been very similar and in not a few instances the same men who acted as the agents of espionage and tyranny for the Czar have served the Bolsheviki in the same capacity. Just as under Czarism there was alliance with the Black

Hundreds and with all sorts of corrupt and vicious criminal agents, so we find the same phenomenon recurring under the Bolsheviki. The time has not yet arrived for the compilation of the full record of Bolshevism in this particular, but enough is known to justify the charge here made. That agents-provocateurs, spies, informers, police agents, and pogrom-makers formerly in the service of the Czar have been given positions of trust and honor by Lenine and Trotzky unfortunately admits of no doubt whatever.

It was stated at a meeting of Russians held in Paris in the summer of 1917 that one of the first Russian regiments which refused to obey orders to advance "contained 120 former political or civil police agents out of 181 refractory soldiers." During the Kerensky régime, at the time when Lenine was carrying on his propaganda through *Pravda*,[45] Vladimir Bourtzev exposed three notorious agents of the old police terror, provocateurs, who were working on the paper. In August, 1917, the Jewish Conjoint Committee in London published a long telegram from the representative of the Jewish Committee in Petrograd, calling attention to the fact that Lenine's party was working in tacit agreement with the Black Hundreds. The telegram is here given in full:

Extreme Russian reactionaries have allied themselves closely with extreme revolutionaries, and Black Hundreds have entered into tacit coalition with the Lenine party. In the army the former agents and detectives of the political police carry on ardent campaign for defeat, and in the rear the former agents-provocateurs prepare and direct endless troubles.

The motives of this policy on the part of the reactionaries are clear. It is the direct road to a counter-revolution. The troubles, the insurrections, and shocking disorders which follow provoke disgust at the Revolution, while the military defeats prepare the ground for an intervention of the old friend of the Russian Black Hundreds, William II, the counter-revolutionaries work systematically for the defeat of the Russian armies, sometimes openly, cynically.

Thus in their press and proclamations they go so far as to throw the whole responsibility for the war and for the obstacles placed in the way of a peace with Germany on the Jews. It is these "diabolical Jews," they say, who prevent the conclusion of peace and insist on the continuation of the war, because they desire to ruin Russia. Proclamations in this sense have been

206

found, together with a voluminous anti-Semitic literature, in the offices of the party of Lenine Bolsheviki (Maximalists), and particularly at the headquarters of the extreme revolutionaries, Château Knheshinskaja. Salutations. Blank.

That the leaders of the Bolsheviki, particularly Lenine and Trotzky, ever entered into any "agreement" with the Black Hundreds, or took any part in the anti-Semitic campaign referred to, is highly improbable. Unless and until it is supported by ample evidence of a competent nature, we shall be justified in refusing to believe anything of the sort. It is, however, quite probable that provocateurs worming their way into Lenine's and Trotzky's good graces tried to use the Bolshevik agitation as a cover for their own nefarious work. As we have seen already, Lenine had previously been imposed upon by a notorious secret police agent, Malinovsky. But the open association of the Bolsheviki with men who played a despicable rôle under the old régime is not to be denied. The simple-minded reader of Bolshevist literature who believes that the Bolshevik government, whatever its failings, has the merit of being a government by real working-men and working-women, needs to be enlightened. Not only are Lenine and Trotzky not of the proletariat themselves, but they have associated with themselves men whose lives have been spent, not as workers, not even as simple bourgeoisie, but as servants of the terror-system of the Czar. They have associated with themselves, too, some of the most corrupt criminals in Russia. Here are a few of them:

Professor Kobozev, of Riga, joined the Bolsheviki and was active as a delegate to the Municipal Council of Petrograd. According to the information possessed by the Russian revolutionary leaders, this Professor Kobozev used to be a police spy, his special job being to make reports to the police concerning the political opinions and actions of students and faculty members. One of the very first men released from prison by the Bolsheviki was one Doctor Doubrovine, who had been a leader of the Black Hundreds, an organizer of many pogroms. He became an active Bolshevik. Kamenev, the Bolshevik leader, friend of Lenine, is a journalist. He was formerly a member of the old Social Democratic party. Soon after the war broke out he was arrested and behaved so badly that he was censured by his party. Early in the Revolution of 1917 he was accused of serving the secret police at Kiev. Bonno Brouevitch, Military Councilor to the Bolshevik government, was a

207

well-known anti-Semite who had been dismissed from his military office on two occasions, once by the Czar's government and once by the Provisional Government. General Komisarov, another of Lenine's trusted military officials and advisers, was formerly a chief official of the Czar's secret police, known for his terrible persecution of the revolutionists. Accused of high treason by the Provisional Government, he fled, but returned and joined the Lenine-Trotzky forces. Prince Andronikov, associate of Rasputin; (Lenine's "My friend, the Prince"); Orlov, police agent and "denouncer" and secretary of the infamous Protopopov; Postnikov, convicted and imprisoned as a German spy in 1910; Lepinsky, formerly in the Czar's secret police; and Gualkine, friend of the unspeakable Rasputin, are some of the other men who have been closely identified with the "proletarian régime" of the Bolsheviki.[46] The man they released from prison and placed in the important position of Military Commander of Petrograd was Muraviev, who had been chief of the Czar's police and was regarded by even the moderate members of the Provisional Government, both under Lvov and Kerensky, as a dangerous reactionary.[47] Karl Radek, the Bohemian, a notorious leader of the Russian Bolsheviki, who undertook to stir up the German workers and direct the Spartacide revolt, was, according to *Justice*, expelled from the German Social Democratic party before the war as a thief and a police spy.[48] How shall we justify men calling themselves Socialists and proletarian revolutionists, who ally themselves with such men as these, but imprison, harry, and abuse such men and women as Bourtzev, Kropotkin, Plechanov, Breshkovskaya, Tchaykovsky, Spiridonova, Agounov, Larokine, Avksentiev, and many other Socialists like them?

In surveying the fight of the Bolsheviki to establish their rule it is impossible to fail to observe that their chief animus has been directed against other Socialists, rather than against members of the reactionary parties. That this has been the fact they do not themselves deny. For example, the "People's Commissary of Justice," G.I. Oppokov, better known as "Lomov," declared in an interview in January, 1918: "Our chief enemies are not the Cadets. Our most irreconcilable opponents are the Moderate Socialists. This explains the arrests of Socialists and the closing down of Socialist newspapers. Such measures of repression are, however, only temporary."[49] And in the Soviet at Petrograd, July 30, 1918, according to *Pravda*,

Lachevitch, one of the delegates, said: "The Socialist-Revolutionists of the Right and the Mensheviki are more dangerous for the government of the Soviets than the bourgeoisie. But these enemies are not yet exterminated and can move about freely. The proletariat must act. We ought, once for all, to rid ourselves of the Socialist-Revolutionists of the Right and of the Mensheviki."

In this summary of the Bolsheviki war against democracy, it will be observed, no attempt has been made to gather all the lurid and fantastic stories which have been published by sensational journalists. The testimony comes from Socialist sources of the utmost reliability, much of it from official Bolshevist sources. The system of oppression it describes is twin brother to that which existed under the Romanovs, to end which hundreds of thousands of the noblest and best of our humankind gave up their lives. Under the banner of Social Democracy a tyranny has been established as infamous as anything in the annals of autocracy.

"O Liberty, what monstrous crimes are committed in thy great name!"

CHAPTER VII

BOLSHEVIST THEORY AND PRACTICE

I

Utopia-making is among the easiest and most fascinating of all intellectual occupations. Few employments which can be called intellectual are easier than that of devising panaceas for the ills of society, of demonstrating on paper how the rough places of life may be made plain and its crooked ones made straight. And it is not a vain and fruitless waste of effort and of time, as things so easy of achievement often are. Many of the noblest minds of all lands and all ages have found pleasure and satisfaction in the imagining of ideal commonwealths and by so doing have rendered great service to mankind, enriching literature and, what is more important, stimulating the urge and passion for improvement and the faith of men in their power to climb to the farthest heights of their dreams. But the material of life is hard and lacks the plastic quality of inspired imagination. Though there is probably no single evil which exists for which a solution has not been devised in the wonderful laboratory of visioning, the perversity of the subtle and mysterious thing called life is such that many great and grave evils continue to challenge, perplex, and harass our humankind.

Yet, notwithstanding the plain lesson of history and experience, the reminder impressed on every page of humanity's record, that between the glow and the glamour of the vision and its actual realization stretches a long, long road, there are many simple-minded souls to whom the vision gleamed is as the goal attained. They do not distinguish between schemes on paper and ideals crystallized into living realities. This type of mind is far more common than is generally recognized; that is why so many people quite seriously believe that the Bolsheviki have really established in Russia a society which conforms to the generous ideals of social democracy. They have read the rhetorical "decrees" and "proclamations" in which the shibboleths of freedom and democracy abound, and are satisfied. Yet it ought to be plainly evident to any intelligent person that, even if the decrees and proclamations were as sound as they are in fact unsound, and as definite as they are in fact vague, they would afford no real basis for judging Bolshevism as an actual experiment in social polity. There is, in ultimate analysis, only one test to apply to Bolshevism—namely, the test of reality. We must ask what the Bolsheviki did, not what they professed; what was the performance, not what was the promise.

Of course, this does not mean that we are to judge result wholly without regard to aim. Admirable intention is still admirable as intention, even when untoward circumstance defeats it and brings deplorable results. Bolshevism is not merely a body of belief and speculation. When the Bolsheviki seized the government of Russia and began to attempt to carry out their ideas, Bolshevism became a living movement in a world of reality and subject to the acid test of pragmatic criteria. It must be judged by such a matter-of-fact standard as the extent to which it has enlarged or diminished the happiness, health, comfort, freedom, well-being, satisfaction, and efficiency of the greatest number of individuals. Unless the test shows that it has increased the sum of good available for the mass, Bolshevism cannot be regarded as a gain. If, on the contrary, the test shows that it has resulted in sensibly diminishing the sum of good available to the greatest number of people, Bolshevism must be counted as a move in the wrong direction, as so much effort lost. Nothing that can be urged on philosophical or moral grounds for or against the moral or intellectual impulses that prompted it can fundamentally change the verdict. Yet, for all that, it is well to examine the theory which inspires the practice; well to know the manner and method of thinking, and the view of life, from which Bolshevism as a movement of masses of men and women proceeds.

Theoretically, Bolshevism, as such, has no necessary connection with the philosophy or the program of Socialism. Certain persons have established a working relation between Socialism, a program, and Bolshevism, a method. The connection is not inherently logical, but, on the contrary, wholly adventitious. As a matter of fact, Bolshevism can only be linked to the program of Socialism by violently and disastrously weakening the latter and destroying its fundamental character. We shall do well to remember this; to

211

remember that the method of action, and, back of the method, the philosophy on which it rests and from which it springs, are separate and distinct from Socialism. They are incalculably older and they have been associated with vastly different programs. All that is new in Bolshevism is that a very old method of action, and a very old philosophy of action, have been seized upon by a new class which attempts to unite them to a new program.

That is all that is implied in the "dictatorship of the proletariat." Dictatorship by small minorities is not a new political phenomenon. All that is new when the minority attempting to establish its dictatorship is composed of poor, propertyless people, is the fact of their economic condition and status. That is the only difference between the dictatorship of Russia by the Romanov dynasty and the dictatorship of Russia by a small minority of determined, class-conscious working-people. It is not only the precise forms of oppressive power used by them that are identically characteristic of Czarism and Bolshevism, but their underlying philosophy. Both forms of dictatorship rest upon the philosophy of might as the only valid right. Militarism, especially as it was developed under Prussian leadership, has exactly the same philosophy and aims at the same general result, namely, to establish the domination and control of society by a minority class. The Bolsheviki have simply inverted Czarism and Militarism.

What really shocks the majority of people is not, after all, the methods or the philosophy of Bolshevism, but the fact that the Bolsheviki, belonging to a subject class, have seized upon the methods and philosophy of the most powerful ruling classes and turned them to their own account. There is a class morality and a class psychology the subtle influences of which few perceive as a matter of habit, which, however, to a great extent shape our judgments, our sympathies, and our antipathies. Men who never were shocked when a Czar, speaking the language of piety and religion, indulged in the most infamous methods and deeds of terror and oppression, are shocked beyond all power of adequate expression when former subjects of that same Czar, speaking the language of the religion of democracy and freedom, resort to the same infamous methods of terror and oppression.

II

The idea that a revolting proletarian minority might by force impose its rule upon society runs through the history of the modern working class, a note of impatient, desperate, menacing despair. The Bolsheviki say that they are Marxian Socialists; that Marx believed in and advocated the setting up, during the transitory period of social revolution, of the "dictatorship of the proletariat." They are not quite honest in this claim, however; they are indulging in verbal tricks. It is true that Marx taught that the proletarian dominion of society, as a preliminary to the abolition of all class rule of every kind, must be regarded as certain and inevitable. But it is not honest to claim the sanction of his teaching for the seizure of political power by a small class, consisting of about 6 per cent. of the population, and the imposition by force of its rule upon the majority of the population that is either unwilling or passive. That is the negation of Marxian Socialism. *It is the essence of Marx's teaching that the social revolution must come as a historical necessity when the proletariat itself comprises an overwhelming majority of the people.*

Let us summarize the theory as it appears in the *Communist Manifesto*: Marx begins by setting forth the fact that class conflict is as old as civilization itself, that history is very largely the record of conflicts between contending social classes. In our epoch, he argues, class conflict is greatly simplified; there is really only one division, that which divides the bourgeoisie and the proletariat: "Society as a whole is more and more splitting up into great hostile camps, into two great classes directly facing each other, bourgeoisie and proletariat." ... "With the development of industry the proletariat not only increases in numbers; it becomes concentrated in great masses, its strength grows, and it feels that strength more." ... "The proletarian movement is the *self-conscious, independent movement of the immense majority in the interests of the immense majority.*" It is this "immense majority" that is to establish its dominion. Marx expressly points out that "all previous historical movements were movements of minorities, or in the interest of minorities." It is the great merit of the movement of the proletariat, as he conceives it, that it is the "movement of the immense majority, in the interests of the immense majority."

Clearly, when Lenine and his followers say that they take their

213

doctrine of the "dictatorship of the proletariat" from Marx, they pervert the truth; they take from Marx only the phrase, not their fundamental policy. It is not to be denied that there were times when Marx himself momentarily lapsed into the error of Blanqui and the older school of Utopian, conspiratory Socialists who believed that they could find a short cut to social democracy; that by a surprise stroke, carefully prepared and daringly executed, a small and desperate minority could overthrow the existing social order and bring about Socialism. As Jaurès has pointed out,[50] the mind of Marx sometimes harked back to the dramatic side of the French Revolution, and was captivated by such episodes as the conspiracy of Babeuf and his friends, who in their day, while the proletariat was a small minority, even as it is in Russia now, sought to establish its dominion. But it is well known that after the failure of the Paris Commune, in 1871, Marx once and for all abandoned all belief in this form of the "dictatorship of the proletariat," and in the possibility of securing Socialism through the conspiratory action of minorities. He was even rather unwilling that the *Manifesto* should be republished after that, except as a purely historical document. It was in that spirit of reaction that he and Engels wrote in 1872 that passage—to which Lenine has given such an unwarranted interpretation—in which they say that the Commune had shown that "the working classes cannot simply take possession of the ready-made state machine and set it in motion for their own aims."

It was no less an interpreter of Marx than his great collaborator and friend, Frederick Engels, who, in 1895, stated the reasons for abandoning all belief in the possibility of accomplishing anything through political surprises and through the action of small conscious and determined minorities at the head of unconscious masses:

History proved that we were wrong—we and those who like us, in 1848, awaited the speedy success of the proletariat. It became perfectly clear *that economic conditions all over the Continent were by no means as yet sufficiently matured for superseding the capitalist organization of production.* This was proved by the economic revolution which commenced on the continent of Europe after 1848 and developed in France, Austria-Hungary, Poland, and, recently, also in Russia, and made Germany into an industrial state of the first rank—all on a capitalist basis, *which shows that in 1848 the prevailing conditions were still capable of expansion.* And to-day we have a huge international army of Socialists.... If this mighty proletarian army has not yet reached its goal, if it is destined to gain its ends only in a long drawn out struggle, making headway but slowly, step by step, this only proves how impossible it was in 1848 to change social conditions by forcible means ... the time for small minorities to place themselves at the head of the ignorant masses and resort to force in order to bring about revolutions, is gone. *A complete change in the organization of society can be brought about only by the conscious co-operation of the masses;* they must be alive to the aim in view; they must know what they want. The history of the last fifty years has taught us that.[51]

What Engels had in mind when he stressed the fact that history showed that in 1848 "the prevailing conditions were still capable of expansion" is the central Marxian doctrine of historical inevitability. It is surely less than honest to claim the prestige and authority of Marx's teachings upon the slender basis of a distorted version of his early thought, while completely ignoring the matured body of his doctrines. It may not matter much to the world to-day what Marx thought, or how far Lenine follows his teachings, but it is of importance that the claim set up by Lenine and Trotzky and many of their followers that they are guided by the principles of Marxian Socialism is itself demonstrably an evidence of moral or intellectual obliquity, which makes them very dangerous guides to follow. It is of importance, too, that the claim they make allures many Socialists of trusting and uncritical minds to follow them.

Many times in his long life Marx, together with Engels, found himself engaged in a fierce war against the very things Lenine and Trotzky and their associates have been trying to do. He thundered against Weitling, who wanted to have a "daring minority" seize the power of the state and establish its dictatorship by a *coup d'état.* He was denounced as a "reactionary" by Willich and Kinkel because, in 1850, he rejected with scorn the idea of a sudden seizure of political power through conspiratory action, and had the courage to say that it would take fifty years for the workers "to fit themselves for political power." He opposed Lassalle's idea of an armed insurrection in 1862, because he was certain that the economic development had not yet reached the stage which alone could make a social change possible. He fought with all the fierce impetuousness of his nature every attempt of

215

Bakunin to lead the workers to attempt the seizure of political power and forcibly establish their rule while still a minority.[52] He fought all these men because he had become profoundly convinced that "*no social order ever disappears before all the productive forces for which there is room in it have been developed; and new and higher relations of production never appear before the material conditions of their existence have matured in the womb of the old society.*"[53] No "dictatorship of the proletariat," no action by any minority, however well armed or however desperate, can overcome that great law.

The "dictatorship of the proletariat" in the sense in which that term is used by the Russian Bolshevik leaders, and by those who in other countries are urging that their example be followed, is not a policy of Marxian Socialism. It is not a product of modern conditions. Rather it harks back to the earlier conspiratory Socialism of Blanqui, with its traditions inherited from Robespierre and Babeuf. So far as its advocates are concerned, Marx and the whole modern Socialist movement might as well never have existed at all. They take us back three-quarters of a century, to the era before Marx, to that past so remote in intellectual and moral character, though recent in point of time, when the working class of no country in Europe possessed the right to vote—when the workers were indeed proletarians and not citizens; not only propertyless, but also "without a fatherland."

In truth, it is not difficult to understand how this theory has found acceptance in Russia. It was not difficult to understand why Marx's doctrine of economic evolution was for many years rejected by most Russian Socialists; why the latter took the view that Socialism must be more quickly attained, that capitalism was not a necessary precursor of Socialism in Russia, but that an intelligent leadership of passive masses would successfully establish Socialism on the basis of the old Russian communal institutions. It was quite easy to understand the change that came with Russia's industrial awakening, how the development of factory production gave an impetus to the Marxian theories. And, though it presents a strange paradox, in that it comes at a time when, despite everything, Russian capitalism continues to develop, it is really not difficult to understand how and why pre-Marxian conceptions reappear in that great land of paradoxes. Politically and intellectually the position of the proletariat of Russia before the recent Revolution was that of the proletariat of France in 1848.

But that which baffles the mind of the serious investigator is the readiness of so many presumably intelligent people living in countries where—as in America—wholly different conditions prevail to ignore the differences and be ready to abandon all the democratic advance made by the workers. There is nothing more certain in the whole range of social and political life than the fact that the doctrine that the power of the state must be seized and used by the proletariat against the non-proletarian classes, even for a relatively brief period, *can only be carried out by destroying all the democracy thus far achieved.*

III

The validity of the foregoing contention can scarcely be questioned, except by those to whom phrases are of more consequence than facts, who place theories above realities. The moment the Bolsheviki tried to translate their rhetorical propaganda for the dictatorship of the proletariat into the concrete terms of political reality they found that they were compelled to direct their main opposition, not against the bourgeoisie, or even against capitalism, but against the newly created democracy. In the movement to create a democratic government resting upon the basis of universal, direct, equal, and secret suffrage they saw a peril to their scheme far more formidable than militarism or capitalism. It was for this reason that they set themselves to the task of suppressing the Constituent Assembly. Only political simpletons will seriously regard the Bolshevik attempt to camouflage their motive by pretending that they determined to crush the Constituent Assembly because its members were elected on a register that was "obsolete" and therefore no longer truly represented the people.

The German Spartacides, who were acting in full accord with the Russian Bolsheviki, had not that miserable excuse. Yet they set out by force of arms to *prevent any election being held.* In this they were quite consistent; they wanted to set up a dictatorship, and they knew that the overwhelming mass of the people wanted something very different. At a dinner of the Inter-Collegiate Socialist Society in New York, in December, 1918, a spokesman for the German variety of Bolshevism blandly explained that

"Karl Liebknecht and his comrades know that they cannot hope to get a majority, therefore they are determined that no elections shall be held. They will prevent this by force. After some time, perhaps, when a proletarian régime has existed long enough, and people have become convinced of the superiority of the Socialist way, or at least grown used to it, *and it is safe to do so*, popular elections may be permitted." Incredible as it seems, this declaration was received with cheers by an audience which only a few minutes before had cheered with equal fervor denunciations of "encroachments upon American democracy."

Curiously enough, the precise manner in which the Bolsheviki have acted against democracy was set forth, as far back as 1850, by a German, Johann von Miquel, in a letter to Karl Marx. Miquel was born in Hanover, but his ancestors were of French origin. He studied at Heidelberg and Göttingen, and became associated with the Socialist movement of the period. He settled down to the practice of law, however, and when Hanover was annexed by Prussia he entered the Prussian parliament. After the "dismissal of the pilot," Bismarck, he became Prussian Minister of Finance, holding that position for ten years. Liebknecht referred to him as "my former *comrade in communismo* and present Chancellor *in re*." This Miquel, while he was still a Socialist, in 1850 wrote to Marx as follows:

The workers' party may succeed against the upper middle class and what remains of the feudal element, *but it will be attacked on its flank by the democracy*. We can perhaps give an anti-bourgeois tone to the Revolution for a little while, *we can destroy the essential conditions of bourgeois production*; but we cannot possibly put down the small tradesmen and shopkeeping class, the petty bourgeoisie. My motto is to secure all we can get. We should prevent the lower and middle class from *forming any organizations for as long a time as possible* after the first victory, and especially oppose ourselves in serried ranks to the plan of calling a Constitutional Assembly. Partial terrorism, local anarchy, must replace for us what we lack in bulk.

What a remarkable anticipation of the Bolshevist methods of 1917-18 is thus outlined in this letter, written sixty-seven years before the Bolshevik *coup d'état!* How literally Lenine, Trotzky and Co. have followed Herr von Miquel! They have desperately tried to "give an anti-bourgeois tone to the

Revolution," denouncing as bourgeois reactionaries the men and women whose labors and sacrifices have made the Russian Socialist movement. They have destroyed "the essential conditions" of bourgeois and of any other than the most primitive production. They have set themselves in serried ranks in opposition to "the plan of calling a Constitutional Assembly." They have suppressed not only the organizations of the "lower and middle class," but also those of a great part of the working class, thus going beyond Miquel. Finally, to replace what they lack in bulk, they have resorted to "partial terrorism and local anarchy."

And it is in the name of revolutionary progress, of ultra-radicalism, that we are called upon to revert to the tactics of desperation born of the discouraging conditions of nearly seventy years ago. A new philosophy has taken possession of the easily possessed minds of Greenwich Village philosophers and parlor revolutionists—a new philosophy of progress, according to which revolutionary progress consists in the unraveling by feverish fingers of the fabric woven through years of sacrifice; in abandoning high levels attained for the lower levels from which the struggles of the past raised us; in harking back to the thoughts and the tactics of men who shouted their despairing, defiant cries into the gloom of the blackest period of the nineteenth century!

Universal, secret, equal, and direct suffrage was a fact in Russia, the first great achievement of the Revolution. Upon that foundation, and upon no other, it was possible to build an enduring, comprehensive social democracy. Against that foundation the Bolsheviki hurled their destructive power, creating a discriminating class suffrage, disfranchising a great part of the Russian people—not merely the bourgeoisie, but a considerable part of the working class itself. Chapter XIII of Article 4 of the Constitution of the "Russian Socialist Federated Soviet Republic" sets forth the qualifications for voting, as follows:

THE RIGHT TO VOTE

Chapter Thirteen

64. The right to vote and to be elected to the Soviets is enjoyed by the following citizens, irrespective of religion, nationality, domicile, etc., of the Russian Socialist Federated Soviet Republic, of both sexes, who shall have completed their eighteenth year by the day of election:

a. All who have acquired the means of living through labor that is productive and useful to society, and also persons engaged in housekeeping which enables the former to do productive work—i.e., laborers and employees of all classes who are employed in industry, trade, agriculture, etc.; and peasants and Cossack agricultural laborers who employ no help for the purpose of making profits.

b. Soldiers of the army and navy of the Soviets.

c. Citizens of the two preceding categories who have to any degree lost their capacity to work.

Note 1: Local Soviets may, upon approval of the central power, lower the age standard mentioned herein.

Note 2: Non-citizens mentioned in Paragraph 20 (Article 2, Chapter Five) have the right to vote.

65. The following persons enjoy neither the right to vote nor the right to be voted for, even though they belong to one of the categories enumerated above, namely:

a. Persons who employ hired labor in order to obtain from it an increase in profits.

b. Persons who have an income without doing any work, such as interest from capital, receipts from property, etc.

c. Private merchants, trade, and commercial brokers.

d. Monks and clergy of all denominations.

e. Employees and agents of the former police, the gendarme corps, and the Okhrana (Czar's secret service), also members of the former reigning dynasty.

f. Persons who have in legal form been declared demented or mentally deficient, and also persons under guardianship.

g. Persons who have been deprived by a Soviet of their rights of citizenship because of selfish or dishonorable offenses, for the period fixed by the sentence.

Apparently the Constitution does not provide any standard for determining what labor is "useful and productive to society," and leaves the way open for a degree of arbitrariness on the part of some authority or other that is wholly incompatible with any generally accepted ideal of freedom and democracy. It is apparent from the text of paragraph 64, subdivision "a" of the foregoing chapter that housekeeping as such is not included in the category of "labor that is productive and useful to society," for a separate category is made of it. The language used is that "The right to vote and to be elected to the Soviets is enjoyed by.... All who have acquired the means of living through labor that is productive and useful to society, *and also* persons engaged in housekeeping, which enables the former to do productive work—*i.e.*, laborers and employees of all classes who are employed in industry, trade, agriculture, etc."

This *seems* to mean that persons engaged in housekeeping can only vote if and when they are so engaged in order to enable other persons than themselves to do "productive work." It appears that housekeeping for persons not engaged in such productive work—for children, for example—would not confer the right to vote. It is not possible to tell with certainty what it *does* mean, however, for there is probably not a single person in Russia or in the world who can tell exactly what this precious instrument actually means. What standard is to be established to determine what labor is "productive" and "useful"? Is the journalist, for instance, engaged in useful and productive labor? Is the novelist? is the agitator? Presumably the journalist employed in defending the Soviet Republic against attacks by unfriendly critics would be doing useful work and be entitled to vote, but what about the journalist employed in making the criticisms? Would the wife of the latter, no matter how much she might disagree with her husband's views, be barred from voting, simply because she was "engaged in housekeeping" for one whose labors were not regarded "productive and useful to society"? If the language used means anything at all, apparently she would be so disfranchised.

Upon what ground is it decided that the "private merchant" may not vote? Certainly it is not because his labor is of necessity neither productive nor useful, for paragraph 65 says that even though belonging to one of the categories of persons otherwise qualified to vote, the private merchant may "enjoy neither the right to vote nor to be voted for." The keeper of a little grocery store, even though his income is not greater than that of a mechanic, and despite the fact that his store meets a local need and makes his services, therefore, "useful" in the highest degree, cannot enjoy civic rights, simply because he is a "merchant"! The clergy of all denominations are excluded from the franchise. It does not matter, according to this constitution, that a minister belongs to a church independent of any connection with the state, that he is elected by people who desire his services and is paid by them, that he satisfies them and is therefore doing a "useful service"—if utility means the satisfying of needs—because he is so employed he cannot vote.

It is clearly provided that "peasants and Cossack agricultural laborers who employ no help for the purpose of making profits" can vote and be voted for. But no persons "who employ hired labor in order to obtain from it an increase in profits" may vote or be elected to office, *even though the work they do is productive and useful to society.* A peasant who hires no assistance may vote, but if he decides that by employing a boy to help him he will be able to give better attention to certain crops and make more money, even though he pays the boy every penny that the service is worth, judged by any standard whatever, he loses his vote and his civic status because, forsooth, he has gained in his net income as a result of his enterprise. And this is seriously put forward as the basis of government in a nation needing an intense and universal stimulation of its economic production.

A militant suffragist friend of mine, whose passion for universal suffrage in America is so great that it leads her to join in all sorts of demonstrations protesting against the failure of the United States Senate to pass the Susan B. Anthony amendment—even leading her to join in the public burning of President Wilson's speeches, a queer emulation of the ancient ecclesiastical bigotry of burning heretical books!—manages to unite to her passion for equal and unrestricted suffrage an equally passionate admiration for the Bolsheviki, arch-enemies of equal and unrestricted suffrage. Her case is not exceptional: it is rather typical of the Bolshevik following in England and in America. Such minds are not governed and directed by rational processes, but by emotional impulses, generally of pathological origin.

What the Bolshevik constitution would mean if practically applied to American life to-day can be briefly indicated. The following classes would certainly be entitled to vote and to be elected to office:

1. All wage-earners engaged in the production of goods and utilities regarded by some designated authority as "productive and useful to society."

2. Teachers and educators engaged in the public service.

3. All farmers owning and working their own farms without hired help of any kind.

4. All wage-earners engaged in the public service as employees of the state, subdivisions of the state, or public service corporations-such as postal clerks, street-railway workers, electricians, and so on.

5. Wives and others engaged in keeping the homes of the foregoing, so as to enable them to work.

6. The "soldiers of the army and navy"—whether all officers are included is not clear from the text.

Now let us see what classes would be as certainly excluded from the right to vote and to be voted for.

1. Every merchant from the keeper of a corner grocery store to the owner of a great mercantile establishment.

2. Every banker, every commission agent, every broker, every insurance agent, every real-estate dealer.

3. Every farmer who hires help of any kind—even a single "hand."

4. Every petty contractor, garage-keeper, or other person employing any hired help whatever, including the professional writer who hires a stenographer, the doctor who hires a chauffeur, and the dentist who hires a mechanic assistant.

5. Every clergyman and minister of the Gospel.

6. Every person whose income is derived from inherited wealth or from invested earnings, including all who live upon annuities provided by gift or bequest.

7. Every person engaged in housekeeping for persons included in any of the foregoing six categories—including the wives of such disqualified

223

persons.

There are many occupational groups whose civic status is not so easily defined. The worker engaged in making articles of luxury, enjoyed only by the privileged few, could hardly have a better claim to a vote than the housekeeper of a man whose income was derived from foreign investments, or than the chauffeur of a man whose income was derived from government bonds. All three represent, presumably, types of that parasitic labor which subjects those engaged in it to disfranchisement. Apparently, though not certainly, then, the following would also be disfranchised:

1. All lawyers except those engaged by the public authorities for the public service.

2. All teachers and educators other than those engaged in the public service.

3. All bankers, managers of industries, commercial travelers, experts, and accountants except those employed in the public service, or whose labor is judged by a competent tribunal to be necessary and useful.

4. All editors, journalists, authors of books and plays, except as special provision might be provided for individuals.

5. All persons engaged in occupations which a competent tribunal decided to classify as non-essential or non-productive.

Any serious attempt to introduce such restrictions and limitations of the right of suffrage in America would provoke irresistible revolt. It would be justly and properly regarded as an attempt to arrest the forward march of the nation and to turn its energies in a backward direction. It would be just as reactionary in the political world as it would be in the industrial world to revert back to hand-tool production; to substitute the ox-team for the railway system, the hand-loom for the power-loom, the flail for the threshing-machine, the sickle for the modern harvesting-machine, the human courier for the electric telegraph.

Yet we find a radical like Mr. Max Eastman giving his benediction and approval to precisely such a program in Russia as a substitute for universal suffrage. We find him quoting with apparent approval an article setting forth Lenine's plan, hardly disguised, to disfranchise every farmer who employs even a single hired helper.[54]

Lenine's position is quite clear. "Only the proletariat leading on the poorest peasants (the semi-proletariat as they are called in our program) ... may undertake the steps toward Socialism that have become absolutely unavoidable and non-postponable.... The peasants want to retain their small holdings and to arrive at some place of equal distribution.... So be it. No sensible Socialist will quarrel with a pauper peasant on this ground. If the lands are confiscated, *so long as the proletarians rule in the great centers, and all political power is handed over to the proletariat,* the rest will take care of itself."[55] Yet, in spite of Lenine's insistence that all political power be "handed over to the proletariat," in spite of a score of similar utterances which might be quoted, and, finally, in spite of the Soviet Constitution which so obviously excludes from the right to vote a large part of the adult population, an American Bolshevist pamphleteer has the effrontery to insult the intelligence of his readers by the stupidly and palpably false statement that "even at the present time 95 per cent. in Russia can vote, while in the United States only about 65 per cent. can vote."[56]

Of course it is only as a temporary measure that this dictatorship of a class is to be maintained. It is designed only for the period of transition and adjustment. In time the adjustment will be made, all forms of social parasitism and economic exploitation will disappear, and then it will be both possible and natural to revert to democratic government. Too simple and naïve to be trusted alone in a world so full of trickery and tricksters as ours are they who find any asurance in this promise. They are surely among the most gullible of our humankind!

Of course, the answer to the claim is a very simple one: it is that no class gaining privilege and power ever surrenders it until it is compelled to do so. Every one who has read the pre-Marxian literature dealing with the dictatorship of the proletariat knows how insistent is the demand that the period of dictatorship must be *prolonged as much as possible.* Even Marx himself insisted, on one occasion at least, that it must be maintained as long as possible,[57] and in the letter of Johann von Miquel, already quoted, we find the same thought expressed in the same terms, "as long as possible." But even if we put aside these warnings of human experience and of recorded history, and persuade ourselves that in Russia we have a wholly new phenomenon, a class possessing powers of dictatorship animated by a burning passion to relinquish those powers as quickly as possible, is it not still evident that the social adjustments that must be made to reach the stage where, according to the Bolshevik standards, political democracy can be introduced, must, under the most favorable circumstances conceivable, take many, many years? Even Lenine admits that "a sound solution of the problem of increasing the productivity of labor" (which lies at the very heart of the problem we are now discussing) "requires at least (especially after a most distressing and destructive war) several years."[58]

From the point of view of social democracy the basis of the Bolshevik state is reactionary and unsound. The true Socialist policy is that set forth by Wilhelm Liebknecht in the following words: "The political power which the Social Democracy aims at and which it will win, no matter what its enemies may do, *has not for its object the establishment of the dictatorship of the proletariat, but the suppression of the dictatorship of the bourgeoisie*."[59]

IV

Democracy in government and in industry must characterize any system of society which can be justly called Socialist. Thirteen years ago I wrote, "Socialism without democracy is as impossible as a shadow without light."[60] That seemed to me then, as it seems to-day, axiomatic. And so the greatest Socialist thinkers and leaders always regarded it. "We have perceived that Socialism and democracy are inseparable," declared William Liebknecht, the well-beloved, in 1899.[61] Thirty years earlier, in 1869, he had given lucid expression to the same conviction in these words: "Socialism and democracy are not the same, but they are only different expressions of the same fundamental idea. They belong to each other, round out each other, and can never stand in contradiction to each other. Socialism without democracy is pseudo-Socialism, just as democracy without Socialism is pseudo-democracy."[62] Democracy in industry is, as I have insisted in my writing with unfailing consistency, as inseparable from Socialism as democracy in government.[63] Unless industry is brought within the control of democracy and made responsive to the common will, Socialism is not attained.

Everywhere the organized working class aspires to attain that industrial democracy which is the counterpart of political democracy.

226

Syndicalism, with all its vagaries, its crude reversal to outworn ideas and methods, is, nevertheless, fundamentally an expression of that yearning. It is the same passion that lies back of the Shop Stewards' movement in England, and that inspires the much more patiently and carefully developed theories and plans of the advocates of "Guild Socialism." Motived by the same desire, our American labor-unions are demanding, and steadily gaining, an increasing share in the actual direction of industry. Joint control by boards composed of representatives of employers, employees, and the general public is, to an ever-increasing extent, determining the conditions of employment, wage standards, work standards, hours of labor, choice and conduct of foremen, and many other matters of vital importance to the wage-earners. That we are still a long way from anything like industrial democracy is all too painfully true and obvious, but it is equally obvious that we are struggling toward the goal, and that there is a serious purpose and intention to realize the ideal.

Impelled by the inexorable logic of its own existence as a dictatorship, the Bolshevik government has had to set itself against any and every manifestation of democracy in industry with the same relentless force as it opposed democracy in government. True, owing to the fact that, following the line of industrial evolution, the trade-union movement was not strongly enough developed to even attempt any organization for the expression of industrial democracy comparable to the Constituent Assembly. It is equally true, however, that had such an organization existed the necessity to suppress it, as the political organization was suppressed, would have proceeded inevitably and irresistibly from the creation of a dictatorship. *There cannot be, in any country, as co-existent forces, political dictatorship and industrial democracy.* It is also true that such democratic agencies as there were existing the Bolsheviki neglected.

That the Bolsheviki did not establish industrial democracy in its fullest sense is not to be charged to their discredit. Had Bolshevism never appeared, and had the Constituent Assembly been permitted to function unmolested and free, it would have taken many years to realize anything like a well-rounded industrial democracy, for which a highly developed industrial system is absolutely essential. The leaders of the Bolshevik movement recognized from the first that the time had not yet arrived for even attempting to set up a Socialist commonwealth based on the social ownership and democratic control of industry. Lenine frankly declared that "Socialism cannot now prevail in Russia,"[64] and Trotzky said, a month after the *coup d'état*: "We are not ready yet to take over all industry.... For the present, we expect of the earnings of a factory to pay the owner 5 or 6 per cent. yearly on his actual investment. What we aim at now is *control* rather than *ownership*."[65] He did not tell Professor Ross, who records this statement, on what grounds the owner of the property thus controlled by the Soviet government, and who thus becomes a partner of the government, is to be excluded from the exercise of the franchise. But let that pass.

When the Bolsheviki seized the power of the state, they found themselves confronted by a terrific task. Russia was utterly demoralized. An undeveloped nation industrially, war and internal strife had wrought havoc with the industrial life she had. Her railways were neglected and the whole transportation system, entirely inadequate even for peace needs, had, under the strain of the war, fallen into chaos. After the March Revolution, as a natural consequence of the intoxication of the new freedom, such disciplines as had existed were broken down. Production fell off in a most alarming manner. During the Kerensky régime Skobelev, as Minister of Labor, repeatedly begged the workers to prove their loyalty to the Revolution by increased exertion and faithfulness in the workshops and factories. The Bolsheviki, on their part, as a means of fighting the Provisional Government, preached the opposite doctrine, that of sabotage. In every manner possible they encouraged the workers to limit production, to waste time and materials, strike for trivial reasons, and, in short, do all that was possible to defeat the effort to place industry upon a sound basis.

When they found themselves in possession of the powers of government the Bolshevik leaders soon had to face the stern realities of the conditions essential to the life of a great nation. They could not escape the necessity of intensifying production. They had not only promised peace, but bread, and bread comes only from labor. Every serious student of the problem has realized that the first great task of any Socialist society must be *to increase the productivity of labor*. It is all very well for a popular propaganda among the masses to promise a great reduction in the hours of labor and, at the same time, a great improvement in the standards of living. The translation of such promises into actual achievements must prove to be an enormous task. To build the better homes, make the better and more abundant clothing, shoes, furniture, and other things required to fulfil the promise, will require a great deal of labor, and such an organization of industry upon a basis of efficiency as no nation has yet developed. If the working class of this or any other country should take possession of the existing organization of production, there would not be enough in the fund now going to the capitalist class to satisfy the requirements of the workers, *even if not a penny of compensation were paid to the expropriated owners.* Kautsky, among others, has courageously faced this fact and insisted that "it will be one of the imperative tasks of the Social Revolution not simply to continue, but to increase production; the victorious proletariat must extend production rapidly if it is to be able to satisfy the enormous demands that will be made upon the new régime."[66]

From the first
this problem had to be faced by the Bolshevik government. We find Lenine insisting that the workers must be inspired with "idealism, self-sacrifice, and persistence" to turn out as large a product as possible; that the productivity of labor must be raised and a high level of industrial performance as the duty of every worker be rigorously insisted upon. It is not enough to have destroyed feudalism and the monarchy:

In every Socialist revolution, however, the main task of the proletariat, and of the poorest peasantry led by it—and, hence, also in the Socialist revolution in Russia inaugurated by us on November 7, 1917, consists in the positive and constructive work of establishing an extremely complex and delicate net of newly organized relationships covering the systematic production and distribution of products which are necessary for the existence of tens of millions of people. The successful realization of such a revolution depends on the original historical creative work of the majority of the population, and first of all of the majority of the toilers. *The victory of the Socialist revolution will not be assured unless the proletariat and the poorest peasantry manifest sufficient consciousness, idealism, self-sacrifice, and persistence.* With the creation of a new—the Soviet—type of state, offering to the oppressed toiling masses the opportunity to participate actively in the free construction of a new society, we have solved only a small part of the difficult task. *The main difficulty is in the economic domain; to raise the productivity of labor, to establish strict*

229

and universal accounting and control of production and distribution, and actually to socialize production.[67]

Lenine recognizes, as every thoughtful person must, that this task of organizing production and distribution cannot be undertaken by "the proletariat and the poorest peasants." It requires a vast amount of highly developed technical knowledge and skill, the result of long training and superior education. This kind of service is so highly paid, in comparison with the wages paid to the manual workers, that it lifts those who perform the service and receive the high salaries into the ranks of the bourgeoisie. Certainly, even though they are engaged in performing work of the highest value and the most vital consequence, the specialists, experts, and directing managers of industry are not of the "working class," as that term is commonly employed. And no matter how we may speculate upon the possible attainment of approximate equality of income in some future near or remote, the fact is that the labor of such men can only be secured by paying much more than is paid to the manual workers.

Quite wisely, the Bolshevik government decided that it must have such services, no matter that they must be highly paid for; that they could only be rendered by the hated bourgeoisie and that, in consequence, certain compromises and relations with the bourgeoisie became necessary the moment the services were engaged. The Bolshevik government recognized the imperative necessity of the service which only highly paid specialists could give and wisely decided that no prejudice or theory must be permitted to block the necessary steps for Russia's reconstruction. In a spirit of intelligent opportunism, therefore, they subordinated shibboleths, prejudices, dogmas, and theories to Russia's necessity. The sanity of this opportunistic attitude is altogether admirable, but it contrasts strangely with the refusal to co-operate with the bourgeoisie in establishing a stable democratic government—no less necessary for Russia's reconstruction and for Socialism. As a matter of fact, the very promptitude and sanity of their opportunism when faced by responsibility, serves to demonstrate the truth of the contention made in these pages, that in refusing to co-operate with others in building up a permanently secure democratic government, they were actuated by no high moral principle, but simply by a desire to gain power. The position of Russia to-day would have been vastly different if the wisdom manifested in the following paragraphs had governed Lenine and his associates in the days when Kerensky was trying to save Russian democracy:

Without the direction of specialists of different branches of knowledge, technique, and experience, the transformation toward Socialism is impossible, for Socialism demands a conscious mass movement toward a higher productivity of labor in comparison with capitalism and on the basis which had been attained by capitalism. Socialism must accomplish this movement forward in its own way, by its own methods—to make it more definite, by Soviet methods. But the specialists are inevitably bourgeois on account of the whole environment of social life which made them specialists.... In view of the considerable delay in accounting and control in general, although we have succeeded in defeating sabotage, we have *not yet* created an environment which would put at our disposal the bourgeois specialists. Many sabotagers are coming into our service, but the best organizers and the biggest specialists can be used by the state either in the old bourgeois way (that is, for a higher salary) or in the new proletarian way (that is, by creating such an environment of universal accounting and control which would inevitably and naturally attract and gain the submission of specialists). We were forced now to make use of the old bourgeois method and agree to a very high remuneration for the services of the biggest of the bourgeois specialists. All those who are acquainted with the facts understand this, but not all give sufficient thought to the significance of such a measure on the part of the proletarian state. *It is clear that the measure is a compromise, that it is a defection from the principles of the Paris Commune and of any proletarian rule, which demand the reduction of salaries to the standard of remuneration of the average workers*—principles which demand that "career hunting" be fought by deeds, not words.

Furthermore, it is clear that such a measure is not merely a halt in a certain part and to a certain degree of the offensive against capitalism (for capitalism is not a quantity of money, but a definite social relationship), *but also a step backward by our Socialist Soviet state*, which has from the very beginning proclaimed and carried on a policy of reducing high salaries to the standard of wages of the average worker.

... The corrupting influence of high salaries is beyond question—both on the Soviets ... and on the mass of the workers. But all thinking and honest workers and peasants will agree with us and will admit that we are unable to

231

get rid at once of the evil heritage of capitalism.... The sooner we ourselves, workers and peasants, learn better labor discipline and a higher technique of toil, making use of the bourgeois specialists for this purpose, the sooner we will get rid of the need of paying tribute to these specialists.[68]

We find the same readiness to compromise and to follow the line of least resistance in dealing with the co-operatives. From 1906 onward there had been an enormous growth of co-operatives in Russia. They were of various kinds and animated by varied degrees of social consciousness. They did not differ materially from the co-operatives of England, Belgium, Denmark, Italy, or Germany except in the one important particular that they relied upon bourgeois Intellectuals for leadership and direction to a greater extent than do the co-operatives in the countries named. They were admirably fitted to be the nuclei of a socialized system of distribution. Out of office the Bolsheviki had sneered at these working-class organizations and denounced them as "bourgeois corruptions of the militant proletariat." Necessity and responsibility soon forced the adoption of a new attitude toward them. The Bolshevik government had to accept the despised co-operatives, and even compromise Bolshevist principles as the price of securing their services:

A Socialist state can come into existence only as a net of production and consumption communes, which keep conscientious accounts of their production and consumption, economize labor, steadily increasing its productivity and thus making it possible to lower the workday to seven, six, or even less hours. Anything less than rigorous, universal, thorough accounting and control of grain and of the production of grain, and later also of all other necessary products, will not do. We have inherited from capitalism mass organizations which can facilitate the transition to mass accounting and control of distribution—the consumers' co-operatives. They are developed in Russia less than in the more advanced countries, but they comprise more than 10,000,000 members. The decree on consumers' associations which was recently issued is extremely significant, showing clearly the peculiarity of the position and of the problem of the Socialist Soviet Republic at the present time.

The decree is an agreement with the bourgeois co-operatives and with the workmen's co-operatives adhering to the bourgeois standpoint. The agreement or compromise consists, firstly, in the fact that the representatives of these institutions not only participated in the deliberations on this decree, but had practically received a determining voice, for parts of the decree which met determined opposition from these institutions were rejected. Secondly and essentially, the compromise consists in the rejection by the Soviet authority of the principle of free admission to the co-operatives (the only consistent principle from the proletarian standpoint), and that the whole population of a given locality should be *united in a single co-operative.* The defection from this, the only Socialist principle, which is in accord with the problem of doing away with classes, allows the existence of working-class co-operatives (which in this case call themselves working-class co-operatives only because they submit to the class interests of the bourgeoisie). Lastly, the proposition of the Soviet government completely to exclude the bourgeoisie from the administration of the co-operatives was also considerably weakened, and only owners of capitalistic commercial and industrial enterprises are excluded from the administration.

If the proletariat, acting through the Soviets, should successfully establish accounting and control on a national scale, there would be no need for such compromise. Through the Food Departments of the Soviets, through their organs of supply, we would unite the population in one co-operative directed by the proletariat, without the assistance from bourgeois co-operatives, without concessions to the purely bourgeois principle which compels the labor co-operatives to remain side by side with the bourgeois co-operatives instead of wholly subjecting these bourgeois co-operatives, fusing both?[69]

V

It is no mood of captious, unfriendly criticism that attention is specially directed to these compromises. Only political charlatans, ineffective quacks, and irresponsible soap-box orators see crime against the revolutionary program of the masses in a wise and honest opportunism. History will not condemn the Bolsheviki for the give-and-take, compromise-where-necessary policy outlined in the foregoing paragraphs. Its condemnation will be directed rather against their failure to act in that spirit from the moment the first Provisional Government arose. Had they joined with the other Socialists and established a strong Coalition Government, predominantly Socialist, but including representatives of the most liberal and democratic elements of the bourgeoisie, it would have been possible to bring the problems of labor organization and labor discipline under democratic direction. It would not have been possible to establish complete industrial democracy, fully developed Socialism, nor will it be possible to do this for many years to come.

But it would have been easy and natural for the state to secure to the workers a degree of economic assurance and protection not otherwise possible. It would have been possible, too, for the workers' organizations, recognized by and co-operating with the state, to have undertaken, in a large degree, the control of the conditions of their own employment which labor organizations everywhere are demanding and gradually gaining. The best features of "Guild Socialism" could nowhere have been so easily adopted.[70] But instead of effort in these directions, we find the Bolsheviki resorting to the *Taylor System of Scientific Management enforced by an individual dictator whose word is final and absolute, to disobey whom is treason*! There is not a nation in the world with a working-class movement of any strength where it would be possible to introduce the industrial servitude here described:

The most conscious vanguard of the Russian proletariat has already turned to the problem of increasing labor discipline. For instance, the central committee of the Metallurgical Union and the Central Council of the Trades Unions have begun work on respective measures and drafts of decrees. This work should be supported and advanced by all means. *We should immediately introduce piece work and try it out in practice. We should try out every scientific and progressive suggestion of the Taylor System*; we should compare the earnings with the general total of production, or the exploitation results of railroad and water transportation, and so on.

The Russian is a poor worker in comparison with the workers of the advanced nations, and this could not be otherwise under the régime of the Czar and other remnants of feudalism. The last word of capitalism in this respect, the Taylor System—as well as all progressive measures of capitalism—combine the refined cruelty of bourgeois exploitation and a number of most valuable scientific attainments in the analysis of mechanical

234

motions during work, in dismissing superfluous and useless motions, in determining the most correct methods of the work, the best systems of accounting and control, etc. The Soviet Republic must adopt valuable and scientific and technical advance in this field. *The possibility of Socialism will be determined by our success in combining the Soviet rule and the Soviet organization of management with the latest progressive measures of capitalism. We must introduce in Russia the study and the teaching of the Taylor System and its systematic trial and adaptation.* While working to increase the productivity of labor, we must at the same time take into account the peculiarities of the transition period from capitalism to Socialism, which require, on one hand, that we lay the foundation for the Socialist organization of emulation, and, on the other hand, *require the use of compulsion so that the slogan of the dictatorship of the proletariat should not be weakened by the practice of a too mild proletarian government.*

The resolution of the last (Moscow) Congress of the Soviets advocates, as the most important problem at present, the creation of "efficient organization" and higher discipline. Such resolutions are now readily supported by everybody. But that their realization requires compulsion, and *compulsion in the form of a dictatorship*, is ordinarily not comprehended. And yet, it would be the greatest stupidity and the most absurd opportunism to suppose that the transition from capitalism to Socialism is possible without compulsion and dictatorship. The Marxian theory has long ago criticized beyond misunderstanding this petty bourgeois-democratic and anarchistic nonsense. And Russia of 1917-18 confirms in this respect the Marxian theory so clearly, palpably, and convincingly that only those who are hopelessly stupid or who have firmly determined to ignore the truth can still err in this respect. Either a Kornilov dictatorship (if Kornilov be taken as Russian type of a bourgeois Cavaignac) or a dictatorship of the proletariat—no other alternative is possible for a country which is passing through an unusually swift development with unusually difficult transitions and which suffers from desperate disorganization created by the most horrible war.[71]

This dictatorship is to be no light affair, no purely nominal force, but a relentless iron-hand rule. Lenine is afraid that the proletariat is too soft-hearted and lenient. He says:

But "dictatorship" is a great word. And great words must not be used in vain. A dictatorship is an iron rule, with revolutionary daring and swift and merciless in the suppression of the exploiters as well as of the thugs (hooligans). And our rule is too mild, quite frequently resembling jam rather than iron.[72]

And so the dictatorship of the proletariat becomes the *dictatorship of a single person*, a super-boss and industrial autocrat. We must learn to combine the stormy, energetic breaking of all restraint on the part of the toiling masses *with iron discipline during work, with absolute submission to the will of one person, the Soviet director, during work*.[73]

As I copy these words from Lenine's book my memory recalls the days, more than twenty years ago, when as a workman in England and as shop steward of my union I joined with my comrades in breaking down the very things Lenine here proposes to set up in the name of Socialism. "Absolute submission to the will of one person" is not a state toward which free men will strive. Not willingly will men who enjoy the degree of personal freedom existing in democratic nations turn to this:

With respect to ... the significance of individual dictatorial power from the standpoint of the specific problems of the present period, we must say that every large machine industry—which is the material productive source and basis of Socialism—requires an absolute and strict unity of the will which directs the joint work of hundreds, thousands, and tens of thousands of people. This necessity is obvious from the technical, economical, and historical standpoint, and has always been recognized by all those who had given any thought to Socialism, as its prerequisite. But how can we secure a strict unity of will? *By subjecting the will of thousands* to the will of one.

This subjection, *if the participants in the common work are ideally conscious and disciplined*, may resemble the mild leading of an orchestra conductor; but may take the acute form of a dictatorship—if there is no ideal discipline and consciousness. But at any rate, *complete submission to a single will is absolutely necessary for the success of the processes of work which is organized on the type of large machine industry*. This is doubly true of the railways. And just this transition from one political problem to another, which in appearance has no resemblance to the first, constitutes the peculiarity of the present period. The Revolution has just broken the oldest, the strongest, and the heaviest chains

236

to which the masses were compelled to submit. So it was yesterday. And to-day, the same Revolution (and indeed in the interest of Socialism) demands the *absolute submission* of the masses to the *single will* of those who direct the labor process. It is self-evident that it can be realized only after great upheavals, crises, returns to the old; only through the greatest strain of the energy of the proletarian vanguard which is leading the people to the new order....

To the extent to which the principal problem of the Soviet rule changes from military suppression to administration, suppression and compulsion will, *as a rule, be manifested in trials, and not in shooting on the spot.* And in this respect the revolutionary masses have taken, after November 7, 1918, the right road and have proved the vitality of the Revolution, when they started to organize their own workmen's and peasants' tribunals, before any decrees were issued dismissing the bourgeois-democratic judicial apparatus. *But our revolutionary and popular tribunals are excessively and incredibly weak. It is apparent that the popular view of the courts—which was inherited from the régime of the landowners and the bourgeoisie—as not their own, has not yet been completely destroyed.* It is not sufficiently appreciated that the courts serve to attract all the poor to administration (for judicial activity is one of the functions of state administration); that the court is *an organ of the rule of the proletariat and of the poorest peasantry; that the court is a means of training in discipline.* There is a lack of appreciation of the simple and obvious fact that, if the chief misfortunes of Russia are famine and unemployment, these misfortunes cannot be overcome by any outbursts of enthusiasm, but only by thorough and universal organization and discipline, in order to increase the production of bread for men and fuel for industry, to transport it in time, and to distribute it in the right way. That therefore *responsibility* for the pangs of famine and unemployment falls on *every one who violates the labor discipline in any enterprise and in any business.* That those who are responsible should be discovered, tried, and *punished without mercy.* The petty bourgeois environment, which we will have to combat persistently now, shows particularly in the lack of comprehension of the economic and political connection between famine and unemployment and the *prevailing dissoluteness in organization and discipline*—in the firm hold of the view of the small proprietor that "nothing matters, if only I gain as much as possible."

237

A characteristic struggle occurred on this basis in connection with the last decree on railway management, the decree which granted dictatorial (or "unlimited") power to individual directors. The conscious (and mostly, probably, unconscious) representatives of petty bourgeois dissoluteness contended that the granting of "unlimited" (*i.e.*, dictatorial) power to individuals was a defection from the principle of board administration, from the democratic and other principles of the Soviet rule. Some of the Socialist-Revolutionists of the left wing carried on a plainly demagogic agitation against the decree on dictatorship, appealing to the evil instincts and to the petty bourgeois desire for personal gain. The question thus presented is of really great significance; firstly, the question of principle is, in general, the appointment of individuals endowed with unlimited power, the appointment of dictators, in accord with the fundamental principles of the Soviet rule; secondly, in what relation is this case—this precedent, if you wish—to the special problems of the Soviet rule during the present concrete period? Both questions deserve serious consideration.[74]

With characteristic ingenuity Lenine attempts to provide this dictatorship with a theoretical basis which will pass muster as Marxian Socialism. He uses the term "Soviet democracy" as a synonym for democratic Socialism and says there is "absolutely no contradiction in principle" between it and "the use of dictatorial power of individuals." By what violence to reason and to language is the word *democracy* applied to the system described by Lenine? To use words with such scant respect to their meanings, established by etymology, history, and universal agreement in usage, is to invite and indeed compel the contempt of minds disciplined by reason's practices. As for the claim that there is no contradiction in principle between democratic Socialism and the exercise of dictatorial power by individuals, before it can be accepted every Socialist teacher and leader of any standing anywhere, the programs of all the Socialist parties, and their practice, must be denied and set aside. Whether democratic Socialism be wise or unwise, a practical possibility or an unrealizable idea, at least it has nothing in common with such reactionary views as are expressed in the following:

That the dictatorship of individuals has very frequently in the history of revolutionary movements served as an expression and means of realization of the dictatorship of the revolutionary classes is confirmed by the

238

undisputed experience of history. With bourgeois democratic principles, the dictatorship of individuals has undoubtedly been compatible. But this point is always treated adroitly by the bourgeois critics of the Soviet rule and by their petty bourgeois aides. On one hand, they declared the Soviet rule simply something absurd and anarchically wild, carefully avoiding all our historical comparisons and theoretical proofs that the Soviets are a higher form of democracy; nay, more, the beginning of a *Socialist* form of democracy. On the other hand, they demand of us a higher democracy than the bourgeois and argue: with your Bolshevist (*i.e.*, Socialist, not bourgeois) democratic principles, with the Soviet democratic principles, individual dictatorship is absolutely incompatible.

Extremely poor arguments, these. If we are not Anarchists, we must admit the necessity of a state—that is, of *compulsion,* for the transition from capitalism to Socialism. The form of compulsion is determined by the degree of development of the particular revolutionary class, then by such special circumstances as, for instance, the heritage of a long and reactionary war, and then by the forms of resistance of the bourgeoisie and the petty bourgeoisie. *There is therefore absolutely no contradiction in principle between the Soviet (Socialist) democracy and the use of dictatorial power of individuals.* The distinction between a proletarian and a bourgeois dictatorship consists in this: that the first directs its attacks against the exploiting minority in the interests of the exploited majority; and, further, in this, that the first is accomplished (also through individuals) not only by the masses of the exploited toilers, but also by the organizations which are so constructed that they arouse these masses to historical creative work (the Soviets belong to this kind of organization).[75]

This, then, is Bolshevism, not as it is seen and described by unfriendly "bourgeois" writers, but as it is seen and described by the acknowledged intellectual and political leader of the Bolsheviki, Nikolai Lenine. I have not taken any non-Bolshevist authority; I have not even restated his views in a summary of my own, lest into the summary might be injected some reflexes of my own critical thought. Bolshevism is revealed in all its reactionary repulsiveness as something between which and absolute, individual dictatorial power there is "absolutely no contradiction in principle." It will not avail for our American followers and admirers of the Bolsheviki to plead that these things are temporary, compromises with the ideal due to the extraordinary circumstances prevailing in Russia, and to beg a mitigation of the severity of our judgment on that account.

The answer to the plea is twofold: in the first place, they who offer it must, if they are sincere, abandon the savagely critical attitude they have seen fit to adopt toward our own government and nation because with "extraordinary conditions prevailing" we have had introduced conscription, unusual restrictions of movement and of utterance, and so forth. How else, indeed, can their sincerity be demonstrated? If the fact that extraordinary conditions justified Lenine and his associates in instituting a régime so tyrannical, what rule of reason or of morals must be invoked to refuse to count the extraordinary conditions produced in our own nation by the war as justification for the special measures of military service and discipline here introduced?

But there is a second answer to the claim which is more direct and conclusive. It is not open to argument at all. It is found in the words of Lenine himself, in his claim that there is absolutely no contradiction between the principle of individual dictatorship, ruling with iron hand, and the principle upon which Soviet government rests. There has been no compromise here, for if there is no contradiction in principle no compromise could have been required. Lenine is not afraid to make or to admit making compromises; he admits that compromises have been made. It was a compromise to employ highly salaried specialists from the bourgeoisie, "a defection from the principles of the Paris Commune and of any proletarian rule," as he says. It was a compromise, another "defection from the only Socialist principle," to admit the right of the co-operatives to determine their own conditions of membership. Having made these declarations quite candidly, he takes pains to assure us that there was no such defection from principle in establishing the absolute rule of an individual dictator, that there was absolutely no contradiction in principle in this.[76]

Moreover, there is no reason for regarding this dictatorship as a temporary thing, if Lenine himself is to be accepted as an authoritative spokesman. Obviously, if there is nothing in the principle of an absolute individual dictatorship which is in contradiction to the Bolshevik ideal, there can be no Bolshevik principle which necessarily requires for its realization the ending of such dictatorship. Why, therefore, may it not be continued indefinitely? Certainly, if the dictatorship is abolished it will not be—if Lenine is to be seriously considered—on account of its incompatibility with Bolshevik principles.

VI

The Bolshevik government of Russia is credited by many of its admirers in this country with having solved the great land problem and with having satisfied the land-hunger of the peasants. It is charged, moreover, that the bitter opposition to the Bolsheviki is mainly due to agitation by the bourgeoisie, led by the expropriated landowners, who want to defeat the Revolution and to have their former titles to the land restored. Of course, it is true that, so far as they dare to do so, the former landowners actively oppose the Bolsheviki. No expropriated class ever acted otherwise, and it would be foolish to expect anything else. But any person who believes that the opposition of the great peasant Socialist organizations, and especially of the Socialist-Revolutionists, is due to the confiscation of the land, either consciously or unconsciously, is capable of believing anything and quite immune from rationality.

The facts in the case are, briefly, as follows: First, as Professor Ross has pointed out,[77] the land policy of the Bolshevik government was a compromise of the principles long advocated by its leaders, a compromise made for political reasons only. Second, as Marie Spiridonova abundantly demonstrated at an All-Russian Soviet Conference in July, 1918, the Bolshevik government did not honorably live up to its agreement with the Socialist-Revolutionists of the Left. Third, so far as the land problem was concerned there was not the slightest need or justification for the Bolshevik *coup d'état*, for the reason that the problem had already been solved on the precise lines afterward followed in the Soviet decree and the leaders of the peasants were satisfied. We have the authority of no less competent a witness than Litvinov, Bolshevist Minister to England, that "the land measure had been 'lifted' bodily from the program of the Socialist-Revolutionists."[78] Each of these statements is amply sustained by evidence which cannot be disputed or overcome.

That the "land decree" which the Bolshevik government promulgated was a compromise with their long-cherished principles admits of no doubt whatever. Every one who has kept informed concerning Russian revolutionary movements during the past twenty or twenty-five years knows that during all that time one of the principal subjects of controversy among Socialists was the land question and the proper method of solving it. The "Narodniki," or peasant Socialists, later organized into the Socialist-Revolutionary party, wanted distribution of the land belonging to the big estates among the peasant communes, to be co-operatively owned and managed. They did not want land nationalization, which was the program of the Marxists—the Social Democrats. This latter program meant that, instead of the land being divided among the peasants' communal organizations, it should be owned, used, and managed by the state, the principles of large-scale production and wage labor being applied to agriculture in the same manner as to industry.

The attitude of the Social Democratic party toward the peasant Socialists and their program was characterized by that same certainty that small agricultural holdings were to pass away, and by the same contemptuous attitude toward the peasant life and peasant aspirations that we find in the writings of Marx, Engels, Liebknecht, and many other Marxists.[79] Lenine himself had always adopted this attitude. He never trusted the peasants and was opposed to any program which would give the land to them as they desired. Mr. Walling, who spent nearly three years in Russia, including the whole period of the Revolution of 1905-06, writes of Lenine's position at that time:

Like Alexinsky, Lenine awaits the agrarian movement ... and hopes that a railway strike with the destruction of the lines of communication and *the support of the peasantry* may some day put the government of Russia into the people's hands. However, I was shocked to find that this important leader also, though he expects a full co-operation with the peasants on equal terms, *during the Revolution*, feels toward them a very *deep distrust*, thinking them to a large extent bigoted and blindly patriotic, and fearing that they may some day shoot down the working-men as the French peasants did during the Paris

242

Commune.

The chief basis for this distrust is, of course, the prejudiced feeling that the peasants are not likely to become good Socialists. *It is on this account that Lenine and all the Social Democratic leaders place their hopes on a future development of large agricultural estates in Russia and the increase of the landless agricultural working class, which alone they believe would prove truly Socialist.*[80]

The Russian Social Democratic Labor party, to which Lenine belonged, and of which he was an influential leader, adopted in 1906 the following program with regard to land ownership:

1. Confiscation of Church, Monastery, Appanage, Cabinet,[81] and private estate lands, *except small holdings*, and turning them over, together with the state lands, to the great organs of local administration, which have been democratically elected. Land, however, which is necessary as a basis for future colonization, together with the forests and bodies of water, which are of national importance, are to pass into the control of the democratic state.

2. Wherever conditions are unfavorable for this transformation, the party declares itself in favor of a division among the peasants of such of the private estates as already have the petty farming conditions, or which may be necessary to round out a reasonable holding.

This program was at the time regarded as a compromise. It did not wholly suit anybody. The peasant leaders feared the amount of state ownership and management involved. On the other hand, the extreme left wing of the Social Democrats—Lenine and his friends—wanted the party to proclaim itself in favor of *the complete nationalization of all privately owned land, even that of the small peasant owners*, but were willing, provided the principle were this stated, to accept, as a temporary expedient, division of the land in certain exceptional instances. On the other hand, the Socialist-Revolutionists wanted, not the distribution of lands among a multitude of private owners, as is very generally supposed, but its socialization. Their program provided for "the socialization of all privately owned lands—that is, the taking of them out of the private ownership of persons into the public ownership and *their management by democratically organized leagues of communities with the purpose of an equitable utilization*." They wanted to avoid the creation of a great army of what they described as "wage-slaves of the state" and, on the other hand, they

243

wanted to build upon the basis of Russian communism and, as far as possible, prevent the extension of capitalist methods—and therefore of the class struggle—into the agrarian life of Russia.

When the Bolsheviki came into power they sought first of all to split the peasant Socialist movement and gain the support of its extreme left wing. For this reason they agreed to adopt the program of the Revolutionary Socialist party. It was Marie Spiridonova who made that arrangement possible. It was, in fact, a political deal. Lenine and Trotzky, on behalf of the Bolshevik government, agreed to accept the land policy of the Socialist-Revolutionists, and in return Spiridonova and her friends agreed to support the Bolsheviki. There is abundant evidence of the truth of the following account of Professor Ross:

Among the first acts of the Bolsheviki in power was to square their debt to the left wing of the Social Revolutionists, their ally in the *coup d'état*. The latter would accept only one kind of currency—the expropriation of the private landowners without compensation and the transfer of all land into the hands of the peasant communes. The Bolsheviki themselves, as good Marxists, took no stock in the peasants' commune. As such, pending the introduction of Socialism, they should, perhaps, have nationalized the land and rented it to the highest bidder, regardless of whether it was to be tilled in small parcels without hired labor or in large blocks on the capitalistic plan. The land edict of November does, indeed, decree land nationalism; however, the vital proviso is added that "the use of the land must be equalized—that is, according to local conditions and according to the ability to work and the needs of each individual," and further that "the hiring of labor is not permitted." The administrative machinery is thus described: "All the confiscated land becomes the land capital of the nation. Its distribution among the working-people is to be in charge of the local and central authorities, beginning with the organized rural and urban communities and ending with the provincial central organs." Such is the irony of fate. *Those who had charged the rural land commune with being the most serious brake upon Russia's progress, and who had stigmatized the People-ists as reactionaries and Utopians, now came to enact into law most of their tenets—the equalization of the use of land, the prohibition of the hiring of labor, and everything else!*[82]

The much-praised land policy of the Bolsheviki is, in fact, not a

244

Bolshevik policy at all, but one which they have accepted as a compromise for temporary political advantage. "Claim everything in sight," said a noted American politician on one occasion to his followers. Our followers of the Bolsheviki, taught by a very clever propaganda, seem to be acting upon that maxim. They claim for the Bolsheviki everything which can in the slightest manner win favor with the American public, notwithstanding that it involves claiming for the Bolsheviki credit to which they are not entitled. As early as May 18, 1917, it was announced by the Provisional Government that the "question of the transfer of the land to the toilers" was to be left to the Constituent Assembly, and there was never a doubt in the mind of any Russian Socialist how that body would settle it; never a moment when it was doubted that the Constituent Assembly would be controlled by the Socialist-Revolutionary party. When Kerensky became Prime Minister one of the first acts of his Cabinet was to create a special committee for the purpose of preparing the law for the socialization of the land and the necessary machinery for carrying the law into effect. The All-Russian Peasants' Congress had, as early as May, five months before the Bolshevik counter-revolution, adopted the land policy for which the Bolsheviki now are being praised by their admirers in this country. That policy had been crystallized into a carefully prepared law which had been approved by the Council of Ministers. The Bolsheviki did no more than to issue a crudely conceived "decree" which they have never at any time had the power to enforce in more than about a fourth of Russia—in place of a law which would have embraced all Russia and have been secure and permanent.

On July 16, 1918, Marie Spiridonova, in an address delivered in Petrograd, protested vehemently against the manner in which the Bolshevik government was departing from the policy it had agreed to maintain with regard to the land, and going back to the old Social Democratic ideas. She declared that she had been responsible for the decree of February, which provided for the socialization of the land. That measure provided for the abolition of private property in land, and placed all land in the hands of and under the direction of the peasant communes. It was the old Socialist-Revolutionist program. But the Bolshevik government had not carried out the law of February. Instead, it had resorted to the Social Democratic method of nationalization. In the western governments, she said,

245

"great estates were being taken over by government departments and were being managed by officials, on the ground that state control would yield better results than communal ownership. Under this system the peasants were being reduced to the state of slaves paid wages by the state. Yet the law provided that these estates should be divided among the peasant communes to be tilled by the peasants on a co-operative system."[83] Spiridonova protested against the attitude of the Bolsheviki toward the peasants, against dividing them into classes and placing the greater part of them with the bourgeoisie. She insisted that the peasants be regarded as a single class, co-operating with the industrial proletariat, yet distinct from it and from the bourgeoisie. For our present purpose, it does not matter whether the leaders of the Bolsheviki were right or wrong in their decision that state operation was better than operation by village co-operatives. Our sole concern here and now is the fact that they did not keep faith with the section of the peasants they had won over to their side, and the fact that, as this incident shows, we cannot regard the formal decrees of the Soviet Republic as descriptions of realities.

The Bolsheviki remain to-day, as at the beginning, a counter-revolutionary power imposing its rule upon the great mass of the Russian people by armed force. There can be little doubt that if a free election could be had immediately upon the same basis as that on which the Constituent Assembly was elected—namely, universal, secret, equal, direct suffrage, the Bolsheviki would be overwhelmingly beaten. There can be little doubt that the great mass of the peasantry would support, as before, the candidates of the Socialist-Revolutionary party. It is quite true that some of the leaders of that party have consented to work with the Bolshevik government. Compromises have been effected; the Bolsheviki have conciliated the peasants somewhat, and the latter have, in many cases, sought to make the best of a bad situation. Many have adopted a passive attitude. But there can be no greater mistake than to believe that the Bolsheviki have solved the land question to the satisfaction of the peasants and so won their allegiance.

VII

This survey of the theories and practices of the Bolsheviki would invite criticism and distrust if the peace program which culminated in the shameful surrender to Germany, the "indecent peace" as the Russians call it, were passed over without mention. And yet there is no need to tell here a story with which every one is familiar. By that humiliating peace Russia lost 780,000 square kilometers of territory, occupied by 56,000,000 inhabitants. She lost one-third of her total mileage of railways, amounting to more than 13,000 miles. She lost, also, 73 per cent. of her iron production; 89 per cent. of her coal production, and many thousands of factories of various kinds. These latter included 268 sugar-refineries, 918 textile-factories, 574 breweries, 133 tobacco-factories, 1,685 distilleries, 244 chemical-factories, 615 paper-mills, and 1,073 machine-factories.[84] Moreover, it was not an enduring peace and war against Germany had to be resumed.

In judging the manner in which the Bolsheviki concluded peace with Germany, it is necessary to be on guard against prejudice engendered by the war and its passions. The tragi-comedy of Brest-Litovsk, and the pitiable rôle of Trotzky, have naturally been linked together with the manner in which Lenine and his companions reached Russia with the aid of the German Government, the way in which all the well-known leaders of the Bolsheviki had deliberately weakened the morale of the troops at the front, and their persistent opposition to all the efforts of Kerensky to restore the fighting spirit of the army—all these things combined have convinced many thoughtful and close observers that the Bolsheviki were in league with the Germans against the Allies. Perhaps the time is not yet ripe for passing final judgment upon this matter. Certainly there were ugly-looking incidents which appeared to indicate a close co-operation with the Germans.

There was, for example, the acknowledged fact that the Bolsheviki on seizing the power of government immediately entered into negotiations with the notorious "Parvus," whose rôle as an agent of the German Government is now thoroughly established. "Parvus" is the pseudonym of one of the most sinister figures in the history of the Socialist movement, Dr. Alexander Helfandt. Born at Odessa, of German-Jewish descent, he studied in Germany and in the early eighteen-nineties attained prominence as a prolific and brilliant contributor to the German Socialist review, *Die Neue Zeit*. He was early "exiled" from Russia, but it was suspected by a great many Socialists that in reality his "exile" was simply a device to cover employment in the Russian Secret Service as a spy and informer, for which the prestige he had gained in Socialist circles was a valuable aid. When the Revolution of 1905 broke out Helfandt returned to Russia under the terms of the amnesty declared at that time. He at once joined the Leninist section of the Social Democratic party, the Bolsheviki. A scandal occurred some time later, when the connection of "Parvus" with the Russian Government was freely charged against him. Among those who attacked him and accused him of being an agent-provocateur were Tseretelli, the Socialist-Revolutionist, and Miliukov, the leader of the Cadets.

Some years later, at the time of the uprisings in connection with the Young Turk movement, "Parvus" turned up in Constantinople, where he was presumably engaged in work for the German Government. This was commonly believed in European political circles, though denied at the time by "Parvus" himself. One thing is certain, namely, that although he was notoriously poor when he went there—his financial condition was well known to his Socialist associates—he returned at the beginning of 1915 a very rich man. He explained his riches by saying that he had, while at Constantinople, Bucharest, and Sofia, successfully speculated in war wheat. He wrote this explanation in the German Socialist paper, *Die Glocke*, and drew from Hugo Hasse the following observation: "I blame nobody for being wealthy; I only ask if it is the rôle of a Social Democrat to become a profiteer of the war."[85] Very soon we find this precious gentleman settled in Copenhagen, where he established a "Society for Studying the Social Consequences of the War," which was, of course, entirely pro-German. This society is said to have exercised considerable influence among the Russians in Copenhagen and to have greatly influenced many Danish Socialists to take Germany's side. According to *Pravda*, the Bolshevik organ, the German Government, through the intermediary of German Social Democrats, established a working relation with Danish trade-unions and the Danish Social Democratic party, whereby the Danish unions got the coal needed in Copenhagen at a figure below the market price. Then the Danish party sent its leader, Borgdjerg, to Petrograd as an emissary to place before the Petrograd Soviet the terms of peace of the German Majority Socialists, which were, of course, the terms of the German Government. We find "Parvus" at the same time, as he is engaged in this sort of intrigue, associated with one Furstenberg in shipping drugs into Russia and food from Russia into Germany.[86] According to Grumbach,[87] he sought to induce prominent Norwegian Socialists to act as intermediaries to inform certain Norwegian syndicates that Germany would grant them a monopoly of coal consignments if the Norwegian Social Democratic press would adopt a more friendly attitude toward Germany and the Social Democratic members in the Norwegian parliament would urge the stoppage or the limitation of fish exports to England.

During this period "Parvus" was bitterly denounced by Plechanov, by Alexinsky and other Russian Socialists as an agent of the Central Powers. He was denounced also by Lenine and Trotzky and by *Pravda*. Lenine described him as "the vilest of bandits and betrayers." It was therefore somewhat astonishing for those familiar with these facts to read the following communication, which appeared in the German Socialist press on November 30, 1917, and, later, in the British Socialist organ, *Justice*:

Stockholm, November 20.—The Foreign Relations Committee of the Bolsheviki makes the following communication: "The German comrade, 'Parvus,' has brought to the Bolshevik Committee at Stockholm the congratulations of the *Parteivorstand* of the Majority Social Democrats, who declare their solidarity with the struggles of the Russian proletariat and with its request to begin pourparlers immediately on the basis of a democratic peace without annexations and indemnities. The Foreign Relations Committee of the Bolsheviki has transmitted these declarations to the Central Committee at Petrograd, as well as to the Soviets."

When Hugo Hasse questioned Philipp Scheidemann about the negotiations which were going on through "Parvus," Scheidemann replied that it was the Bolsheviki themselves who had invited "Parvus" to come to Stockholm for the purpose of opening up negotiations. This statement was denounced as a lie by Karl Radek in *Pravda*. Some day, doubtless, the truth will be known; for the present it is enough to note the fact that as early as November the Bolsheviki were negotiating through such a discredited agent of the Central Powers as Dr. Alexander Helfandt, otherwise "Parvus," the well-known Marxist! Such facts as this, added to those previously noticed,

249

tended inevitably to strengthen the conviction that Lenine and Trotsky were the pliant and conscious tools of Germany all the time, and that the protests of Trotzky at Brest-Litovsk were simply stage-play.

But for all that, unless and until official, documentary evidence is forthcoming which proves them to have been in such relations with the German Government and military authorities, they ought not to be condemned upon the chain of suspicious circumstances, strong as that chain apparently is. The fact is that they had to make peace, and make it quickly. Kerensky, had he been permitted to hold on, would equally have had to make a separate peace, and make it quickly. Only one thing could have delayed that for long—namely, the arrival of an adequate force of Allied troops on the Russian front to stiffen the morale and to take the burden of fighting off from the Russians. Of that there was no sign and no promise or likelihood. Kerensky knew that he would have had to make peace, at almost any cost and on almost any terms, if he remained in power. If the Bolsheviki appear in the light of traitors to the Allies, it should be remembered that pressure of circumstances would have forced even such a loyal friend of the Allies as Kerensky certainly proved himself to be to make a separate peace, practically on Germany's terms, in a very little while. It was not a matter of months, but of weeks at most, probably of days.

Russia had to have peace. The nation was war-weary and exhausted. The Allies had not understood the situation—indeed, they never have understood Russia, even to this day—and had bungled right along. What made it possible for the Bolsheviki to assert their rule so easily was the fact that they promised immediate peace, and the great mass of the Russian workers wanted immediate peace above everything else. They were so eager for peace that so long as they could get it they cared at the time for nothing. Literally nothing else mattered. As we have seen, the Bolshevik leaders had strenuously denied wanting to make a "separate peace." There is little reason for doubting that they were sincere in this in the sense that what they wanted was a *general* peace, if that could be possibly obtained. Peace they had to have, as quickly as possible. If they could not persuade their Allies to join with them in making such a general peace, they were willing to make a *separate* peace. That is quite different from *wanting* a separate peace from the first. There was, indeed, in the demand made at the beginning of December upon the Allies to restate their war aims within a period of seven days an arrogant and provocative tone which invited the suspicion that the ultimatum—for such it was—had not been conceived in good faith; that it was deliberately framed in such a manner as to prevent compliance by the Allies. And it may well be the fact that Lenine and Trotzky counted upon the inevitable refusal to convince the Russian people, and especially the Russian army, that the Allied nations were fighting for imperialistic ends, just as the Bolsheviki had always charged. The Machiavellian cunning of such a policy is entirely characteristic of the conspirator type.

On December 14th the armistice was signed at Brest-Litovsk, to last for a period of twenty-eight days. On December 5th, the Bolsheviki had published the terms upon which they desired to effect the armistice. These terms, which the Germans scornfully rejected, provided that the German forces which had been occupied on the Russian front should not be sent to other fronts to fight against the Allies, and that the German troops should retire from the Russian islands held by them. In the armistice as it was finally signed at Brest-Litovsk there was a clause which, upon its face, seemed to prove that Trotzky had kept faith with the Allies. The clause provided that there should be no transfer of troops by either side, for the purpose of military operations, during the armistice, from the front between the Baltic and the Black Sea. This, however, was, from the German point of view, merely a *pro forma* arrangement, a "scrap of paper." Grumbach wrote to *L'Humanité* that on December 20th Berlin was full of German soldiers from the Russian front en route to the western front. He said that he had excellent authority for saying that this had been called to the attention of Lenine and Trotzky by the Independent Social Democrats, but that, "nevertheless, they diplomatically shut their eyes."[88] It is more than probable that, in the circumstances, neither Lenine nor Trotzky cared much if at all for such a breach of the terms of the armistice, but, had their attitude been otherwise, what could they have done? They were as helpless as ever men were in the world, as subsequent events proved.

As one reads the numerous declamatory utterances of Trotzky in those critical days of early December, 1917, the justice of Lenine's scornful description of his associate as a "man who blinds himself with revolutionary phrases" becomes manifest. It is easy to understand the strained relations that existed between the two men. His "neither war nor peace" gesture—it was no more!—his dramatic refusal to sign the stiffened peace terms, his desire to call all Russia to arms again to fight the Germans, his determination to create a vast "Red Army" to renew the war against Germany, and his professed willingness to "accept the services of American officers in training that army," all indicated a mind given to illusions and stone blind to realities. Lenine at least knew that the game was up. He knew that the game into which he had so coolly entered when he left Switzerland, and which he had played with all his skill and cunning, was at an end and that the Germans had won. The Germans behaved with a perfidy that is unmatched in modern history, disregarded the armistice they had signed, and savagely hurled their forces against the defenseless, partially demobilized and trusting Russians. There was nothing left for the Bolsheviki to do. They had delivered Russia to the Germans. In March the "indecent peace" was signed, with what result we know. Bolshevism had been the ally of Prussian militarism. Consciously or unconsciously, willingly or unwillingly, Lenine, Trotzky, and the other Bolshevik leaders had done all that men could do to make the German military lords masters of the world. Had there been a similar movement in France, England, the United States, or even Italy, to-day the Hohenzollerns and Habsburgs would be upon their thrones, realizing the fulfilment of the Pan-German vision.

VIII

In view of the fact that so many of our American pacifists have glorified the Bolsheviki, it may be well to remind them, if they have forgotten, or to inform them, if they do not know it, that their admiration is by no means reciprocated. Both Lenine and Trotzky have spoken and written in terms of utter disdain of pacifist movements in general and of the pacifists of England and America in particular. They have insisted that, *in present society*, disarmament is really a reactionary proposal. The inclusion in the Constitution, which they have forced upon Russia by armed might, of *permanent universal compulsory military service* is not by accident. They believe that only when all nations have become Socialist nations will it be a proper policy for Socialists to favor disarmament. It would be interesting to know how our

American admirers and defenders of Bolshevism, who are all anti-conscriptionists and ultra-pacifists, so far as can be discovered, reconcile their position with that of the Bolsheviki who base their state, not as a temporary expedient, *but as a matter of principle*, upon universal, compulsory military service! What, one wonders, do these American Bolsheviki worshipers think of the teaching of these paragraphs from an article by Lenine?[89]

Disarmament is a Socialistic ideal. In Socialist society there will be no more wars, which means that disarmament will have been realized. But he is not a Socialist who expects the realization of Socialism *without* the social revolution and the dictatorship of the proletariat. Dictatorship is a government power, depending directly upon force, and, in the twentieth century, force means, not fists and clubs, but armies. To insert "disarmament" into our program is equivalent to saying, we are opposed to the use of arms. But such a statement would contain not a grain of Marxism, any more than would the equivalent statement, we are opposed to the use of force.

A suppressed class which has no desire to learn the use of arms, and to bear arms, deserves nothing else than to be treated as slaves. We cannot, unless we wish to transform ourselves into mere bourgeois pacifists, forget that we are living in a society based on classes, and that there is no escape from such a society, except by the class struggle and the overthrow of the power of the ruling class.

In every class society, whether it be based on slavery, serfdom, or, as at the present moment, on wage-labor, the class of the oppressors is an armed class. Not only the standing army of the present day, but also the present-day popular militia—even in the most democratic bourgeois republics, as in Switzerland—means an armament of the bourgeoisie against the proletariat....

How can you, in the face of this fact, ask the revolutionary Social Democracy to set up the "demand" of "disarmament"? *To ask this is to renounce completely the standpoint of the class struggle, to give up the very thought of revolution.* Our watchword must be: to arm the proletariat so that it may defeat, expropriate, and disarm the bourgeoisie. This is the only possible policy of the revolutionary class, a policy arising directly from the *actual evolution* of

253

capitalistic militarism, in fact, dictated by the evolution. Only after having disarmed the bourgeoisie can the proletariat, without betraying its historic mission, cast all weapons to the scrap-heap; and there is no doubt that the proletariat will do this, but only then, and not by any possibility before then.

How is it possible for our extreme pacifists, with their relentless opposition to military force in all its forms to conscription, to universal military service, to armaments of all kinds, even for defensive purposes, and to voluntarily enlisted armies even, to embrace Bolshevism with enthusiasm, resting as it does upon the basis of the philosophy so frankly stated by Lenine, is a question for which no answer seems wholly adequate. Of course, what Lenine advocates is class armament within the nation, for civil war—the war of the classes. But he is not opposed to national armaments, as such, nor willing to support disarmament as a national policy *until the time comes when an entirely socialized humanity finds itself freed from the necessity of arming against anybody*. There is probably not a militarist in America to-day who, however bitterly opposed to disarmament as a present policy, would not agree that if, in some future time, mankind reaches the happy condition of universal Socialism, disarmament will then become practicable and logical. It would not be difficult for General Wood to subscribe to that doctrine, I think. It would not have been difficult for Mr. Roosevelt to subscribe to it.

Not only is Lenine willing to support national armaments, and even to fight for the defense of national rights, whenever an attack on these is also an attack on proletarian rights—which he believes to be the case in the continued war against Germany, he goes much farther than this *and provides a theoretical justification for a Socialist policy of passive acceptance of ever-increasing militarism*. He draws a strangely forced parallel between the Socialist attitude toward the trusts and the attitude which ought to be taken toward armaments. We know, he argues, that trusts bring great evils. Against the evils we struggle, but how? Not by trying to do away with the trusts, for we regard the trusts as steps in progress. We must go onward, through the trust system to Socialism. In a similar way we should not deplore "the militarization of the populations." If the bourgeoisie militarizes all the men, and all the boys, nay, even all the women, why—so much the better! "Never will the women of an oppressed class that is really revolutionary be content" to demand disarmament. On the contrary, they will encourage their sons to bear the arms and "learn well the business of war." Of course, this knowledge they will use, "not in order that they may shoot at their brothers, the workers of other countries, as they are doing in the present war ... but in order that they may struggle against the bourgeoisie in their own country, in order that they may put an end to exploitation, poverty, and war, not by the path of good-natured wishes, but by the path of victory over the bourgeoisie and of disarmament of the bourgeoisie."[90]

Universally the working class has taken a position the very opposite of this. Universally we find the organized working class favoring disarmament, peace agreements, and covenants in general opposing extensions of what Lenine describes as "the militarization of populations." For this universality of attitude and action there can only be one adequate explanation—namely, the instinctive class consciousness of the workers. But, according to Lenine, this instinctive class consciousness is all wrong; somehow or other it expresses itself in a "bourgeois" policy. The workers ought to welcome the efforts of the ruling class to militarize and train in the arts of war not only the men of the nations, but the boys and even the women as well. Some day, if this course be followed, there will be two great armed classes in every nation and between these will occur the decisive war which shall establish the supremacy of the most numerous and powerful class. Socialism is thus to be won, not by the conquests of reason and of conscience, but by brute force.

Obviously, there is no point of sympathy between this brutal and arrogant gospel of force and the striving of modern democracy for the peaceful organization of the world, for disarmament, a league of nations, and, in general, the supplanting of force of arms by the force of reason and morality. There is a Prussian quality in Lenine's philosophy. He is the Treitschke of social revolt, brutal, relentless, and unscrupulous, glorying in might, which is, for him, the only right. And that is what characterizes the whole Bolshevik movement: it is the infusion into the class strife and struggles of the world the same brutality and the same faith that might is right which made Prussian militarism the menace it was to civilization.

And just as the world of civilized mankind recognized Prussian militarism as its deadly enemy, to be overcome at all costs, so, too, Bolshevism must be overcome. And that can best be done, not by attempting to drown it in blood, but by courageously and consistently setting ourselves to the task of removing the social oppression, the poverty, and the servitude which produce the desperation of soul that drives men to Bolshevism. The remedy for Bolshevism is a sane and far-reaching program of constructive social democracy.

POSTSCRIPTUM: A PERSONAL STATEMENT

This book is the fulfilment of a promise to a friend. Soon after my return from Europe, in November, I spent part of a day in New York discussing Bolshevism with two friends. One of these is a Russian Socialist, who has lived many years in America, a citizen of the United States, and a man whose erudition and fidelity to the working-class movement during many years have long commanded my admiration and reverence. The other friend is a native American, also a Socialist. A sincere Christian, he has identified his faith in the religion of Jesus and his faith in democratic Socialism. The two are not conflicting forces, or even separate ones, but merely different and complementary aspects of the same faith. He is a man who is universally loved and honored for his nobility of character and his generous idealism. While in Europe I had spent much time consulting with Russian friends in Paris, Rome, and other cities, and had collected a considerable amount of authentic material relating to Bolshevism and the Bolsheviki. I had not the slightest intention of using this material to make a book; in fact, my plans contemplated a very different employment of my time. But, in the course of the discussion, my American Socialist friend asked me to "jot down" for him some of the things I had said, and, especially, to write, in a letter, what I believed to be the psychology of Bolshevism. This, in an unguarded moment, I undertook to do.

When I set out, a few days later, to redeem my promise, I found that, in order to make things intelligible, it was absolutely necessary to explain the historical backgrounds of the Russian revolutionary movement, to describe the point of view of various persons and groups with some detail, and to quote quite extensively from the documentary material I had gathered. Naturally, the limits of a letter were quickly outgrown and I found that my response to my friend's innocent request approached the length of a small volume. Even so, it was quite unsatisfactory. It left many things unexplained and much of my own thought obscure. I decided then to rewrite the whole thing and make a book of it, thus making available for what I hope will be a large number of readers what I had at first intended only for a dear friend.

I am very conscious of the imperfections of the book as it stands. It has been written under conditions far from favorable, crowded into a very busy life. My keenest critics will, I am sure, be less conscious of its defects than I am. It is, however, an earnest contribution to a very important discussion, and, I venture to hope, with all its demerits, a useful one. If it aids a single person to a clearer comprehension of the inherent wrongfulness of the Bolshevist philosophy and method, I shall be rewarded.

So here, my dear Will, is the fulfilment of my promise.

APPENDICES

I. An Appeal To The Proletariat By The Petrograd Workmen's And Soldiers' Council

II. How The Russian Peasants Fought For A Constituent Assembly—a Report To The International Socialist Bureau

III. Former Socialist Premier Of Finland On Bolshevism

APPENDIX I

AN APPEAL TO THE PROLETARIAT BY THE PETROGRAD WORKMEN'S AND SOLDIERS' COUNCIL

Comrades:

Proletarians and Working-people of all Countries:

We, Russian workers and soldiers, united in the Petrograd Workmen's and Soldiers' Delegate Council, send you our warmest greetings and the news

257

of great events. The democracy of Russia has overthrown the century-old despotism of the Czars and enters your ranks as a rightful member and as a powerful force in the battle for our common liberation. Our victory is a great victory for the freedom and democracy of the world. The principal supporter of reaction in the world, the "gendarme of Europe," no longer exists. May the earth over his grave become a heavy stone! Long live liberty, long live the international solidarity of the proletariat and its battle for the final victory!

Our cause is not yet entirely won. Not all the shadows of the old régime have been scattered and not a few enemies are gathering their forces together against the Russian Revolution. Nevertheless, our conquests are great. The peoples of Russia will express their will in the Constitutional convention which is to be called within a short time upon the basis of universal, equal, direct, and secret suffrage. And now it may already be said with certainty in advance that the democratic republic will triumph in Russia. The Russian people is in possession of complete political liberty. Now it can say an authoritative word about the internal self-government of the country and about its foreign policy. And in addressing ourselves to all the peoples who are being destroyed and ruined in this terrible war, we declare that the time has come in which the decisive struggle against the attempts at conquest by the governments of all the nations must be begun. The time has come in which the peoples must take the matter of deciding the questions of war and peace into their own hands.

Conscious of its own revolutionary strength, the democracy of Russia declares that it will fight with all means against the policy of conquest of its ruling classes, and it summons the peoples of Europe to united, decisive action for peace. We appeal to our brothers, to the German-Austrian coalition, and above all to the German proletariat. The first day of the war you were made to believe that in raising your weapons against absolutist Russia you were defending European civilization against Asiatic despotism. In this many of you found the justification of the support that was accorded to the war. Now also this justification has vanished. Democratic Russia cannot menace freedom and civilization.

We shall firmly defend our own liberty against all reactionary threats, whether they come from without or within. The Russian Revolution will not retreat before the bayonets of conquerors, and it will not allow itself to be trampled to pieces by outside military force. We call upon you to throw off the yoke of your absolutist régime, as the Russian people has shaken off the autocracy of the Czars. Refuse to serve as the tools of conquest and power in the hands of the kings, Junkers, and bankers, and we shall, with common efforts, put an end to the fearful butchery that dishonors humanity and darkens the great days of the birth of Russian liberty.

Working-men of all countries! In fraternally stretching out our hands to you across the mountains of our brothers' bodies, across the sea of innocent blood and tears, across the smoking ruins of cities and villages, across the destroyed gifts of civilization, we summon you to the work of renewing and solidifying international unity. In that lies the guaranty of our future triumph and of the complete liberation of humanity.

Working-men of all countries, unite!

Tchcheidze, *the President.*

Petrograd, *April, 1917.*

APPENDIX II

HOW THE RUSSIAN PEASANTS FOUGHT FOR A CONSTITUENT ASSEMBLY[91]

A report to the International Socialist Bureau by Inna Rakitnikov, Vice-President of the Executive Committee of the Soviet of Delegates, placing themselves upon the grounds of the defense of the Constituent Assembly.

With a letter-preface by the citizen, E. Roubanovitch, member of the International Socialist Bureau.

To the Executive Committee of the International Socialist Bureau:

Dear Comrades,—The citizen Inna Rakitnikov has lately come from Petrograd to Paris for personal reasons that are peculiarly tragic. At the time of her departure the Executive Committee of the Second Soviet of Peasant Delegates of All-Russia, of which she is one of the vice-presidents, requested her to make to the International Socialist Bureau a detailed report of the fights that this organization had to make against the Bolsheviki in order to realize the convocation of the Constituent Assembly.

This is the report under the title of a document that I present here, without commentary, asking you to communicate it without delay to all the sections of the International. Two words of explanation, only: First, I wish to draw your attention to the fact that this is the second time that the Executive Committee of the Soviet of the Peasants of All-Russia addresses itself publicly to the International.

At the time of my journey to Stockholm in the month of September, 1917, I made, at a session of the Holland, Scandinavian committee, presided over by Branting, a communication in the name of the Executive Committee of the Soviet of Peasants. I handed over on this occasion to our secretary, Camille Huysmans, an appeal to the democrats of the entire world, in which the Executive Committee indicated clearly its position in the questions of the world war and of agrarian reform, and vindicated its place in the Workers' and Socialist International family.

I must also present to you the author of this report. The citizen Rakitnikov, a member of the Russian Revolutionary Socialist party, has worked for a long time in the ranks of this party as a publicist and organizer and propagandist, especially among the peasants. She has known long years of prison, of Siberia, of exile. Before and during the war until the beginning of the Revolution she lived as a political fugitive in Paris. While being a partizan convinced of the necessity of national defense of invaded countries against the imperialistic aggression of German militarism—in which she is in perfect accord with the members of our party such as Stepan Sletof, Iakovlef, and many other voluntary Russian republicans, all dead facing the enemy in the ranks of the French army—the citizen Rakitnikov belonged to the international group. I affirm that her sincere and matured testimony cannot be suspected of partizanship or of dogmatic partiality against the Bolsheviki, who, as you know, tried to cover their follies and their abominable crimes against the plan of the Russian people, and against all the other Socialist parties, under the lying pretext of internationalist ideas, ideas which they have, in reality, trampled under foot and betrayed.

Yours fraternally,

E. Roubanovitch,

June 28, 1918.

Member of the B.S.I.

"The Bolsheviki who promised liberty, equality, peace, etc., have not been ashamed to follow in the footsteps of Czarism. It is not liberty; it is tyranny." (Extract from a letter of a young Russian Socialist, an enthusiast of liberty who died all too soon.)

I

Organization of the Peasants after the Revolution in Soviets of Peasant Delegates

A short time after the Revolution of February the Russian peasants grouped themselves in a National Soviet of Peasant Delegates at the First Congress of the Peasants of All-Russia, which took place at Petrograd. The Executive Committee of this Soviet was elected. It was composed of well-known leaders of the Revolutionary Socialist party and of peasant delegates sent from the country. Without adhering officially to the Revolutionary Socialist party, the Soviet of Peasant Delegates adopted the line of conduct of this party. While co-ordinating its tactics with the party's, it nevertheless remained an organization completely independent. The Bolsheviki, who at this Congress attempted to subject the peasants to their influence, had not at the time any success. The speeches of Lenine and the other members of this party did not meet with any sympathy, but on the contrary provoked lively protest. The Executive Committee had as its organ

261

the paper *Izvestya of the National Soviet of Peasant Delegates*. Thousands of copies of this were scattered throughout the country. Besides the central national Soviet there existed local organizations, the Soviets, the government districts who were in constant communication with the Executive Committee staying at Petrograd.

From its foundation the Executive Committee exercised great energy in the work of the union and the organization of the peasant masses, and in the development of the Socialist conscience in their breasts. Its members spread thousands and hundreds of thousands of copies of pamphlets of the Revolutionary Socialist party, exposing in simple form the essence of Socialism and the history of the International explaining the sense and the importance of the Revolution in Russia, the history of the fight that preceded it, showing the significance of the liberties acquired. They insisted, above all, on the importance of the socialization of the soil and the convocation of the Constituent Assembly. A close and living tie was created between the members of the Executive Committee staying at Petrograd and the members in the provinces. The Executive Committee was truly the expression of the will of the mass of the Russian peasants.

The Minister of Agriculture and the principal agrarian committee were at this time occupied in preparing the groundwork of the realization of socialization of the soil; the Revolutionary Socialist party did not cease to press the government to act in this sense. Agrarian committees were formed at once to fight against the disorganized recovery of lands by the peasants, and to take under their control large properties where exploitation based on the co-operative principle was in progress of organization; agricultural improvements highly perfected would thus be preserved against destruction and pillage. At the same time agrarian committees attended to a just distribution among the peasants of the lands of which they had been despoiled.

The peasants, taken in a body, and in spite of the agrarian troubles which occurred here and there, awaited the reform with patience, understanding all the difficulties which its realization required and all the impossibilities of perfecting the thing hastily. The Executive Committee of the Soviet of Peasants' Delegates played in this respect an important rôle. It did all it could to explain to the peasants the complexity of the problem in order to prevent them from attempting anything anarchistic, or to attempt a disorganized recovery of lands which could end only with the further enrichment of peasants who were already rich.

Such was, in its general aspect, the action of the National Soviet of Peasants' Delegates, which, in the month of August, 1917, addressed, through the intermediary of the International Socialist Bureau, an appeal to the democracies of the world. In order to better understand the events which followed, we must consider for a moment the general conditions which at that time existed in Russia, and in the midst of which the action of this organization was taking place.

II

The Difficulties of the Beginning of the Revolution

The honeymoon of the Revolution had passed rapidly. Joy gave place to cares and alarms. Autocracy had bequeathed to the country an unwieldy heritage: the army and the whole mechanism of the state were disorganized. Taking advantage of the listlessness of the army, the Bolshevist propaganda developed and at the same time increased the desire of the soldiers to fight no more. The disorganization was felt more and more at the front; at the same time anarchy increased in the interior of the country; production diminished; the productiveness of labor was lowered, and an eight-hour day became in fact a five or six-hour day. The strained relations between the workers and the administration were such that certain factories preferred to close. The central power suffered frequent crises; the Cadets, fearing the responsibilities, preferred to remain out of power.

All this created a state of unrest and hastened the preparations for the election of the Constituent Assembly, toward which the eyes of the whole country were turned. Nevertheless, the country was far from chaos and from the anarchy into which further events plunged it. Young Russia, not accustomed to liberty, without experience in political life and autonomous action, was far from that hopeless state to which the Bolsheviki reduced it some months later. The people had confidence in the Socialists, in the Revolutionary Socialist party, which then held sway everywhere, in the municipalities, the zemstvos, and in the Soviets; they had confidence in the Constituent Assembly which would restore order and work out the laws. All that was necessary was to combat certain characteristics and certain peculiarities of the existence of the Russian people, which impelled them toward anarchy, instead of encouraging them, as did the Bolsheviki, who, in this respect, followed the line of least resistance.

The Bolshevist propaganda did all within its power to weaken the Provisional Government, to discredit it in the eyes of the people, to increase the licentiousness at the front and disorganization in the interior of the country. They proclaimed that the "Imperialists" sent the soldiers to be massacred, but what they did not say is that under actual conditions it was necessary for a revolutionary people to have a revolutionary army to defend its liberty. They spoke loudly for a counter-revolution and for counter-revolutionaries who await but the propitious moment to take hold of the government, while in reality the complete failure of the insurrection of Kornilov showed that the counter-revolution could rest on nothing, that there was no place for it then in the life of Russia.

In fine, the situation of the country was difficult, but not critical. The united efforts of the people and all the thousands of forces of the country would have permitted it to come to the end of its difficulties and to find a solution of the situation.

III

The Insurrection of Kornilov

But now the insurrection of Kornilov broke out. It was entirely unexpected by all the Socialist parties, by their central committees, and, of course, by the Socialist Ministers. Petrograd was in no way prepared for an attack of this kind. In the course of the evening of the fatal day when Kornilov approached Petrograd, the central committee of the Revolutionary

Socialist party received by telephone, from the Palace of Hiver, the news of the approach of Kornilovien troops. This news revolutionized everybody. A meeting of all the organizations took place at Smolny; the members of the party alarmed by the news, and other persons wishing to know the truth about the events, or to receive indications as to what should be done, came there to a reunion. It was a strange picture that Smolny presented that night. The human torrent rushed along its corridors, committees and commissions sat in its side apartments. They asked one another what was happening, what was to be done. News succeeded news. One thing was certain. Petrograd was not prepared for the fight. It was not protected by anything, and the Cossacks who followed Kornilov could easily take it.

The National Soviet of Peasants' Delegates in the session that it held that same night at No. 6 Fontaka Street adopted a resolution calling all the peasants to armed resistance against Kornilov. The Central Executive Committee with the Soviet of Workmen's and Soldiers' Delegates established a special organization which was to defend Petrograd and to fight against the insurrection. Detachments of volunteers and of soldiers were directed toward the locality where Kornilov was, to get information and to organize a propaganda among the troops that followed the General, and in case of failure to fight hand to hand. As they quit in the morning they did not know how things would turn; they were rather pessimistic with regard to the issue of the insurrection for the Socialists.

The end of this conspiracy is known. The troops that followed Kornilov left him as soon as they found out the truth. In this respect, everything ended well, but this event had profound and regrettable circumstances.

The acute deplorable crisis of the central power became chronic. The Cadets, compromised by their participation in the Kornilov conspiracy, preferred to remain apart. The Socialist-Revolutionists did not see clearly what there was at the bottom of the whole affair. *It was as much as any one knew at the moment.* Kerensky, in presence of the menace of the counter-revolution on the right and of the growing anarchy on the extreme left, would have called to Petrograd a part of the troops from the front to stem the tide. Such was the rôle of different persons in this story. It is only later, when all the documents will be shown, that the story can be verified, but at all events it is beyond doubt that the Revolutionary Socialist party was in no wise mixed in this conspiracy. The conspiracy of Kornilov completely freed the hands of the Bolsheviki. In the Pravda, and in other Bolshevist newspapers, complaints were read of the danger of a new counter-revolution which was developing with the complicity of Kerensky acting in accord or in agreement with the traitor Cadets. The public was excited against the Socialist-Revolutionists, who were accused of having secretly helped this counter-revolution. The Bolsheviki alone, said its organs, had saved the Revolution; to them alone was due the failure of the Kornilov insurrection.

The Bolsheviki agitation assumed large proportions. Copies of the *Pravda*, spread lavishly here and there, were poisoned with calumny, campaigns against the other parties, boasting gross flatteries addressed to the soldiers and appeals to trouble. Bolsheviki meetings permeated with the same spirit were organized at Petrograd, Moscow, and other cities. Bolshevist agitators set out for the front at the same time with copies of the *Pravda* and other papers, and the Bolsheviki enjoyed, during this time—as Lenine himself admits—complete liberty. Their chiefs, compromised in the insurrection of June 3d, had been given their freedom.

Their principal watchword was "Down with the war!" "Kerensky and the other conciliators," they cried, "want war and do not want peace. Kerensky will give you neither peace, nor land, nor bread, nor Constituent Assembly. Down with the traitor and the counter-revolutionists! They want to smother the Revolution. We demand peace. We will give you peace, land to the peasants, factories and work to the workmen!" Under this simple form the agitation was followed up among the masses and found a propitious ground, first among the soldiers who were tired of war and athirst for peace. In the Soviet of the Workmen's and Soldiers' Delegates of Petrograd the Bolshevist party soon found itself strengthened and fortified. Its influence was also considerable among the sailors of the Baltic fleet. Cronstadt was entirely in their hands. New elections of the Central Executive Committee of the Soviet of Workmen's and Soldiers' Delegates soon became necessary; they gave a big majority to the Bolsheviki. The old bureau, Tchcheidze at its head, had to leave; the Bolsheviki triumphed clamorously.

To fight against the Bolsheviki the Executive Committee of the

National Soviet of Peasants' Delegates decided at the beginning of December to call a Second General Peasants' Congress. This was to decide if the peasants would defend the Constituent Assembly or if they would follow the Bolsheviki. This Congress had, in effect, a decisive importance. It showed what was the portion of the peasant class that upheld the Bolsheviki. It was principally the peasants in soldiers' dress, the "déclassé soldiers," men taken from the country life by the war, from their natural surroundings, and desiring but one thing, the end of the war. The peasants who had come from the country had, on the contrary, received the mandate to uphold the Constituent Assembly. They firmly maintained their point of view and resisted all the attempts of the Bolsheviki and the "Socialist-Revolutionists of the Left" (who followed them blindly) to make their influence prevail. The speech of Lenine was received with hostility; as for Trotzky, who, some time before, had publicly threatened with the guillotine all the "enemies of the Revolution," they prevented him from speaking, crying out: "Down with the tyrant! Guillotineur! Assassin!" To give his speech Trotzky, accompanied by his faithful "capotes," was obliged to repair to another hall.

The Second Peasants' Congress was thus distinctly split into two parties. The Bolsheviki tried by every means to elude a straight answer to the question, "Does the Congress wish to uphold the Constituent Assembly?" They prolonged the discussion, driving the peasants to extremities by every kind of paltry discussion on foolish questions, hoping to tire them out and thus cause a certain number of them to return home. The tiresome discussions carried on for ten days, with the effect that a part of the peasants, seeing nothing come from it, returned home. But the peasants had, in spite of all, the upper hand; by a roll-call vote 359 against 314 pronounced themselves for the defense without reserve of the Constituent Assembly.

Any work in common for the future was impossible. The fraction of the peasants that pronounced itself for the Constituent Assembly continued to sit apart, named its Executive Committee, and decided to continue the fight resolutely. The Bolsheviki, on their part, took their partizans to the Smolny, declared to be usurpers of the Soviet of Peasants' Delegates who pronounced themselves for the defense of the Constituante, and, with the aid of soldiers, ejected the former Executive Committee from their premises and took possession of their goods, the library, etc.

267

The new Executive Committee, which did not have at its disposition Red Guards, was obliged to look for another place, to collect the money necessary for this purpose, etc. Its members were able, with much difficulty, to place everything upon its feet and to assure the publication of an organ (the *Izvestya* of the National Soviet of Peasants' Delegates determined to defend the Constituent Assembly), to send delegates into different regions, and to establish relations with the provinces, etc.

Together with the peasants, workmen and Socialist parties and numerous democratic organizations prepared themselves for the defense of the Constituent Assembly: The Union of Postal Employees, a part of the Union of Railway Workers, the Bank Employees, the City Employees, the food distributors' organizations, the teachers' associations, the zemstvos, the co-operatives. These organizations believed that the *coup d'état* of October 25th was neither legal nor just; they demanded a convocation with brief delay of the Constituent Assembly and the restoration of the liberties that were trampled under foot by the Bolsheviki.

These treated them as *saboteurs*, "enemies of the people," deprived them of their salaries, and expelled them from their lodgings. They ordered those who opposed them to be deprived of their food-cards. They published lists of strikers, thus running the risk of having them lynched by the crowds. At Saratov, for example, the strike of postal workers and telegraphers lasted a month and a half. The institutions whose strike would have entailed for the population not only disorganization, but an arrest of all life (such as the railroads, the organizations of food distributers), abstained from striking, only asking the Bolsheviki not to meddle with their work. Sometimes, however, the gross interference of the Bolsheviki in work of which they understood nothing obliged those opposed to them, in spite of everything, to strike. It is to be noted also that the professors of secondary schools were obliged to join the strike movements (the superior schools had already ceased to function at this time) as well as the theatrical artistes: a talented artist, Silotti, was arrested; he declared that even in the time of Czarism nobody was ever uneasy on account of his political opinions.

IV

The Bolsheviki and the Constituent Assembly

At the time of the accomplishment of their *coup d'état*, the Bolsheviki cried aloud that the ministry of Kerensky put off a long time the convocation of the Constituante (which was a patent lie), that they would never call the Assembly, and that they alone, the Bolsheviki, would do it. But according as the results of the elections became known their opinions changed.

In the beginning they boasted of their electoral victories at Petrograd and Moscow. Then they kept silent, as if the elections had no existence whatever. But the *Pravda* and the *Izvestya* of the Soviet of Workmen's and Soldiers' Delegates continued to treat as caluminators those who exposed the danger that was threatening the Constituent Assembly at the hands of the Bolsheviki. They did not yet dare to assert themselves openly. They had to gain time to strengthen their power. They hastily followed up peace pourparlers, to place Russia and the Constituent Assembly, if this met, before an accomplished fact.

They hastened to attract the peasants to themselves. That was the reason which motived the "decree" of Lenine on the socialization of the soil, which decree appeared immediately after the *coup d'état*. This decree was simply a reproduction of a Revolutionary Socialists' resolution adopted at a Peasants' Congress. What could the socialization of the soil be to Lenine and all the Bolsheviki in general? They had been, but a short time before, profoundly indifferent with regard to this Socialist-Revolutionist "Utopia." It had been for them an object of raillery. But they knew that without this "Utopia" they would have no peasants. And they threw them this mouthful, this "decree," which astonished the peasants. "Is it a law? Is it not a law? Nobody knows," they said.

It is the same desire to have, cost what it may, the sympathy of the peasants that explains the union of the Bolsheviki with those who are called the "Socialist-Revolutionists of the Left" (for the name Socialist-Revolutionist spoke to the heart of the peasant), who played the stupid and shameful rôle of followers of the Bolsheviki, with a blind weapon between their hands.

269

A part of the "peasants in uniform" followed the Bolsheviki to Smolny. The Germans honored the Bolsheviki by continuing with them the pourparlers for peace. The Bolshevist government had at its disposal the Red Guards, well paid, created suddenly in the presence of the crumbling of the army for fear of remaining without the help of bayonets. These Red Guards, who later fled in shameful fashion before the German patrols, advanced into the interior of the country and gained victories over the unarmed populace. The Bolsheviki felt the ground firm under their feet and threw off the mask. A campaign against the Constituent Assembly commenced. At first in *Pravda* and in *Izvestya* were only questions. What will this Constituent Assembly be? Of whom will it be composed? It is possible that it will have a majority of servants of the bourgeoisie—Cadets Socialist-Revolutionists. *Can we confide to such a Constituent Assembly the destinies of the Russian Revolution? Will it recognize the power of the Soviets?* Then came certain hypocritical "ifs." "If," yes, "if" the personnel of the Constituent Assembly is favorable to us; "if" it will recognize the power of the Soviets, it can count on their support. *If not—it condemns itself to death.*

The Socialist-Revolutionists of the Left in their organ, *The Flag of Labor*, repeated in the wake of the Bolsheviki, "We will uphold the Constituent Assembly in *the measure we—*"

Afterward we see no longer questions or prudent "ifs," but distinct answers. "The majority of the Constituent Assembly is formed," said the Bolsheviki, "of Socialist-Revolutionists and Cadets—that is to say, enemies of the people. This composition assures it of a counter-revolutionary spirit. Its destiny is therefore clear. Historic examples come to its aid. *The victorious people has no need of a Constituent Assembly. It is above the Constituante.* It has gone beyond it." The Russian people, half illiterate, were made to believe that in a few weeks they had outgrown the end for which millions of Russians had fought for almost a century; that they no longer had need of the most perfect form of popular representation, such as did not exist even in the most cultivated countries of western Europe. To the Constituent Assembly, legislative organ due to equal, direct, and secret universal suffrage, they opposed the Soviets, with their recruiting done by hazard and their elections to two or three degrees,[92] the Soviets which were the revolutionary organs

270

and not the legislative organs, and whose rôle besides none of those who fought for the Constituent Assembly sought to diminish.

V

The Fight Concentrates Around the Constituent Assembly

This was a maneuver whose object appeared clearly. The defenders of the Constituent Assembly had evidence of what was being prepared. The peasants who waited with impatience the opening of the Constituent Assembly sent delegates to Petrograd to find out the cause of the delay of the convocation. These delegates betook themselves to the Executive Committee of the Soviet of Peasants' Delegates (11 Kirillovskaia Street), and to the Socialist-Revolutionist fraction of the members of the Constituante (2 Bolotnai Street). This last fraction worked actively at its proper organization. A bureau of organization was elected, commissions charged to elaborate projects of law for the Constituante. The fraction issued bulletins explaining to the population the program which the Socialist-Revolutionists were going to defend at the Constituante. Active relations were undertaken with the provinces. At the same time the members of the fraction, among whom were many peasants and workmen, followed up an active agitation in the workshops and factories of Petrograd, and among the soldiers of the Preobrajenski Regiment and some others. The members of the Executive Committee of the Soviet of Peasants' Delegates worked in concert with them. It was precisely the opinion of the peasants and of the workmen which had most importance in the fight against the Bolsheviki. They, the true representatives of the people, were listened to everywhere; people were obliged to reckon with them.

It was under these conditions that the Democratic Conference met. Called by the Provisional Government, it comprised representatives of the Soviets, of parties, of organizations of the army, peasant organizations, co-operatives, zemstvos, agricultural committees, etc. Its object was to solve the question of power until the meeting of the Constituent Assembly.

At this conference the Bolsheviki formed only a small minority; but they acted as masters of the situation, calling, in a provocative manner, all those who were not in accord with them, "Kornilovist, counter-revolutionaries, traitors!" Because of this attitude the conference, which ought to have had the character of an assembly deciding affairs of state, took on the character of a boisterous meeting, which lasted several days of unending twaddle. What the Bolsheviki wanted was a verbal victory—to have shouted more loudly than their opponents. The same speeches were repeated every day. Some upheld a power exclusively Socialist, others—the majority composed of delegates from different corners of the country—sanctioned an agreement with all the democratic elements.

The provincial delegates, having come with a view to serious work, returned to their homes, carrying with them a painful impression of lost opportunities, of useless debates.

There remained but a few weeks before the convocation of the Constituent Assembly. Those who voted against a government exclusively Socialist did not think that, under the troublesome conditions of the time, they could expose the country to the risk of a dispersion of strength; they feared the possible isolation of the government in face of certain elements whose help could not be relied on. But they did not take into account a fact which had resulted from the Kornilovist insurrection: the natural distrust of the working masses in presence of all the non-Socialists, of those who—not being in immediate contact with them—placed themselves, were it ever so little, more on the right.

The Democratic conference resulted in the formation of a Pre-Parliament. There the relations, between the forces in presence of each other, were about the same. Besides the Bolsheviki soon abandoned the Pre-Parliament, for they were already preparing their insurrection which curtailed the dissolution of that institution.

"We are on the eve of a Bolshevik insurrection"—such was, at this time, the opinion of all those who took part in political life. "We are rushing to it with dizzy rapidity. The catastrophe is inevitable." But what is very characteristic is this, that, while preparing their insurrection, the Bolsheviki, in their press, did not hesitate to treat as liars and calumniators all those who spoke of the danger of this insurrection, and that on the eve of a conquest of

272

power (with arms ready) premeditated and well prepared in advance.

During the whole period that preceded the Bolshevik insurrection a great creative work was being carried on in the country in spite of the undesirable phenomena of which we have spoken above.

1. With great difficulty there were established organs of a local, autonomous administration, volost and district zemstvos, which were to furnish a basis of organization to the government zemstvos. The zemstvo of former times was made up of only class representatives; *the elections to the new zemstvos were effected by universal suffrage, equal, direct, and secret.* These elections were a kind of schooling for the population, showing it the practical significance of universal suffrage, and preparing it for the elections to the Constituent Assembly. At the same time they laid the foundation of a local autonomous administration.

2. Preparations for the election to the Constituent Assembly were made; an agitation, an intense propaganda followed; preparations of a technical order were made. This was a difficult task because of the great number of electors, the dispersion of the population, the great number of illiterate, etc. Everywhere special courts had been established, in view of the elections, to train agitators and instructors, who afterward were sent in great numbers into the country.

3. *At the same time the ground was hurriedly prepared for the law concerning the socialization of the soil.* The abandonment of his post by Tchernov, Minister of Agriculture, did not stop this work. The principal agricultural committee and the Minister of Agriculture, directed by Rakitnikov and Vikhiliaev, hastened to finish this work before the convocation of the Constituent Assembly. The Revolutionary Socialist party decided to keep for itself the post of Minister of Agriculture; for the position they named S. Maslov, who had to exact from the government an immediate vote on the law concerning the socialization of the soil. *The study of this law in the Council of Ministers was finished. Nothing more remained to be done but to adopt and promulgate it. Because of the excitement of the people in the country, it was decided to do this at once, without waiting for the Constituent Assembly.* Finally, to better realize the conditions of the time, it must be added that the whole country awaited anxiously the elections to the Constituent Assembly. All believed that this was going to settle the life of Russia.

VI

The Bolshevist Insurrection

It was under these conditions that the Bolshevist *coup d'état* happened. In the capitals as well as in the provinces, it was accomplished by armed force; at Petrograd, with the help of the sailors of the Baltic fleet, of the soldiers of the Preobrajenski, Semenovski, and other regiments, in other towns with the aid of the local garrisons. Here, for example, is how the Bolshevist *coup d'état* took place at Saratov. I was a witness to these facts myself. Saratov is a big university and intellectual center, possessing a great number of schools, libraries, and divers associations designed to elevate the intellectual standard of the population. The zemstvo of Saratov was one of the best in Russia. The peasant population of this province, among whom the Revolutionary Socialist propaganda was carried on for several years by the Revolutionary Socialist Party, is wide awake and well organized. The municipality and the agricultural committees were composed of Socialists. The population was actively preparing for the elections to the Constituent Assembly; the people discussed the list of candidates, studied the candidates' biographies, as well as the programs of the different parties.

On the night of October 28th, by reason of an order that had come from Petrograd, the Bolshevik *coup d'état* broke out at Saratov. The following forces were its instruments: the garrison which was a stranger to the masses of the population, a weak party of workers, and, in the capacity of leaders, some Intellectuals who, up to that time, had played no rôle in the public life of the town.

It was indeed a military *coup d'état*. The city hall, where sat the Socialists, who were elected by equal, direct, and secret universal suffrage, was surrounded by the soldiers; machine-guns were placed in front and the bombardment began. This lasted a whole night; some were wounded, some killed. The municipal judges were arrested. Soon after a Manifesto solemnly announced to the population that the "enemies of the people," the

274

"counter-revolutionaries," were overthrown; that the power at Saratov was going to pass into the hands of the Soviet (Bolshevist) of the Workmen's and Soldiers' Delegates.

The population was perplexed; the people thought that they had sent to the Town Hall Socialists, men of their choice. Now these men were declared "enemies of the people," were shot down or arrested by other Socialists. What did all this mean? And the inhabitant of Saratov felt a fear stealing into his soul at the sight of this violence; he began to doubt the value of the Socialist idea in general. The faith of former times gave place to doubt, disappointment, and discouragement. The *coup d'état* was followed by divers other manifestations of Bolshevist activity—arrests, searches, confiscation of newspapers, ban on meetings. Bands of soldiers looted the country houses in the suburbs of the city; a school for the children of the people and the buildings of the children's holiday settlement were also pillaged. Bands of soldiers were forthwith sent into the country to cause trouble there.

The sensible part of the population of Saratov severely condemned these acts in a series of Manifestos signed by the Printers' Union, the mill workers, the City Employees' Union, Postal and Telegraph Employees, students' organizations, and many other democratic associations and organizations.

The peasants received the *coup d'état* with distinct hostility. Meetings and reunions were soon organized in the villages. Resolutions were voted censuring the *coup d'état* of violence, deciding to organize to resist the Bolsheviki, and demanding the removal of the Bolshevist soldier members from the rural communes. The bands of soldiers, who were sent into the country, used not only persuasion, but also violence, trying to force the peasants to give their votes for the Bolshevik candidates at the time of the elections to the Constituent Assembly; they tore up the bulletins of the Socialist-Revolutionists, overturned the ballot-boxes, etc.

But the Bolshevik soldiers were not able to disturb the confidence of the peasants in the Constituent Assembly, and in the Revolutionary Socialist party, whose program they had long since adopted, and whose leaders and ways of acting they knew, the inhabitants of the country proved themselves in all that concerned the elections wide awake to the highest degree. There were hardly any abstentions, *90 per cent. of the population took part in the voting.* The day of the voting was kept as a solemn feast; the priest said mass; the peasants dressed in their Sunday clothes; they believed that the Constituent Assembly would give them order, laws, the land. In the government of Saratov, out of fourteen deputies elected, there were twelve Socialist-Revolutionists; there were others (such as the government of Pensa, for example) that elected *only* Socialist-Revolutionists. The Bolsheviki had the majority only in Petrograd and Moscow and in certain units of the army. The elections to the Constituent Assembly were a decisive victory for the Revolutionary Socialist party.

Such was the response of Russia to the Bolshevik *coup d'état*. To violence and conquest of power by force of arms, the population answered by the elections to the Constituent Assembly; the people sent to this assembly, not the Bolsheviki, but, by an overwhelming majority, Socialist-Revolutionists.

VII

The Fight Against the Bolsheviki

But the final result of the elections was not established forthwith. In many places the elections had to be postponed. The Bolshevik *coup d'état* had disorganized life, had upset postal and telegraphic communications, and had even destroyed, in certain localities, the electoral mechanism itself by the arrest of the active workers. The elections which began in the middle of November were not concluded till toward the month of January.

In the mean time, in the country a fierce battle was raging against the Bolsheviki. It was not, on the part of their adversaries, a fight for power. If the Socialist-Revolutionists had wished they could have seized the power; to do that they had only to follow the example of those who were called "the Revolutionary Socialists of the Left." Not only did they not follow their example, but they also excluded them from their midst. A short time after the Bolshevik insurrection, when the part taken in this insurrection by certain Revolutionary Socialists of the Left was found out, the Central Committee of the Revolutionary Socialist party voted to exclude them from the party for

276

having violated the party discipline and having adopted tactics contrary to its principles. This exclusion was confirmed afterward by the Fourth Congress of the party, which took place in December, 1917.

Soon after the *coup d'état* of October the question was among all parties and all organizations: "What is to be done? How will the situation be remedied?" The remedy included three points. First, creation of a power composed of the representatives of all Socialist organizations, with the "Populist-Socialists" on the extreme right, and with the express condition that the principal actors in the Bolshevik *coup d'état* would not have part in the Ministry. Second, immediate establishment of the democratic liberties, which were trampled under foot by the Bolsheviki, without which any form of Socialism is inconceivable. Third, convocation without delay of the Constituent Assembly.

Such were the conditions proposed to the Bolsheviki in the name of several Socialist parties (the Revolutionary Socialist party, the Mensheviki, the Populist-Socialists, etc.), and of several democratic organizations (Railroad Workers' Union, Postal and Telegraphic Employees' Union, etc.). The Bolsheviki, at this time, were not sure of being able to hold their position; certain Commissaries of the People, soon after they were installed in power, handed in their resignation, being terrified by the torrents of blood that were shed at Moscow and by the cruelties which accompanied the *coup d'état*. The Bolsheviki pretended to accept the pourparlers, but kept them dragging along so as to gain time. In the mean time they tried to strengthen themselves in the provinces, where they gained victories such as that of Saratov; they actively rushed the pourparlers for peace; they had to do it at all cost, even if, in doing it, they had to accept the assistance of the traitor and spy, by name Schneur, for they had promised peace to the soldiers.

For this it sufficed them to have gained some victories in the provinces, and that the Germans accepted the proposition of pourparlers of peace ("the German generals came to meet us in gala attire, wearing their ribbons and decorations," with triumph announced in their appeal to the Russian people the representatives of this "Socialist" government Schneur & Co.), for this the Bolsheviki henceforth refused every compromise and all conference with the other parties. For the other parties—those who did not recognize the Bolshevik *coup d'état* and did not approve of the violence that was perpetrated—there was only one alternative, the fight.

It was the Revolutionary Socialist party and the National Soviet of Peasants' Delegates that had to bear the brunt of this fight, which was carried on under extremely difficult conditions. All the non-Bolshevik newspapers were confiscated or prosecuted and deprived of every means of reaching the provinces; their editors' offices and printing establishments were looted. After the creation of the "Revolutionary Tribunal," the authors of articles that were not pleasing to the Bolsheviki, as well as the directors of the newspapers, were brought to judgment and condemned to make amends or go to prison, etc.

The premises of numerous organizations were being constantly pillaged; the Red Guard came there to search, destroying different documents; frequently objects which were found on the premises disappeared. Thus were looted the premises of the Central Committee of the Revolutionary Socialist party (27 Galernaia Street), and, several times, the offices of the paper *Dielo Narvda* (22 Litcinaia Street), as well as the office of the "League for the Defense of the Constituent Assembly," the premises of the committees of divers sections of the Revolutionary Socialist party, the office of the paper *Volia Naroda*, etc.

Leaders of the different parties were arrested. The arrest of the whole Central Committee of the Revolutionary Socialist party was to be carried out as well as the arrest of all the Socialist-Revolutionists, and of all the Mensheviki in sight. The Bolshevist press became infuriated, exclaiming against the "counter-revolution," against their "complicity" with Kornilov and Kalodine.

All those who did not adhere to the Bolsheviki were indignant at the sight of the crimes committed, and wished to defend the Constituent Assembly. Knowingly, and in a premeditated manner, the Bolshevist press excited the soldiers and the workmen against all other parties. And then when the unthinking masses, drunk with flattery and hatred, committed acts of lynching, the Bolshevist leaders expressed sham regrets! Thus it was after the death of Doukhonine, who was cut to pieces by the sailors; and thus it was after the dastardly assassination of the Cadets, Shingariev and Kokochkine, after the shootings *en masse* and the drowning of the officers.

It was under these conditions that the fight was carried on; and the brunt of it, as I have already stated, was sustained by the Revolutionary Socialist party and the National Soviet of Peasants' Delegates, and it was against these two that the Bolsheviki were particularly infuriated. "Now it is not the Cadets who are dangerous to us," said they, "but the Socialist-Revolutionists—these traitors, these enemies of the people." The most sacred names of the Revolution were publicly trampled under foot by them. Their cynicism went so far as to accuse Breshkovskaya, "the Grandmother of the Russian Revolution," of having sold out to the Americans. Personally I had the opportunity to hear a Bolshevist orator, a member of the Executive Committee of the Soviet of Workmen's and Soldiers' Delegates, express this infamous calumny at a meeting organized by the Preobrajenski Regiment. The Bolsheviki tried, by every means, to crush the party, to reduce it to a clandestine existence. But the Central Committee declared that it would continue to fight against violence—and that in an open manner; it continued to issue a daily paper, only changing its title, as in the time of Czarism, and thus continued its propaganda in the factories, and helped to form public opinion, etc.

At the Fourth Congress of the party, which took place in December, the delegates from the provinces, where the despotism of the Bolsheviki was particularly violent, raised the question of introducing terrorist methods in the fight against the Bolsheviki. "From the time that the party is placed in a fight under conditions which differ nothing from those of Czarism, ancient methods are to be resumed; violence must be opposed to violence," they said. But the Congress spurned this means; the Revolutionary Socialist party did not adopt the methods of terrorism; it could not do it, because the Bolsheviki were, after all, followed by the masses—unthinking, it is true, but the masses, nevertheless. It is by educating them, and not by the use of violence, that they are to be fought against. Terrorist acts could bring nothing but a bloody suppression.

VIII

The Second Peasant Congress

In the space of a month a great amount of work was accomplished. A breach was made in the general misunderstanding. Moral help was assured to the Constituent Assembly on the part of the workmen and part of the soldiers of Petrograd. There was no longer any confidence placed in the Bolsheviki. Besides, the agitation was not the only cause of this change. The workers soon came to understand that the Bolshevik tactics could only irritate and disgust the great mass of the population, that the Bolsheviki were not the representatives of the workers, that their promises of land, of peace, and other earthly goods were only a snare. The industrial production diminished more and more; numerous factories and shops closed their doors and thousands of workmen found themselves on the streets. The population of Petrograd, which, at first, received a quarter of a pound of bread per day (a black bread made with straw), had now but one-eighth of a pound, while in the time of Kerensky the ration was half a pound. The other products (oatmeal, butter, eggs, milk) were entirely lacking or cost extremely high prices. One ruble fifty copecks for a pound of potatoes, six rubles a pound of meat, etc. The transportation of products to Petrograd had almost ceased. The city was on the eve of famine.

The workers were irritated by the violence and the arbitrary manner of the Bolsheviki, and by the exploits of the Red Guard, well paid, enjoying all the privileges, well nourished, well clothed, and well shod in the midst of a Petrograd starving and in rags.

Discontent manifested itself also among the soldiers of the Preobrajenski and Litovsky regiments, and others. In this manner in the day of the meeting of the Constituent Assembly they were no longer very numerous. What loud cries, nevertheless, they had sent forth lately when Kerensky wished to send the Preobrajenski and Seminovski regiments from Petrograd! "What? Send the revolutionary regiments from Petrograd? To make easier the surrender of the capital to the counter-revolution?" The soldiers of the Preobrajenski Regiment organized in their barracks frequent meetings, where the acts of the Bolsheviki were sharply criticized; they started a paper, *The Soldiers' Cloak*, which was confiscated.

On the other hand, here is one of the resolutions voted by the workers of the Putilov factory:

The Constituent Assembly is the only organ expressing the will of the entire people. It alone is able to reconstitute the unity of the country.

The majority of the deputies to the Constituent Assembly who had for some time been elected had arrived in Petrograd, and the Bolsheviki always retarded the opening. The Socialist-Revolutionist fraction started conferences with the other fractions on the necessity for fixing a day for the opening of the Constituante, without waiting the good pleasure of the Commissaries of the People. They chose the date, December 27th, but the opening could not take place on that day, the Ukrainian fraction having suddenly abandoned the majority to join themselves to the Bolsheviki and the Revolutionary Socialists of the Left. Finally, the government fixed the opening of the Constituent Assembly for the 5th (18th) of January.

Here is a document which relates this fight for the date of the opening of the Constituante:

Bulletin of Members of the Constituent Assembly Belonging to the Socialist-Revolutionist Fraction. No. 5, Dec. 31, 1917.

To All the Citizens:

The Socialist-Revolutionist fraction of the Constituent Assembly addresses the whole people the present exposé of the reasons for which the Constituent Assembly has not been opened until this day: it warns them, at the same time, of the danger which threatens the sovereign rights of the people.

Let it be thus placed in clear daylight, the true character of those who, under pretext of following the well-being of the workers, forge new chains for liberated Russia, those who attempt to assassinate the Constituent Assembly, which alone is able to save Russia from the foreign yoke and from the despotism which has been born within.

Let all the citizens know that the hour is near when they must be ready to rise like one man for the defense of their liberty and their Constituent Assembly.

For, citizens, your salvation is solely in your own hands.

Citizens! you know that on the day assigned for the opening of the

Constituent Assembly, November 28th, all the Socialist-Revolutionist deputies who were elected had come to Petrograd. You know that neither violence of a usurping power nor arrests of our comrades, by force of arms which were opposed to us at the Taurida Palace, could prevent us from assembling and fulfilling our duty.

But the civil war which has spread throughout the country retarded the election to the Constituent Assembly and the number of deputies elected was insufficient.

It was necessary to postpone the opening of the Constituent Assembly.

Our fraction utilized this forced delay by an intensive preparatory work. We elaborated, in several commissions, projects of law concerning all the fundamental questions that the Constituante would have to solve. We adopted the project of our fundamental law on the question of the land; we elaborated the measures which the Constituante would have to take from the very first day in order to arrive at a truly democratic peace, so necessary to our country; we discussed the principles which should direct the friendly dwelling together of all the nationalities which people Russia and assure each people a national point of view, the free disposition of itself, thus putting an end to the fratricidal war.

Our fraction would have been all ready for the day of the opening of the Constituante, in order to commence, from the first, a creative work and give to the impoverished country peace, bread, land, and liberty.

At the same time, we did our utmost to accelerate the arrival of the deputies and the opening of the Assembly.

During this time events became more and more menacing every day, the Bolshevik power was more rapidly leading our country to its fall. From before the time when the Germans had presented their conditions of peace the Bolsheviki had destroyed the army, suppressed its provisioning, and stripped the front, while at the same time by civil war and the looting of the savings of the people they achieved the economic ruin of the country. Actually, they recognized themselves that the German conditions were unacceptable and invited the reconstruction of the army. In spite of this, these criminals do not retire; they will achieve their criminal work.

Russia suffers in the midst of famine, of civil war, and enemy invasion which threatens to reach even the heart of the country.

No delay is permissible.

Our fraction fixed on the 27th of December the last delay for the opening of the Constituante; on this day more than half of the deputies could have arrived in Petrograd. We entered into conference with the other fractions. The Ukrainians, some other national fractions, and the Menshevik Social Democrats adhered to our resolution. The Revolutionary Socialists of the Left hypocritically declared themselves partizans of an early opening of the Constituante. But behold, the Council of the so-called "Commissaries of the People" fixed the opening for the 5th of January. *At the same time they called for the 8th of January a Congress of the Soviets of Workmen's and Soldiers' Delegates, thus hoping to be able to trick and to cover with the name of this Congress their criminal acts.* The object of this postponement is clear; they did not even hide it and threatened to dissolve the Constituent Assembly in case that it did not submit to the Bolshevik Congress of Soviets. The same threat was repeated by those who are called Socialist-Revolutionists of the Left.

The delegation of the Ukrainian Revolutionary Socialists abandoned us also and submitted to the order for the convocation on January 5th, considering that the fight of the Bolshevik power against the Constituent Assembly is an internal question, which interests only Greater Russia.

Citizens! We shall be there, too, on January 5th, so that the least particle of responsibility for the sabotage of the Constituent Assembly may not fall upon us.

But we do not think that we can suspend our activity with regard to the speediest possible opening of the Constituent Assembly.

We address an energetic appeal to all the deputies; in the name of the fatherland, in the name of the Revolution, in the name of the duty which devolves upon you by reason of your election, come, all, to Petrograd! On the 1st of January all the deputies present will decide on the day for the opening of the Constituent Assembly.

We appeal to you, citizens! Remind your elected representatives of their duty.

And remember that your salvation is solely in your own hands, a mortal danger threatens the Constituent Assembly; be all ready to rise in its defense!

The Revolutionary Socialist Fraction of the Constituent Assembly.

On the 3d of January the League for the Defense of the Constituent Assembly held a meeting at which were present 210 delegates, representing the Socialist parties as well as various democratic organizations and many factories—that of Putilov, that of Oboukhov, and still others from the outskirts of Narva, from the districts of Viborg, Spassky, and Petrogradsky, from the Isle Vassily. It was decided to organize for January 5th a peaceful display in honor of the opening of the Constituent Assembly.

The Bolsheviki answered this by furious articles in the *Pravda*, urging the people not to spare the counter-revolutionaries, these bourgeoisie who intend, by means of their Constituante, to combat the revolutionary people. They advised the people of Petrograd not to go out on the streets that day. "We shall act without reserve," they added.

Sailors were called from Cronstadt; cruisers and torpedo-boats came. An order was issued to the sailors and to the Red Guards who patrolled all the works of the Taurida, to make use of their arms if any one attempted to enter the palace. For that day unlimited powers were accorded to the military authorities. At the same time an assembly of the representatives of the garrison at Petrograd, fixed for that day, was proscribed, and the newspaper, *The Soldiers' Cloak*, was suppressed.

A Congress of Soviets was called for the 8th of January. They prepared the dissolution of the Constituent Assembly and they wanted to place the Congress before the accomplished fact. The Executive Committee of the Soviet of Peasants' Delegates, and the Central Executive Committee of the Soviets of Workmen's and Soldiers' Delegates chosen at the first elections answered by the two following appeals:

Peasant Comrades!

The Bolsheviki have fixed the 5th of January for the opening of the Constituent Assembly; for the 8th of January they call the III Congress of the Soviets of Workmen's and Soldiers' Delegates, and for the 13th the Peasant Congress.

The peasants are, by design, relegated to the background.

An outrage against the Constituent Assembly is being prepared.

In this historic moment the peasants cannot remain aloof.

The Provisional Executive Committee of the National Soviet of

Peasants' Delegates, which goes on duty as a guard to the Constituent Assembly, has decided to call, on the 8th of January, also, the Third National Congress of the Soviets of Peasants' Delegates. The representation remains the same as before. Send your delegates at once to Petrograd, Grand Bolotnai, 2A.

The fate of the Constituent Assembly is the fate of Russia, the fate of the Revolution.

All up for the defense of the Constituent Assembly, for the defense of the Revolution—not by word alone, but by acts!

[Signed] *The Provisional Executive Committee of the National Soviet of Peasants' Delegates, upholding the principle of the defense of the Constituent Assembly.*

Appeal of the Central Executive Committee of the Soviets of Workmen's and Soldiers' Delegates, Chosen at the First Elections

To all the Soviets of Workmen's and Soldiers' Delegates, to all the Committees of the Army and of the Navy, to all the organizations associated with the Soviets and Committees, to all the members of the Socialist-Revolutionist and Menshevist Social Democratic fractions who left the Second Congress of Soviets:

Comrades, workmen, and soldiers! Our cry of alarm is addressed to all those to whom the work of the Soviets is dear. Know that a traitorous blow threatens the revolutionary fatherland, the Constituent Assembly, and even the work of the Soviets. Your duty is to prepare yourselves for their defense.

The Central Executive Committee, nominated at the October Congress, calls together for the 8th of January a Congress of Soviets, destined to bungle the Constituent Assembly.

Comrades! The Second Congress of Soviets assembled at the end of October, under conditions particularly unfavorable, at the time that the Bolshevik party, won over by its leaders to a policy of adventure, a plot unbecoming a class organization, executed at Petrograd a *coup d'état* which gave it power; at a time when certain groups with the same viewpoint disorganized even the method of convocation of the Second Congress, thus openly aspiring to falsify the results; at this same Congress the regular representatives of the army were lacking (only two armies being represented), and the Soviets of the provinces were very insufficiently represented (only about 120 out of 900). Under these conditions it is but natural that the Central Executive Committee of the Soviets chosen at the first election would not recognize the right of this Congress to decide the politics of the Soviets.

However, in spite of the protestations, and even of the departure of a great number of delegates (those of the Revolutionary Socialist fraction, Mensheviki, and Populist-Socialists), a new Executive Committee of the Soviets was elected. To consider this last as the central director of all the Soviets of the country was absolutely impossible. The delegates who remained in the Congress formed only an assembly of a group with a little fraction of the Revolutionary Socialists of the Left, who had given their adhesion to them. Thus the Central Committee named by their Conference could not be considered except as representatives of these two groups only.

Bringing to the organization of Soviets an unheard-of disorder, establishing by their shameful methods of fighting its domination over the Soviets, some of which were taken by surprise, the others terrorized and broken in their personnel, deceiving the working class and the army by its short-sighted policy of adventure, the new Executive Committee during the two months that have since passed has attempted to subject all the Soviets of Russia to its influence. It succeeded in part in this, in the measure in which the confidence of the groups which constituted it in the policy was not yet exhausted. But a considerable portion of the Soviets, as well as fractions of other Soviets, fractions composed of the most devoted and experienced fighters, continued to follow the only true revolutionary road; to develop the class organization of the working masses, to direct their intellectual and political life, to develop the political and social aspects of the Revolution, to exert, by all the power of the working class organized into Soviets, the necessary pressure to attain the end that it proposed. The questions of peace and of war, that of the organization of production and of food-supply, and that of the fight for the Constituent Assembly are in the first place. The policy of adventure of the groups which seized the power is on the eve of failure. Peace could not be realized by a rupture with the Allies and an entente with the imperialistic orb of the Central Powers. By reason of this failure of the policy of the Commissaires of the People, of the disorganization of production (which, among other things, has had as a result the creation of hundreds of thousands of unemployed), by reason of the civil war kindled in the country and the absence of a power recognized by the whole people, the Central Powers tend to take hold in the most cynical fashion of a whole series of western provinces (Poland, Lithuania, Courland), and to subject the whole country to their complete economic, if not political, domination.

The question of provisioning has taken on an unheard-of acuteness; the gross interference in the functioning of organs already created for this object, and the civil war kindled everywhere throughout the country, have completely demoralized the provisioning of wheat in regions where they had none, the north and the army are found on the eve of famine.

Industry is dying. Hundreds of factories and workshops are stopped. The short-sighted policy of the Commissaries has caused hundreds of workmen to be thrown on the streets and become unemployed. The will of the entire people is threatened with being violated. The usurpers who in October got hold of the power by launching the word of order for a swift convocation of the Constituent Assembly strive hard, now that the elections are over, to retain the power in their hands by arresting the deputies and dissolving the Constituante itself.

All that which the country holds of life, and in the first place all the working class and all the army, ought to rise with arms in their hands to defend the popular power represented by the Constituante, which must bring peace to the people and consolidate by legislative means the revolutionary conquests of the working class.

In bringing this to your knowledge, the Central Committee chosen at the first elections invites you, Comrades, to place yourself immediately in agreement with it.

Considering the Congress of October as incompetent, the Central Committee chosen at the first elections has decided to begin a preparatory work in view of the convocation of a new Congress of the Soviets of Workmen's and Soldiers' Delegates.

In the near future, while the Commissaires of the People, in the persons of Lenine and Trotzky, are going to fight against the sovereign power of the Constituent Assembly, we shall have to intervene with all our energy in the conflict artificially encited by the adventurers, between that

Assembly and the Soviets. *It will be our task to aid the Soviets in taking consciousness of their rôle, in defining their political lines, and in determining their functions and those of the Constituante.*

Comrades! The convocation of the Congress for the 8th of January is dictated by the desire to provoke a conflict between the Soviets and the Constituante, and thus botch this last. Anxious for the fate of the country, the Executive Committee chosen at the first elections decides to convoke at Petrograd for the 8th of January an extraordinary assembly of *all the Soviets, all the Committees of the Army and the Navy, all the fractions of the Soviets and military committees, all the organizations that cluster around the Soviets and the Committees that are standing upon the ground of the defense of the Constituante.* The following are the Orders of the Day:

1. The power of the Constituent Assembly.
2. The fight for the general democratic peace and the re-establishment of the International.
3. The immediate problems of the policy of the Soviets.

Comrades! Assure for this extraordinary assembly of Soviets the most complete representation of all the organizations of workmen and soldiers. Establish at once election centers. We have a fight to uphold.

In the name of the Revolution, all the reason and all the energy ought to be thrown into the balance.

The Central Executive Committee of Soviets of Workmen's and Soldiers' Delegates chosen at the first elections.

25 December, 1917.

IX

The Manifestation of January 5th at Petrograd

From eleven o'clock in the morning cortèges, composed principally of working-men bearing red flags and placards with inscriptions such as

288

"Proletarians of All Countries, Unite!" "Land and Liberty!" "Long Live the Constituent Assembly!" etc., set out from different parts of the city. The members of the Executive Committee of the Soviet of Peasants' Delegates had agreed to meet at the Field, of Mars where a procession coming from the Petrogradsky quarter was due to arrive. It was soon learned that a part of the participants, coming from the Viborg quarter, had been assailed at the Liteiny bridge by gunfire from the Red Guards and were obliged to turn back. But that did not check the other parades. The peasant participants, united with the workers from Petrogradsky quarter, came to the Field of Mars; after having lowered their flags before the tombs of the Revolution of February and sung a funeral hymn to their memory, they installed themselves on Liteinaia Street. New manifestants came to join them and the street was crowded with people. At the corner of Fourstatskaia Street (one of the Streets leading to the Taurida Palace) they found themselves all at once assailed by shots from the Red Guards.

The Red Guard fired *without warning*, something that never before happened, even in the time of Czarism. The police always began by inviting the participators to disperse. Among the first victims was a member of the Executive Committee of the Soviet of Peasants' Delegates, the Siberian peasant, Logvinov. An explosive bullet shot away half of his head (a photograph of his body was taken; it was added to the documents which were transferred to the Commission of Inquiry). Several workmen and students and one militant of the Revolutionary Socialist party, Gorbatchevskaia, were killed at the same time. Other processions of participants on their way to the Taurida Palace were fired into at the same time. On all the streets leading to the palace, groups of Red Guards had been established; they received the order "Not to spare the cartridges." On that day at Petrograd there were one hundred killed and wounded.

It must be noted that when, at a session of the Constituent Assembly, in the Taurida Palace, they learned of this shooting, M. Steinberg, Commissioner of Justice, declared in the corridor that it was a lie, that he himself had visited the streets of Petrograd and had found everywhere that "all was quiet." Exactly as the Ministers of Nicholas Romanov after the suppressions said "Lie. Lie," so cried the Bolsheviki and the Revolutionary Socialists of the Left, in response to the question formally put on the subject of the shooting by a member of the Constituent Assembly.

The following day the Bolshevik organs and those of the Revolutionary Socialists of the Left passed over these facts in silence. This silence they kept also on the 9th of January, the day on which literally all Petrograd assembled at the funeral of the victims. Public indignation, however, obliged them in the end to admit that there had been some small groups of participants and to name a Commission of Inquiry concerning the street disorders which had taken place on January 5th. This Commission was very dilatory in the performance of its duty and it is very doubtful if they ever came to any decision.

Analogous manifestations took place at Moscow, at Saratov and other cities; everywhere they were accompanied by shootings. The number of victims was particularly considerable at Moscow.

X

At the Taurida Palace on the Day of the Opening of the Constituent Assembly

The Taurida Palace on that day presented a strange aspect. At every door, in the corridors, in the halls, everywhere soldiers and sailors and Red Guards armed with guns and hand-grenades, who at every turn demanded your pass. It was no easy matter to get into the palace. Nearly all the places reserved for the public were occupied by the Bolsheviki and their friends. The appearance of the Taurida Palace was not that of a place where the free representatives of a free people were going to assemble.

The Bolsheviki delayed as much as possible the opening of the session. It was only at four o'clock instead of at midday that they deigned to make up their minds. They and the Revolutionary Socialists of the Left occupied seats of the extreme left; then came the Revolutionary Socialists, the Mensheviki, and the other Socialist fractions. The seats on the right remained vacant. The few Cadets that had been chosen preferred not to come. In this manner the Constituent Assembly was composed at this first and last session solely of Socialists. This, however, did not prevent the presence in the corridors and the session hail of a crowd of sailors and Red Guards armed, as if it were a question of an assembly of conspirators, enemies of the Revolution.

From the beginning a fight was started by the election of president. The majority nominated for the office of president Chernov; the Bolsheviki and the Revolutionary Socialists of the Left voted against him. The Bolsheviki did not propose any candidate of their own, and placed before the members the candidacy of a Revolutionary Socialist of the Left, Marie Spiridonova, who was totally incapable of fulfilling this rôle. Afterward several declarations were read—that of the Bolsheviki, that of the Socialist-Revolutionists (read by Chernov), that of the Mensheviki (read by Tseretelli). The partizans of each fraction greeted the reading of their own declaration with deafening applause (for the audience was one of "comrades" and did not hesitate to take part in the debates); cat-calls and shouts greeted the orators of the opposing fractions. Each word of the declarations of the Socialist-Revolutionists and of the Mensheviki (declarations which every Socialist could sign) was received with a round of hisses, shouts, deafening cries, exclamations of contempt for the Bolsheviki, the sailors, and the soldiers. The speech of Chernov—president and member of a detested party—had above all the honor of such a greeting. As for Tseretelli, he was at first greeted by an inconceivable din, but was able afterward—his speech was so full of profound sense—to capture the attention of the Bolsheviki themselves.

A general impression that was extremely distressing came from this historic session. The attitude of the Bolsheviki was grossly unbecoming and provocative of disdain. It indicated clearly that the dissolution of the Constituante was, for them, already decided. Lenine, who continually kept contemptuous silence, wound up by stretching himself upon his bench and pretending to sleep. Lunotcharsky from his ministerial bench pointed contemptuously with his finger toward the white hair of a veteran of the Revolutionary Socialist party. The sailors leveled the muzzles of their revolvers at the Socialist-Revolutionists. The audience laughed, whistled, and shouted.

The Bolsheviki finally left the Assembly, followed, as might be understood, by their servants, the Revolutionary Socialists of the Left. The fractions which remained voted the law proposed by the Socialist-Revolutionists on the transfer of the lands to common ownership (socialization of the soil). The sailors and Red Guards attempted several times to interrupt the session. At five o'clock in the morning they finally demanded with a loud voice that everybody leave.

"We were obliged to go," said, later, the members of the Constituent Assembly at a meeting of the Executive Committee of the Soviet of Peasants' Delegates in recounting these tragic moments, "not that we were afraid of being shot; we were prepared for that, and each one of us expected it, but fear of something else which is far worse: for fear of insults and gross violence. We were only a handful; what was that beside those great big fellows full of malice toward the Constituante and of defiance for the 'enemies of the people,' the 'servants of the bourgeoisie,' which we were in their eyes, thanks to the lies and the calumnies of the Bolsheviki? Careful of our dignity, and out of respect for the place where we were, we could not permit ourselves to be cuffed, nor that they throw us out of the Taurida Palace by force—and that is what would have inevitably happened."

It was thus that the Constituent Assembly ended. The Socialist-Revolutionist fraction maintained an attitude of surprising calm and respectful bearing, not allowing itself to be disturbed by any provocation. The correspondents of foreign newspapers congratulated the members and said to them that in this session to which the Bolsheviki had wished to give the character of "any-old-kind-of-a-meeting" all the fractions maintained a truly parliamentary attitude.

The Bolshevik terror became rife. *All the newspapers that tried to open the eyes of the people as to what was happening were confiscated.* Every attempt to circulate the *Dielo Naroda* or other newspapers of the opposition was severely punished. The volunteer venders of these papers were arrested, cruelly struck down by rifle butts, and sometimes even shot. The population, indignant, gathered in groups on the streets, but the Red Guards dispersed all assemblages.

XI

The Dissolution of the Third All-Russian Peasants' Congress

This is the course of the events which followed the dissolution of the Constituante. On the 8th of January the members of the Constituante assembled at Bolotnaia; two were arrested; the premises of the fraction were occupied by the Red Guards. On the 9th of January took place the funeral of the victims, in which all Petrograd took part. The Bolsheviki this time did not dare to shoot into the magnificent procession preceded by a long line of coffins. The 10th of January they dispersed the Third All-Russian Congress of Peasants which had placed itself on the side of the Constituent Assembly. The Congress had been at first arranged for the 8th of January (the same day as the Bolshevik Congress of the Soviets), but, because of the events, it was postponed to the 10th. The peasants who had come to this Congress knew perfectly well that they would have a fight to uphold, perhaps even to give their lives. Their neighbors, their co-villagers, wept when they saw them set out, as if it were a question of men condemned to death. That alone suffices to show to what degree were conscious these peasants who had come from all corners of the country to prepare themselves for the defense of the Constituent Assembly.

As soon as the Congress was opened sailors and Red Guards, armed with guns and hand-grenades, broke into the premises (11 Kirillovskaia Street), surrounded the house, poured into the corridors and the session hall, and ordered all persons to leave.

"In whose name do you order us, who are Delegates to the Peasants' Congress of All-Russia, to disperse?" asked the peasants.

"In the name of the Baltic fleet," the soldiers replied.

The peasants refused; cries of protest were raised. One by one the peasant delegates ascended the tribune to stigmatize the Bolsheviki in speeches full of indignation, and to express the hopes that they placed in the Constituent Assembly.

The sailors listened. They had come to disperse a counter-revolutionary Congress, and these speeches troubled them. One sailor, not able to stand it any longer, burst into tears.

"Let me speak!" he shouted to the president. "I hear your speeches, peasant comrades, and I no longer understand anything.... What is going on? We are peasants, and you, too, are peasants. But we are of this side, and you are of the other.... Why? Who has separated us? For we are brothers.... But it is as if a barrier had been placed between us." He wept and, seizing his revolver, he exclaimed, "No, I would rather kill myself!"

This session of the Congress presented a strange spectacle, disturbed by men who confessed that they did not know why they were there; the peasants sang revolutionary songs; the sailors, armed with guns and grenades, joined them. Then the peasants knelt down to sing a funeral hymn to the memory of Logvinov, whose coffin was even yesterday within the room. The soldiers, lowering their guns, knelt down also.

The Bolshevik authorities became excited; they did not expect such a turn to events. "Enough said," declared the chief; "we have come not to speak, but to act. If they do not want to go to Smolny, let them get out of here." And they set themselves to the task.

In groups of five the peasants were conducted down-stairs, trampled on, and, on their refusal to go to Smolny, pushed out of doors during the night in the midst of the enormous city of which they knew nothing.

Members of the Executive Committee were arrested, the premises occupied by sailors and Red Guards, the objects found therein stolen.

The peasants found shelter in the homes of the inhabitants of Petrograd, who, indignant, offered them hospitality; a certain number were lodged in the barracks of the Preobrajenski Regiment. The sailors, who but a few minutes before had sung a funeral hymn to Logvinov, and wept when they saw that they understood nothing, now became the docile executors of the orders of the Bolsheviki. And when they were asked, "Why do you do this?" they answered as in the time, still recent, of Czarism: "It is the order. No need to talk."

It was thus there was manifested the habit of servile obedience, of arbitrary power and violence, which had been taking root for several centuries; under a thin veneer of revolution one finds the servile and violent man of yesterday.

In the midst of these exceptional circumstances the peasants gave proof of that obstinacy and energy in the pursuit of their rights for which they are noted. Thrown out in the middle of the night, robbed, insulted, they decided, nevertheless, to continue their Congress. "How, otherwise, can we go home?" said they. "We must come to an understanding as to what is to be done."

The members of the Executive Committee who were still free succeeded in finding new premises (let it be noted that among others the workmen of the big Oboukhovsky factory offered them hospitality), and during three days the peasants could assemble secretly by hiding themselves from the eyes of the Red Guard, and the spies in various quarters of Petrograd, until such time as the decisions were given on all great questions. *A procès-verbal was prepared concerning all that had taken place on Kirillovskaia Street. A declaration was made protesting against the acts of the Bolshevik government.* This declaration was to be read at the Taurida Palace when the Soviets were in congress by delegates designated for that purpose. The Bolsheviki, however, would not permit the delegates to enter the Taurida Palace.

Here are the texts of the declaration and of the procès-verbal:

At the Third National Congress of Soviets of Peasants' Delegates grouped around the principle of the defense of the Constituent Assembly, this declaration was sent to the Congress of Workmen's, Soldiers' and Peasants' Delegates called together by the Bolshevist government at the Taurida Palace:

At the Second National Peasants' Congress the 359 delegates who had come together for the defense of the Constituent Assembly continued the work of the Congress and elected a provisional Executive Committee, independently of the 354 delegates who had opposed the power of the Constituent Assembly and adhered to the Bolsheviki.

We, peasant delegates, having come to Petrograd, more than 300 in number, to participate in a Congress called by the Provisional Executive Committee, which is that of those of the Soviets which acknowledge the principle of the defense of the Constituent Assembly, declare to our electors, to the millions of the peasant population, and to the whole country, that the actual government which is called "The Government of the Peasants and Workmen" has established in their integrity the violence, the arbitrariness, and all the horrors of the autocratic régime which was overthrown by the great Revolution of February. All the liberties attained by that Revolution and won by innumerable sacrifices during several generations are scouted and trodden under foot. Liberty of opinion does not exist; men who under the government of the Czar had paid by years of prison and exile for their devotedness to the revolutionary cause are now again thrown into the dungeons of fortresses without any accusation whatever, of anything of which they might be guilty, being made to them. Again spies and informers are in action. Again capital punishment is re-established in its most horrible forms; shooting on the streets and assassinations without judgment or examination. *Peaceful processions, on their way to salute the Constituent Assembly, are greeted by a fusillade of shots upon the orders of the autocrats of Smolny. The liberty of the press does not exist; the papers which displease the Bolsheviki are suppressed, their printing plants and offices looted, their editors arrested.*

The organizations which, during the preceding months, were established with great difficulty—zemstvos, municipalities, agricultural and food committees—are foolishly destroyed in an excess of savage fanaticism.

The Bolsheviki even try to kill the supreme representation, the only one legitimately established, of the popular will—the Constituent Assembly.

To justify this violence and this tyranny they try to allege the well-being of the people, but we, peasant workers, we see well that their policy will only tighten the cord around the workers' necks, while the possibility of a democratic peace becomes more remote every day; matters have come to the point where the Bolsheviki proclaim a further mobilization—of salaried volunteers, it is true—to renew the hostilities. They strive to represent the war with Ukraine and with the Cossacks under the aspect of a war of classes; it is not, however, the bourgeoisie, but the representatives of the working classes who are killed on one side and on the other. They promised the Socialist régime, and they have only destroyed the production of the factories so as to leave the population without product and throw the workers into an army of unemployed; the horrible specter of famine occupies the void left by the broken organizations of food-supply; millions of the money of the people are squandered in maintaining a Red Guard—or sent to Germany to keep up the agitation there, while the wives and the widows of our soldiers no longer receive an allowance, there being no money in the Treasury, and are obliged to live on charity.

The Russian country is threatened with ruin. Death knocks at the doors of the hovels of the workmen.

By what forces have the Bolsheviki thus killed our country? Twelve days before the organization of the autonomous administration was achieved and the elections to the Constituent Assembly begun, at the time when there had been organized all the autonomous administrations of volosts, districts, governments, and cities, chosen by equal, direct, and secret universal suffrage, thus assuring the realization of the will of the people and justifying the confidence of the population—even then they seized the power and established a régime which subjects all the institutions of the country to the unlicensed power of the Commissaries of the People. *And these Commissaries rely upon the Soviets, which were chosen at elections that were carried out according to rank, with open balloting and inequality of vote, for therein the peasants count only as many representatives as the workmen of the cities, although in Russia their number is sixty times greater.*

Absence of control permits every abuse of power; absence of secret voting permits that into these Soviets at these suspicious elections some enter who are attracted by the political rôle of these institutions; the defeat of inequality in the suffrage restrains the expression of the will of the peasants, and, accordingly, these cannot have confidence in this system of government. The tyranny that presided at these elections was such that the Bolsheviki themselves pay no attention to the results, and declare that the Soviets that are opposed to themselves are bourgeoisie and capitalists. We, representing the peasant workers, must declare in the name of our constituents: if anything can save Russia, it can only be the re-establishment of the organs of local autonomous administration, chosen by equal, direct, and secret universal suffrage and the resumption, without delay, of the work of the Constituent Assembly.

The Constituent Assembly alone can express the exact will of the working-people, for the system of election which governs it includes every measure of precaution against violence, corruption, and other abuses, and assures the election of deputies chosen by the majority; now, in the country, the majority is composed of the working class.

Millions of peasants delegated us to defend the Constituante, but this was dissolved as soon as it began to work for the good of the people. The work of the Constituante was interrupted at the time that it was discussing the law concerning land, when a new agricultural régime was being elaborated for the country. For this reason, and for this alone, the Constituante adopted only the first articles of this law, articles which established the definite transfer of all the land to the hands of the workers, without any ransom. The other articles of this law, which concerned the order of the apportionment of lots, its forms, its methods of possession, etc., could not be adopted, although they were completely elaborated in the commission and nothing remained but to sanction them.

We, peasants assembled in Congress, we, too, have been the object of violence and outrages, unheard of even under the Czarist régime. Red Guards and sailors, armed, invaded our premises. We were searched in the rudest manner. Our goods and the provisions which we had brought from home were stolen. Several of our comrade-delegates and all the members of the Committee were arrested and taken to Peter and Paul Fortress. We ourselves were, late at night, put out of doors in a city which we did not know, deprived of shelter under which to sleep. All that, to oblige us either to go to Smolny, where the Bolshevist government called another Congress, or to return to our homes without having attained any result. But violence could not stop us; secretly, as in the time of Czarist autocracy, we found a place to assemble and to continue our work.

In making known these facts to the country and the numerous millions of the peasant population, we call upon them to stigmatize the revolting policy practised by the Bolshevik government with regard to all those who are not in accord with it. Returned to our villages, dispersed in every corner of immense Russia, we shall use all our powers to make known to the mass of peasants and to the entire country the truth concerning this government of violence; to make known in every corner of the fatherland that the actual government, which has the hardihood to call itself "Government of the Workmen and Peasants," in reality shoots down workmen and peasants and shamelessly scoffs at the country. We shall use all our strength to induce the population of peasant workers to demand an account from this government of violence, as well as from their prodigal children, their sons and brothers, who in the army and navy give aid to these autocrats in the commission of violence.

In the name of millions of peasants, by whom we were delegated, we demand that they no longer obstruct the work of the Constituent Assembly. We were not allowed to finish the work for which we had come; at home we shall continue this work. We shall employ all our strength to effect, as soon as possible, the convocation of a new National Congress of Peasants' Delegates united on the principle of the defense of the Constituante, and that in a place where we need not fear a new dissolution. Lately we fought against autocracy and Czarist violence; we shall fight with no less energy against the new autocrats who practise violence, whoever they may be, and whatever may be the shibboleths by which they cover their criminal acts. We shall fight for the Constituent Assembly, because it is in that alone that we see the salvation of our country, that of the Revolution, and that of Land and Liberty.

Charged by our constituents to defend the Constituent Assembly, we cannot participate in a Congress called by those who have dissolved it; who have profaned the idea which to the people is something sacred; who have shot down the defenders of true democracy; who have shed the sacred blood of our Logvinov, member of the Executive Committee of peasant deputies, who on the 5th of January was killed by an explosive bullet during a peaceful manifestation, bearing the flag "Land and Liberty." Comrade-peasants who have come by chance to this Congress declare to these violators that the only Executive Committee that upholds the idea of the defense of the Constituante forms a center around which are grouped all the peasant workers. We call the entire mass of peasants to the work that is common to all—the fight for "Land and Liberty," for the true government of the people. "We all come from the people, children of the same family of workers," and we all have to follow a route that leads to happiness and liberty. Now this road, which leads to "Land and Liberty," goes through the Constituent Assembly alone. The Constituent Assembly was dissolved, but it was chosen by the entire people, and it ought to live.

Long live the Constituent Assembly!
Down with violence and tyranny!
All power to the people, through the agency of the
Constituent Assembly!

[Signed] The Third National Congress of Soviets of Peasant Delegates, United on the Principle of the Defense of the Constituent Assembly.

Procès-verbal of the Session of the III National Congress of Soviets Of Peasants' Delegates, United on the Principle of the Defense of the Constituent Assembly

The Provisional Executive Committee of Soviets of Peasants' Delegates nominated by the fraction of the Second National Congress of these Soviets, which, to the number of 359 delegates, was organized on the basis of the principle of the defense of the Constituent Assembly, had addressed to all the Soviets an appeal inviting those who believe in the defense of the Constituante to send representatives to the Third Congress, fixed by the Committee for the 8th of January, and destined to offset the Congress called for the 12th of January by the Committee of that fraction of the Congress which, to the number of 314 votes, took sides against the power of the Constituent Assembly and joined the Bolsheviki.

The Peasants' Congress, meeting by districts and by governments, as well as the local executive committees of Soviets which have chosen us, knew well to which Congress they delegated us and had given us precise mandates, expressing their confidence in the Constituent Assembly and their blame of the Soviets and the Bolshevik organs that impede the work of the Constituante and call the peasants to the Congress of January 12th. These congresses and these committees have charged us to use all our efforts to defend the Constituent Assembly, binding themselves, on their part, in case our efforts were insufficient, to rise in a body for its defense.

By reason of the disorganization of postal and telegraphic communications, and because in different localities the calls of the Committee were held up by the Bolshevist organizations, the instructions concerning the Congress fixed for the 8th of January were not received in many provinces until after considerable delay.

Some minutes before the opening of the Conference, which was to take place on the premises of the Committee (11 Kirillovskaia Street), where the delegates on hand had lodged, there arrived a detachment of sailors and Red Guards armed with guns and bombs, who surrounded the house, guarding all the entrances, and occupied all the apartments. The Executive Committee, performing its duty toward the peasant workers, which duty was to hold their flag with a firm hand, not fearing any violence, and not allowing themselves to be intimidated by the bayonets and the bombs of the enemies of the peasant workers, opened the session at the hour indicated.

The Bolshevist pretorians, however, violating the freedom of assembly, broke into the hall and surrounded the office and members of the Conference with bayonets drawn. Their leader, Kornilov, staff-commandant of the Red Guards of the Rojdestvensky quarter, made a speech to the delegates, in which he said that they were to go to the Smolny Institute, to the Bolshevist Congress, assuring them that they had come to this Congress by mistake; at the end he read a document ordering him to make a search of the premises, to confiscate all papers, and to arrest all who would offer resistance. In reply to this speech the delegates and the members of the Executive Committee spoke in turn; they stigmatized vehemently the criminal policy of the Bolshevist government, which dissolved the Constituent Assembly, the true representation of the popular will, without having given it the time to register a vote on the agricultural law; which shot down workers participating in peaceful negotiations; which deprived the people of the right of assembly to discuss their needs; which destroyed freedom of speech and assembly and trampled in the dust the whole Russian Revolution. The delegates, one after another, tried to explain to the Red Guards that it was not the delegates that were deceived in coming to this conference, but those who were going to Smolny to the Bolshevist Congress, those who, by order of the Bolsheviki, kill the peasants' representatives and dissolve their Congress.

In the midst of these speeches Kornilov declared the Congress dissolved; to this Comrade Ovtchinnikov, president of the Conference, replied that the Congress would not be dissolved except by force, and, besides, that the document read by Kornilov did not authorize him to pronounce its dissolution. Members of the Congress having entered into arguments with the sailors and the Red Guards, concerning the violence inflicted on the peasant delegates, the sound of the rattling of guns was heard and the leader of the pretorians declared that if the Congress would not submit to his orders he would stop at nothing. All the members of the Congress were forthwith searched and thrown out of doors in groups of five, with the idea that, having come from the provinces, and not knowing Petrograd, they would find themselves dispersed in such a way as not to be able to assemble again anywhere, and would be obliged either to betake themselves to the railway and return home or to direct their steps toward Smolny, the address of which was given to each one at the exit. At the same time, without reason, the following were arrested: Minor, a deputy to the Constituent Assembly; Rakitnikov, Ovtchinnikov, Roussine, Sorokine, and Tchernobaiev, members of the Executive Committee of the Soviet of Peasant Delegates; and Chmelev, a soldier. The premises of the Committee, on which were various documents and papers which were to be sent into the country, were occupied by Red Guards, and machine-guns were placed at the entrance. The search ended about nine o'clock in the evening. Some late delegates alone were authorized to spend the night on the premises under the supervision of Red Guards.

An inquiry held among the comrades, who had come for this Third National Peasants' Congress, established that, at the time when the premises of the Executive Committee were seized, January 10, 1918, there were, among the sailors and Red Guards of the detachment that did the work, *German and Austrian prisoners dressed in Russian uniforms*; it also established the fact that many objects had disappeared in the course of the search. The Congress decided: first, to consider as a law the socialization of the soil voted by the Constituent Assembly and to apply the same in the country; second, to consider that the Constituent Assembly, dispersed by brutal force, was nevertheless elected by the whole people and ought to exist and to assemble again as soon as that would be possible; third, to fight everywhere in the provinces in the defense of the organs of autonomous administration, which the Bolsheviki dispersed by armed force. During these few days when the peasants were obliged to assemble in secret and to station patrols to protect their meetings, they followed those methods of conspiracy that the Russian Socialists had been obliged to employ when they fought against the tyranny of autocracy. Returning to their villages, the peasants bore with them the

302

greatest hate for the Bolsheviki, whom they considered the personification of tyranny and violence. And they took with them also a firm resolution to fight against this violence.

The Executive Committee, whose powers were confirmed by the Third Congress, found itself thus, for the second time, deprived of all its goods, its premises, and its pecuniary resources; it found itself obliged to lead a half-clandestine existence, to organize secret assemblies, etc. Miss Spiridonova, who, in this fight against the peasants that rose to the defense of the Constituent Assembly, gave proof of intolerance and peculiar fanaticism, found herself at the head of the "peasants in uniform," sitting at Smolny, *adopting a decree whereby all the moneys that came by post to the Executive Committee of the Soviet of Peasant Delegates defending the Constituent Assembly were to be confiscated.*

The action of the Executive Committee was thus rendered very difficult. But it continued to fight, to publish an organ, to commission delegates, to entertain continued relations with the provinces and the country.

XII

Conclusion

Morally, Bolshevism was killed in the eyes of the workers in the course of these days when a peaceful demonstration was fired upon, the Constituent Assembly dissolved, the Peasant Congress (and, very soon, the Congress of the Agricultural Committees) dispersed. The Central Committee of the Revolutionary Socialist party issued an order for new elections to the Soviets, thinking thus to eliminate automatically the Bolsheviki. And, in truth, when at Petrograd and in the provinces, these elections began, the Revolutionary Socialists and the Mensheviki received the majority and the Bolsheviki were snowed under. But these new elections were thwarted by many circumstances: first, because of the lessening of production the workmen were discharged in a body and quit the factories; second, the Bolsheviki put obstacles in the way of the elections and sometimes openly prohibited them. Nevertheless, wherever they could be held, the results were unfavorable to

303

the Bolsheviki.

Finally, when the working classes clearly saw the shameful rôle played by the Bolsheviki in the matter of peace, when they saw the Bolsheviki humbly beg for peace at any price from the Germans, they understood that it was impossible to continue to tolerate such a government. *The Central Committee of the Revolutionary Socialist party published a Manifesto appealing to an armed fight against the Bolshevik government and the German gangs* that were overrunning the country.

The frightful results of this "peace," so extolled by the Bolsheviki, rendered even the name of the Bolshevist government odious in the eyes of every conscientious and honest man.

But Bolshevism still endures, for it is based on the armed force of the Red Guard, on the supineness of the masses deprived of a political education, and not accustomed to fight or to act, and from ancient habit of submitting to force.

The causes which produced Bolshevism are: first, the accumulation of all the conditions of the historic past of the Russian people; second, their psychic character and their habits; third, the conditions of the present time; and fourth, the general situation of the world—that is to say, the war.

We also note the vague and hesitating policy of the Provisional Government; the lack of political education among the people, ready to follow him who promises the most; small development of civic sentiment; the want of any attachment whatever to the state—that of the Romanov having never given anything to the people and having taken all from them. Czarism took from the miserable peasant his last penny under form of taxes; it took his children from him for war; for the least act of disobedience to authority he was whipped. He wallowed in misery and in ignorance, deprived of every right, human or legal. How could he, this wretched and oppressed peasant develop civic sentiments, a consciousness of his personal dignity? On the other hand, we must take into account the immense weariness caused by the war and by the disorganization which it brought into the whole cycle of existence (to an incomparably greater degree than in western Europe). Such were the causes which had established a favorable scope for Bolshevik propaganda; to introduce their domination they knew how to make use of the shortcomings of the people and the defects of Russian life.

In fine, what is Bolshevism in its essence? *It is an experiment, that is either criminal or that proceeds from a terrible thoughtlessness, tried, without their consent, on the living body of the Russian people.* Thus some attempt to apply their theories, others wish to measure the height of their personal influence, while still others (and they are found in every movement) seek to profit by the circumstances.

Bolshevism is a phenomenon brought about by force; it is not a natural consequence of the progress of the Russian Revolution. Taken all in all, Bolshevism is not Socialism. The Bolshevist *coup d'état* was accomplished contrary to the wish of the majority of the people, who were preparing for the Constituent Assembly.

It was accomplished with the help of armed force, and it is because of this that the Bolshevist régime holds out.

It has against it the whole conscious portion of the peasant and working population and all the Intellectuals.

It has crushed and trampled under foot the liberty that was won by the Russian people.

The Bolsheviki pretend to act in the name of the people. Why, then, have they dissolved the Constituent Assembly elected by the people?

They pretend to have the majority of the people with them. Why, then, this governmental terror that is being used in a manner more cruel even than in the time of Czarism?

They say that, to fight against the bourgeoisie, the use of violence is necessary. But their principal thrusts are directed not against the bourgeoisie, but against the Socialist parties that do not agree with them. And they dare give this caricature the name of Dictatorship of the Proletariat!

Socialism must necessarily be founded on democratic principles. If not, "it cuts off the branch of the tree on which it rests," according to the expression of Kautsky.

Socialism needs constructive elements. It does not limit itself to the destruction of ancient forms of existence; it creates new ones. But

Bolshevism has only destructive elements. It does nothing but destroy, always destroy, with a blind hatred, a savage fanaticism.

What has it established? Its "decrees" are only verbal solutions without sense, skeletons of ideas, or simply a revolutionary phraseology containing nothing real (as for example the famous shibboleth, "neither peace nor war").

During the few months of its reign Bolshevism has succeeded in destroying many things; nearly everything that the effort of the Russian people had established. Life, disorganized almost to its foundations, has become almost impossible in Russia. The railroads do not function, or function only with great difficulty; the postal and telegraphic communications are interrupted in several places. The zemstvos—bases of the life of the country—are suppressed (they are "bourgeois" institutions); the schools and hospitals, whose existence is impossible without the zemstvos, are closed. The most complete chaos exists in the food-supply. The Intellectuals, who, in Russia, had suffered so much from the Czarist tyranny and oppression, are declared "enemies of the people" and compelled to lead a clandestine existence; they are dying of hunger. It is the Intellectuals and not the bourgeois (who are hiding) that suffer most from the Bolshevist régime.

The Soviets alone remain. But the Soviets are not only revolutionary organs, they are "guardians of the Revolution," but in no way legislative and administrative organs.

Bolshevism is an experiment tried on the Russian people. The people are going to pay dearly for it. At least let not this experiment be lost, on them, as well as on other peoples! Let the Socialists of western Europe be not unduly elated by words or by far-fetched judgments. Let them look the cruel reality in the face and examine facts to find out the truth.

A tyranny which is supported by bayonets is always repugnant, wherever it comes from, and under whatever name it may strut. It can have nothing in common with Socialism, which is not only a doctrine of economic necessity, but also a doctrine of superior justice and truth.

"All the societies or individuals adhering to the Internationale will know what must be the basis of their conduct toward all men: Truth, Justice, Morality, without Distinction of Color, Creed, or Nationality," said the statutes that were drawn up by the prime founders of our Internationale.

306

The Executive Committee of the National Soviet of Peasant Delegates Placing themselves on the Grounds of the Defense of the Constituent Assembly, having had to examine, in its session of February 8, 1918, the violence committed by the Bolsheviki, and to pass in review the persecutions that this organization had to suffer from that party and from the government of the Commissaries of the People, decided to bring the violence committed by the Bolsheviki in the name of Socialism to the knowledge of the Socialists of western Europe and of the International Socialist Bureau through the citizen, E. Roubanovitch, representative of the Revolutionary Socialist party at the International Socialist Bureau and intrusted with International relations by the Executive Committee of the First Soviet of Peasants.

The Executive Committee demands the expulsion, from the Socialist family, of the Bolshevist leaders, as well as of those of the Revolutionary Socialists of the Left, who seized the power by force, held it by violence and compromised Socialism in the eyes of the popular masses.

Let our brothers of western Europe be judges between the Socialist peasants who rose in the defense of the Constituent Assembly and the Bolsheviki, who dispersed them by armed force, thus trampling under foot the will of the Russian people.

Inna Rakitnikov,
Vice-President of the Executive Committee of the Soviet of Peasant Delegates, who stand in Defense of the Constituent Assembly.

May 30, 1918.

APPENDIX III

FORMER SOCIALIST PREMIER OF FINLAND ON BOLSHEVISM

The following letter was addressed to Mr. Santeri Nuorteva, who, it will be remembered, was appointed Minister to America by the Revolutionary Government of Finland. The author of the letter, Oskar Tokoi, was the first Socialist Prime Minister in the world. He is a Socialist of long standing, who has always been identified with the radical section of the movement. Mr. Nuorteva, it should be added, is himself a strong supporter of the Bolsheviki, and is their accredited American representative.

Archangel, *September 10, 1918.*

Santeri Nuorteva,

Fitchburg, Mass.:

Dear Comrade,—I deem it my duty to appeal to you and to other comrades in America in order to be able to make clear to you the trend of events here.

The situation here has become particularly critical. We, the Finnish refugees, who, after the unfortunate revolution, had to flee from Finland to Russia, find ourselves to-day in a very tragic situation. A part of the former Red Guardists who fled here have joined the Red Army formed by the Russian Soviet Government; another part has formed itself as a special Finnish legion, allied with the army of the Allied countries; and a third part, which has gone as far as to Siberia, is prowling about there, diffused over many sections of the country, and there have been reports that a part of those Finns have joined the ranks of the Czecho-Slovaks. The Finnish masses, thus divided, may therefore at any time get into fighting each other, which indeed would be the greatest of all misfortunes. It is therefore necessary to take a clear position, and to induce all the Finns to support it, and we hope that you as well, over in America, will support it as much as is in your power.

During these my wanderings I have happened to traverse Russia from one end to another, and I have become deeply convinced that Russia is not able to rise from this state of chaos and confusion by her own strength and of her own accord. The magnificent economic revolution, which the Bolsheviki in Russia are trying now to bring about, is doomed in Russia to complete failure. The economic conditions in Russia have not even approximately reached a stage to make an economic revolution possible, and the low grade of education, as well as the unsteady character of the Russian people, makes it still more impossible.

It is true that magnificent theories and plans have been laid here, but their putting into practice is altogether impossible, principally because of the following reasons: The whole propertied class—which here in Russia, where small property ownership mainly prevails, is very numerous—is opposing and obstructing; technically trained people and specialists necessary in the industries are obstructing; local committees and sub-organs make all systematic action impossible, as they in their respective fields determine things quite autocratically and make everything unsuccessful which should be based on a strong, coherent, and in every respect minutely conceived system as a social production should be based. But even if all these, in themselves unsurmountable obstacles, could be made away with, there remains still the worst one—and that is the workers themselves.

It is already clear that in the face of such economic conditions the whole social order has been upset. Naturally only a small part of the people will remain backing such an order. The whole propertied class belongs to the opponents of the government, including the petty bourgeoisie, the craftsmen, the small merchants, the profiteers. The whole Intellectual class and a great part of the workers are also opposing the government. In comparison with the entire population only a small minority supports the government, and, what is worse to the supporters of the government, are rallying all the hooligans, robbers, and others to whom this period of confusion promises a good chance of individual action. It is also clear that such a régime cannot stay but with the help of a stern terror. But, on the other hand, the longer the terror continues the more disagreeable and hated it becomes. Even a great part of those who from the beginning could stay with the government and who still are sincere Social Democrats, having seen all this chaos, begin to step aside, or to ally themselves with those openly opposing the government. Naturally, as time goes by, there remains only the worst and the most demoralized element. Terror, arbitrary rule, and open brigandage become more and more usual, and the government is not able at all to prevent it. And the outcome is clearly to be foreseen—the unavoidable failure of all this magnificently planned system.

And what will be the outcome of that? My conviction is that as soon as possible we should turn toward the other road—the road of united action. I have seen, and I am convinced that the majority of the Russian people is fundamentally democratic and whole-heartedly detests a reinstitution of autocracy, and that therefore all such elements must, without delay, be made to unite. But it is also clear that at first they, even united, will not be able to bring about order in this country on their own accord. I do not believe that at this time there is in Russia any social force which would be able to organize the conditions in the country. For that reason, to my mind, we should, to begin with, frankly and honestly rely on the help of the Allied Powers. Help from Germany cannot be considered, as Germany, because of her own interests, is compelled to support the Bolshevik rule as long as possible, as Germany from the Bolshevik rule is pressing more and more political and economic advantages, to such an extent even that all of Russia is becoming practically a colony of Germany. Russia thus would serve to compensate Germany for the colonies lost in South Africa.

A question presents itself at once whether the Allied Powers are better. And it must be answered instantly that neither would they establish in Russia any Socialist society. Yet the democratic traditions of these countries are some surety that the social order established by them will be a democratic one. It is clear as day that the policy of the Allied Powers is also imperialistic, but the geographical and economic position of these countries is such that even their own interests demand that Russia should be able to develop somewhat freely. The problem has finally evolved into such a state of affairs where Russia must rely on the help either of the Allies or Germany; we must choose, as the saying goes, "between two evils," and, things being as badly mixed as they are, the lesser evil must be chosen frankly and openly. It does not seem possible to get anywhere by dodging the issue. Russia perhaps would have saved herself some time ago from this unfortunate situation if she had understood immediately after the February Revolution the necessity of a union between the more democratic elements. Bolshevism undoubtedly has brought Russia a big step toward her misfortune, from which she cannot extricate herself on her own accord.

Thus there exists no more any purely Socialist army, and all the fighting forces and all those who have taken to arms are fighting for the interests of the one or the other group of the Great Powers. The question therefore finally is only this—in the interests of which group one wants to fight. The revolutionary struggles in Russia and in Finland, to my mind, have clearly established that a Socialist society cannot be brought about by the force of arms and cannot be supported by the force of arms, but that a Socialist order must be founded on a conscious and living will by an overwhelming majority of the nations, which is able to realize its will without the help of arms.

But now that the nations of the world have actually been thrown into an armed conflict, and the war, which in itself is the greatest crime of the world, still is raging, we must stand it. We must, however, destroy the originator and the cause of the war, the militarism, by its own arms, and on its ruins we must build, in harmony and in peace—not by force, as the Russian Bolsheviki want—a new and a better social order under the guardianship of which the people may develop peacefully and securely.

I have been explaining to you my ideas, expecting that you will publish them. You over in America are not able to imagine how horrible the life in Russia at the present time is. The period after the French Revolution surely must have been as a life in a paradise compared with this. Hunger, brigandage, arrests, and murders are such every-day events that nobody pays any attention to them. Freedom of assemblage, association, free speech, and free press is a far-away ideal which is altogether destroyed at the present time. Arbitrary rule and terror are raging everywhere, and, what is worst of all, not only the terror proclaimed by the government, but individual terror as well.

My greetings to all friends and comrades.

Oskar Tokoi.

THE END

FOOTNOTES:

[1] Plechanov never formally joined the Menshevik faction, I believe, but his writings showed that he favored that faction and the Mensheviki acknowledged his intellectual leadership.

[2] They had gained one member since the election.

[3] Quoted by Litvinov, *The Bolshevik Revolution: Its Rise and Meaning*, p. 22. Litvinov, it must be remembered, was the Bolshevik Minister to Great Britain. His authority to speak for the Bolsheviki is not to be questioned.

[4] The date is Russian style—March 12th, our style.

311

[5] *The State in Russia—Old and New*, by Leon Trotzky; *The Class Struggle*, Vol. II, No. 2, pp. 213-221.

[6] This document is printed in full at the end of the volume as Appendix. I

[7] The author of the present study is responsible for the use of italics in this document.

[8] Litvinov, *The Bolshevik Revolution: Its Rise and Meaning*, p. 30.

[9] Lenine is not quite accurate in his statement of Marx's views nor quite fair in stating the position of the "opportunists." The argument of Marx in *The Civil War in France* is not that the proletariat must "break down" the governmental machinery, but that it must *modify* it and *adapt* it to the class needs. This is something quite different, of course. Moreover, it is the basis of the policy of the "opportunists." The Mensheviki and other moderate Socialists in Russia were trying to *modify* and *adapt* the political state.

[10] The reference is to Karl Kautsky, the great German exponent of Marxian theory.

[11] *The New International* (American Bolshevik organ), June 30, 1917.

[12] *The New International*, July 23, 1917.

[13] Litvinov, *op. cit.*, p. 31.

[14] *The New International*, April, 1918.

[15] See, *e.g.*, the article by Lenine, *New International*, April, 1918, and Litvinov, *op. cit.*

[16] See my *Syndicalism, Industrial Unionism, and Socialism* for the I.W.W. philosophy.

[17] Bryant, *Six Months in Red Russia*, p. 141.

[18] This appeal is published as Appendix I at the end of this volume.

[19] Certain Soviets of Soldiers at the Front had decided that they would stay in their trenches for defensive purposes, but would obey no commands to go forward, no matter what the military situation.

[20] Figures supplied by the Russian Information Bureau.

[21] "It was with a deep and awful sense of the terrible failure before us that I consented to become Premier at that time," Kerensky told the present writer.

[22] The story was reproduced in *New Europe* (London), September, 1917.

[23] *The New International*, April, 1918.

[24] See p. 254.

[25] See the letter of E. Roubanovitch, Appendix II, p. 331.

[26] *Justice*, London, January 31, 1918.

[27] *Justice*, London, May 16, 1918.

[28] *Vide* Special Memorandum to the International Socialist Bureau on behalf of the Revolutionary Socialist party of Russia.

[29] See Appendix III.

[30] *Pravda*, July 5, 1918.

[31] February, 1918, Protest Against Recognition of Bolshevik Representative by British Labor Party Conference.

[32] Proclamation to People of the Northern Province, etc., December, 1918

[33] *The New International*, April, 1918.

[34] The dates given are according to the Russian calendar.

[35] See the Rakitnikov Memorandum—Appendix.

[36] *The New International*, April, 1918.

[37] The number of votes was over 36,000,000.

[38] *Vide* Rakitnikov report.

[39] Twenty-three members of the Executive Committee were arrested and, without any trial, thrown into the Fortress of Peter and Paul.

[40] From a Declaration of Protest by the Executive Committee of the Third National Congress of Peasants' Delegates (anti-Bolshevist), sent to the Bolshevik Congress of Soviets of Workmen, Soldiers, and Peasants, but not permitted to be read to that assembly.

[41] *L'Ouorier Russe*, May, 1918.

[42] *Idem.*

[43] *Izvestya*, July 28, 1918.

[44] *Pravda*, October 8, 1918 (No. 216).

[45] "Agents-Provocateurs and the Russian Revolution," article in *Justice,*, August 16, 1916, by J. Tchernoff.

[46] Most of the information in this paragraph is based upon an article in the Swiss newspaper *Lausanne Gazette* by the well-known Russian journalist, Serge Persky, carefully checked up by Russian Socialist exiles in Paris.

[47] Joseph Martinek, in the *Cleveland Press*.

[48] *Justice* (London), January 23, 1919.

[49] *Justice*, London, January 31, 1918.

[50] Jean Jaurès, *Studies in Socialism*.

[51] F. Engels, 1895, Preface to Marx's *Civil War in France*.

[52] The reader is referred to my *Sidelights on Contemporary Socialism* and my *Karl Marx: His Life and Works* for a fuller account of these struggles.

[53] Marx, *A Contribution to the Critique of Political Economy*, p. 12.

[54] Editorial entitled "Bolshevik Problems," in *The Liberator*, April, 1918.

[55] The article by Lenine quoted by Mr. Eastman appeared in *The New International*, February, 1918.

[56] *The Bolsheviks and the Soviets*, by Albert Rhys Williams, p. 6.

[57] *Ansprache der Centralbehorde an den Bund, vom Marz, 1850*: Anhang IX der Enthullerngen über den Kommunisten-process Zu Koln, p. 79.

[58] Lenine, *The Soviets at Work*.

[59] Wilhelm Liebknecht, *No Compromise, No Political Trading*, p. 30.

[60] *Socialism: a Summary and Interpretation of Socialist Principles*, by John Spargo, p. 215 (1st edition Macmillan, 1916).

[61] Liebknecht, *No Compromise, No Political Trading*, p. 16.

[62] Liebknecht, *No Compromise, No Political Trading*, p. 28.

[63] This subject is treated in the following, among others, of my books:
Socialism: a Summary and Interpretation of Socialist Principles; *Applied Socialism*; *Syndicalism, Industrial Unionism, and Socialism*; *Elements of Socialism* (Spargo and Arner), and *Social Democracy Explained*.

[64] *The New International*, July 23, 1917.

[65] Conversation with Trotzky reported by E.A. Ross, *Russia in Upheaval*, p. 208.

[66] Kautsky, *The Social Revolution*, p. 137.

[67] Lenine, *The Soviets at Work*.

[68] Lenine, *op. cit.*

[69] Lenine, *op. cit.*

[70] The best expositions of Guild Socialism are *Self-Government in Industry*, by G.D.H. Cole, and *National Guilds*, by S.G. Hobson, edited by A.R.

Orage.

[71] Lenine, *op. cit.*

[72] Lenine, *op. cit.*

[73] Lenine, *op. cit.*

[74] Lenine, *op. cit.*

[75] Lenine, *op. cit.*

[76] Of course, Trotzky's statement to Professor Ross about paying the capitalists "5 or 6 per cent. a year" was frankly a compromise.

[77] E.A. Ross, *Russia in Upheaval*, pp. 206-207.

[78] Litvinov, *The Bolshevik Revolution: Its Rise and Meaning*, p. 39.

[79] Marx and Engels speak of the "idiocy of rural life" from which capitalism, through the concentration of agriculture and the abolition of small holdings, would rescue the peasant proprietors (*Communist Manifesto*). In *Capital* Marx speaks of the manner in which modern industry "annihilates the peasant, *the bulwark of the old society*" (Vol. I, p. 513). Liebknecht says that in 1848 it was the *city* which overthrew the corrupt citizen king and the *country* which overthrew the new republic, chose Louis Bonaparte and prepared the way for the Empire. "The French peasantry created an empire through their blind fear of proletarian Socialism" (*Die Grund und Bodenfrage*). Kautsky wrote, "Peasants who feel that they are not proletarians, but true peasants, are not only not to be won over to our cause, *but belong to our most dangerous adversaries*" (*Dat Erfurter Programm und die Land-agitation*). It would be easy to compile a volume of such utterances.

[80] Walling, *Russia's Message*, p. 118. The italics are mine.

[81] "Cabinet lands" are the crown lands, property of the Czar and royal family.

[82] Ross, *op. cit.*, pp. 206-207.

[83] *Justice*, London, August 1, 1917.

[84] The figures given are quoted by Sack, in *The Birth of Russian Democracy*, and were originally published by the Bolshevist Commissaire of Commerce.

[85] *Parvus et le Parti Socialiste Danois*, by P.G. La Chesnais.

[86] La Chesnais, *op. cit.*

[87] In "*L'Humanité*," article condensed in *Justice*, January 31, 1918.

[88] International Notes, *Justice*, January 3, 1918.

[89] *The Disarmament Cry*, by N. Lenine, in *The Class Struggle*, May-June, 1918.

[90] *The "Disarmament" Cry*, by N. Lenine, *The Class Struggle*, May-June, 1918.

[91] Most, if not all, dates in this document are given as in the Russian calendar, which is thirteen days behind ours.

[92] This refers, doubtless, to the different basis for voting applied to the peasants and the industrial workers, as provided in the Soviet Constitution.